The River Nene

The Rivers and Waterways of Britain and Ireland Past and Present

The River Nene

From Source to Sea

with

David Phillips

Past and Present

Past & Present Publishing Ltd

First published in October 1997

British Library Cataloguing in Publication Data

A catalogue record for this book is available from the British Library.

ISBN 1 85895 133 X

Half title A lovely view of the river looking upstream towards the overshoot weir above Titchmarsh Mill.

Title page For centuries the Nene has provided a means of communication, while its meadows have provided rich grazing for cattle.

Past & Present Publishing Ltd
Unit 5
Home Farm Close
Church Street
Wadenhoe
Peterborough PE8 5TE
Tel (01832) 720440
Fax (01832) 720531
e-mail: pete@slinkp-p.demon.co.uk

Printed and bound in Great Britain

Maps reproduced by courtesy of the Environment Agency.

All photographs are by the author or from the author's collection unless otherwise credited.

Opposite Ice forming on lock gates on a day when wintry conditions made the river impassable to boat traffic.

Acknowledgements

The love of those closest to me is greater even than my love of rivers, and this book is, therefore, dedicated to them - in particular my partner Michelle, who helped and contributed so much to it, and my parents, William and Dulcie, who first introduced me to the joys of our countryside.

Thanks are also due to the many people and organisations who provided the photographs and information that helped make this book possible.

David Phillips
September 1997

Contents

Foreword 6
Introduction 7

1 The sources 17
2 Northampton to Wellingborough 32
3 Irchester to Thrapston 47
4 Islip to Fotheringay 62
5 Fotheringay to Peterborough 87
6 Down to the sea 109
7 The Old River 126
8 The tributaries:
  Ise, Willow Brook and Harper's Brook 137
9 Fishing 151
10 Messing about on the river 167
11 The nature of the Nene 178

Index 191

Foreword

by
Chris Yates

David Phillips has written a fascinating and finely detailed pen portrait of a lesser-known British river, but because of his familiarity with and delight in the subject he raises its profile almost to the same characterful status as Old Father Thames.

The River Nene, it turns out, is something of a national treasure.

The natural history of the river is graphically described, but David is just as enthusiastic about the people associated with the Nene: kings, countrymen, inventors, poets, fishermen. There is such a rich variety of personalities that the reader becomes reluctant to leave them and continue his voyage downstream.

There are many interesting places to visit, however, from source to sea, and David beautifully recounts his discovery of the Nene's birthplace, all the way down through Northampton, Wellingborough, Peterborough and finally to the sea. The history of these places, and the story of how the river created them, is lucidly described, and by the time the reader reaches journey's end, at the Wash, the Nene has become almost a friend.

Over half a century ago, H. E. Bates, in *Down The River*, made a similar journey along the Nene, but David Phillips's book, while not as personal as Bates's, contains more quirky historical facts and is naturally more relevant to the here and now. Of course we will read all about the Nene's pike, perch, bream and carp. David is a passionate angler and the life below the river's surface is vividly portrayed. But it is the poet John Clare, associated with Northampton, who gets the first and last words.

It is heartening that David, in expressing his delight in the river, should have been so wide ranging in his choice of subjects. He has given us everything from kingfishers to kings, from backwaters to buried treasure, from pike to poets - and the writing glides gently along like the stream.

Chris Yates is a television angling personality, and appeared in the award-winning BBC series A Passion For Angling. *He is also a former record carp captor and is currently editor of the monthly fishing magazine* Waterlog.

Introduction

The past it is a magic word
Too beautiful to last
It looks back like a lovely face
And who can forget the past?
There's music in its childhood
That's known in every tongue
Like the music of the wildwood
All chorus to the song

John Clare

The river of life

The past is a comforting place to visit when the present – and future – appear threatening. Nostalgia is a land to which we all love to return, and nobody knew that better than the Nene valley's own peasant poet, John Clare.

Poor Clare pined away the fading years of his life musing upon the placid waters of the Nene at Northampton as his confused mind drifted back to better times. He remembered this blessed valley before Enclosure Acts, the steam engine and the Industrial Revolution wrenched the countryside from a simplicity that had existed since medieval times. He was scared of the brave new world that was rapidly flooding and drowning the old order.

We'll return to Clare and his immortal lines many times as this book progresses, like the Nene itself, from source to sea. Nostalgia and a regret for what we have lost will be a key theme, but rest assured that this is no myopic view of the past through rose-tinted glasses. There have been many changes down this valley, and a great deal of them have been for the better. But before we get down to specifics, what exactly is a river?

Britain's rivers are her arteries and her heart, pumping the lifeblood upon which our survival depends. Our green and pleasant land would be neither green nor pleasant without the water they provide. Water is, of course, vital for the existence of every living thing. Everything that lives – you and me included – consists mainly of water, and rivers are the natural distributors of that precious liquid. And they do their job very well.

Most of the surface of our planet is covered by water. There's plenty to go round, but it's no good to us if it's all locked up in the great oceans. Luckily, water doesn't just sit there in the Atlantic doing nothing. The ocean is constantly evaporating and the moisture released into the air is carried in clouds by the prevailing westerly winds to our shores. Once it meets land, the water vapour tends to fall as rain. Most falls on high ground, which is where our major rivers start life as little streams, trickling out of the porous underground rock.

From there each stream begins its epic journey back to the sea, carrying the water and nutrients that every plant and animal needs to survive. As it flows, so it grows, joined by lesser tributaries as it proceeds downstream. Eventually, swollen to many times the size at which it began life, the river reaches its estuary and flows out into the sea, where the whole evaporation-precipitation process begins all over again.

Ever since early man first tottered on to two legs and took a good look around the world he was to dominate, he has taken advantage of the many riches that rivers have had to offer. Our earliest hunting ancestors camped close to rivers both for supplies of fresh water and to prey upon the fish and animals that lived there. Later the early farmers planted their crops and raised livestock in the nutrient-rich soil of the river valleys.

Later still, the first of our early settlements grew up around strategic river crossings. The rivers themselves were used as natural defences and, of course, for easy transport to other settlements. Most of these settlements grew and flourished to become our greatest towns and

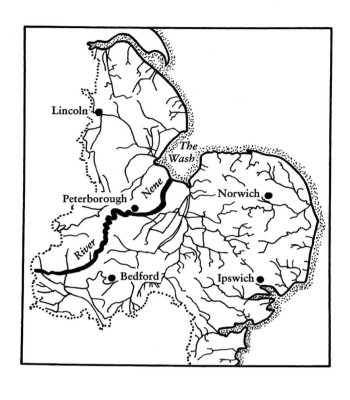

FO

COTTE

OU

Lower Barnv
Oundle

WADENHOE
Wadenhoe Lock

Islip Lock

Woodford
Lock   Th

WOODFORD   De

GREAT ADDINGTON   Lower Rings
Upper Ringstea

LITTLE ADDINGTON

IRTHLINGBOROUGH   Irthlingborough L

Higham Lock

WELLINGBOROUGH
Ditchford Lock

Lower Wellingborough Lock
Upper Wellingborough Lock

GREAT DODDINGTON
EARLS BARTON   Wollaston Lock
Doddington Lock

NORTHAMPTON   Billing
Aquadrome   Barton Lock
Billing   White Mills Lock
Weston Favell   Lock   Whiston Lock
Lock
Northampton Lock   Cogenhoe
Lock
Clifford
Abington   Mill
Rush Mills   Lock   Lock
Grand Union Canal   Lock

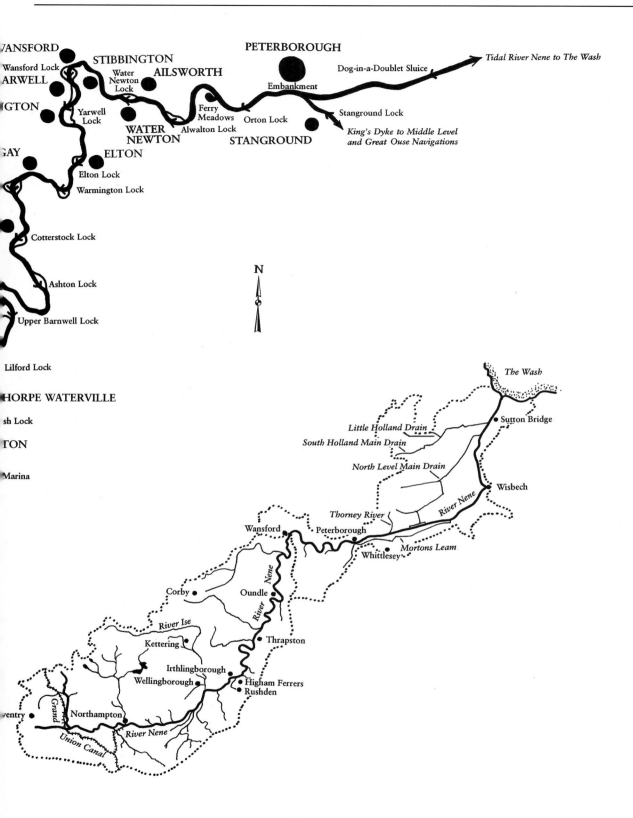

WANSFORD
Wansford Lock
ARWELL
IGTON
Yarwell Lock
GAY
ELTON
Elton Lock
Warmington Lock
Cotterstock Lock
Ashton Lock
Upper Barnwell Lock
Lilford Lock
THORPE WATERVILLE
sh Lock
TON
Marina

STIBBINGTON
Water
Newton
Lock
WATER
NEWTON
AILSWORTH
Ferry
Meadows
Alwalton Lock

PETERBOROUGH
Embankment
Orton Lock
STANGROUND

Dog-in-a-Doublet Sluice
Tidal River Nene to The Wash
Stanground Lock
*King's Dyke to Middle Level
and Great Ouse Navigations*

N

The Wash
Sutton Bridge
Little Holland Drain
South Holland Main Drain
North Level Main Drain
Wisbech
Thorney River
Peterborough
River Nene
Whittlesey
Mortons Leam
Wansford
Corby
Oundle
River Nene
Thrapston
River Ise
Kettering
Irthlingborough
Wellingborough
Higham Ferrers
Rushden
Grand
Union Canal
Northampton
River Nene
ventry

The River Nene after the last Ice Age must have looked much as it did when this photograph was taken in 1991, with the river below Oundle in full flood.

cities, but the rivers upon which they stand have changed much in the interim.

The Rhine connection

Believe it or not, the subject of this book – the River Nene – was once a tributary of the River Rhine. In those far-off times the British Isles themselves did not exist – at least not as islands. They were part of the European continental land mass, and it was the great Ice Ages that alternately joined us to Europe then cast us asunder as the ice advanced and receded. So much water was locked up in ice at the peak of the Ice Ages that sea levels were a couple of hundred feet lower than they are today.

About 10,000 years ago the Nene was a very different river from the one we know today. It was in fact a torrent of meltwater from the mile-thick ice sheet to the north that was slowly disappearing as the last Ice Age receded. The massive floods that ensued ground through the soft limestone, ironstone and boulder clay to gouge out the familiar broad and fertile Nene valley. They also carried down countless millions of tons of sand and gravel, which were deposited on the valley floor to form the rich seams of minerals that are excavated for building materials today.

With the ice gone, the climate warmed. At first the valley was part of an inhospitable tundra where giant elk, mammoths and other long-extinct species of exotic mammals roamed. But as the temperatures crept ever upward, nomadic human settlers moved in from the continent, just before sea levels finally rose high enough to break through the land bridge where the Straits of Dover are today. Britain was now an island – and the Nene was no longer a tributary of the Rhine. She flowed into the newly-flooded North Sea,

which now separated her from her estranged parent river.

The changes since then have been far less dramatic, but at the same time much closer to all of us, because the biggest influence upon the Nene since the last Ice Age has been humankind. We have harnessed her, changed her course, polluted and exploited her. Yet still she bubbles out from her twin sources in the uplands of Northamptonshire, growing in stature as she flows downstream and on through the heart of England for 115 miles before emptying into The Wash.

Man's influence

Over the centuries the Nene's sluggish meandering course has borne witness to great events that were to shape the history of the world. The Romans arrived in the valley and lingered long enough to create massive garrisons and a riverside pottery industry that was renowned throughout their great empire. The rich invaders were able to build lavish villas overlooking the Nene at a time when the climate was mild enough for them to plant vineyards on the gentle slopes of its valley. Later the climate cooled and the Romans headed south in a vain attempt to shore up their declining empire, but they left behind a legacy of influence that would continue to shape lives – and the river itself – long after they had retreated to warmer climes.

Marauding Danes struck terror into the hearts of early settlers as they surged upstream in their warships to lay the foundations of settlements of their own – most of which still exist today. The Normans also found the lush valley to their liking, despite the considerable inconveniences they suffered from their new subjects. Fresh from his triumph over the Saxon

King Harold at the Battle of Hastings in 1066, William the Conqueror's militia headed north to the Fenlands around Peterborough only to suffer a series of setbacks from Hereward the Wake, who didn't accept the notion of being conquered.

Eventually triumphant, William granted much of the Nene valley to his favoured niece, Judith. In the closing years of the 11th century, this spoilt young woman was, through her uncle's generosity, able to enjoy the richest fruits of the land, for this fertile valley yielded the finest crops and grazing, plus some of the best hunting in the kingdom. At that time, of course, the dense oak woods of Rockingham Forest had not been decimated, and provided plentiful timber for building and fuel as well as cover for vast numbers of deer. Meanwhile watermills were built, harnessing the vibrant energy of the river itself for the benefit of all who lived in these parts.

The ordered way of life of the invaders from Normandy soon had an immense influence along the Nene. Northampton, built at the confluence of the river's two source streams, grew quickly to become one of Britain's most prestigious towns. The Middle Ages

There are few better views of the Nene valley than from the hill at Wadenhoe Church.

saw English monarchs open parliaments there, and monasteries flourished throughout the valley until Henry VIII curbed their powers and demolished their cloisters. Grand castles and abbeys alike had been build from the ample supplies of local stone. At Fotheringay there were both, and it was here in the forbidding castle looming over the Nene's quiet, willow-lined banks that a remarkable Scottish queen was cruelly executed.

In the 17th century a decisive battle in the English Civil War was fought at Naseby, at one of the twin sources of the Nene, which must have run red with the blood of thousands of slain Royalist soldiers.

Famous Nene folk

The folk of Northampton and the Nene valley were, on balance, more inclined towards Cromwell and his New Model Army, and the seeds of that non-conformist attitude were later to germinate in the New World, for buried in our churchyards are the ancestors of George Washington, arguably the world's greatest statesman and father of the United States of America. His influence upon a fast-changing new nation was matched only by another great American visionary, Benjamin Franklin, who – needless to say – also had the blood of Nene folk running through his veins.

Those folk were blessed with verve and imagination, not to mention entrepreneurial skills. They recognised the natural wealth of the valley in which they lived, and made their fortunes by exploiting it. The sweet grass of the rich, green water meadows produced livestock second to none, and it wasn't long before a thriving leather industry emerged. In the first half of this century Northamptonshire was still the shoemaking capital of the world.

Another natural resource, ironstone, saw the towns of the Nene valley at an advantage in the Industrial Revolution. Old men can still remember the furnaces and foundries of sleepy little towns like Islip, while the giant steelworks at Corby closed less than two decades ago. Today the night sky no longer glows red from the intense heat of the furnaces, and nature has repossessed the old quarries, but evidence of the wealth of iron ore in the rocks beneath our feet can be seen in the rusty-red stonework of many of our old buildings. Today heavy industry no longer plays a significant role in the Nene valley, no doubt much to the river's relief; the burden that she carried during the height of our industrial past came close to breaking her back.

Pollution perils

Historians with an eye on our imperial past like to remind us of the so-called golden age of the Victorians, but it can be argued that the often squalid search for riches during the 19th century was the most destructive era the country – and its rivers – ever knew. The Industrial Revolution brought the Nene to her knees. The sheer arrogance of the Victorians' attitude towards their environment should make us all feel queasy. In many respects they robbed us all of our birthright.

In the late 17th century, poet John Clare railed against the destruction of the pastoral world he loved so much. Today, through his pained verse, we can transport ourselves back to that lost world. Hopefully we may also appreciate him better than his contemporaries, who first sent him mad, then locked him up in a Northampton asylum.

But it wasn't just Clare who was mad. In setting their cold hearts on ruling the world, our forefathers decided to prove that Mother Nature herself existed only to be tamed. The River Nene was canalised and, in parts, straightened. Shallow riffles and pleasant meanders were obliterated in an attempt to control her sudden floods and open her up to navigation to supply the booming industries inland.

Worse still, below Peterborough the course of the river itself was diverted. Instead of heading south from the city and flowing through Whittlesey Mere – the largest freshwater lake in southern England – an ugly new cut was excavated to the north to shift the waters more quickly to the sea. Today, deep in the heart of the drained Fens, you can still find the old, severed course of the Nene as it twists and turns to no purpose through villages like Benwick and the market town of March, but it is no more than a stagnant shadow of its former self. Even Whittlesey Mere is long gone, pumped dry by a steam engine in a matter of weeks in 1851.

The catastrophic combination of Land Enclosure Acts and the birth of modern industry witnessed an unprecedented migration of the population from countryside to the expanding towns, which could never cope with the pressure created by that superheated Victorian economy. The waste products of both industry and population, from Northampton downstream, spewed virtually uncontrolled into the Nene.

Oddly enough, human sewage in small quantities isn't harmful to a river. As every good gardener knows, a bit of muck is beneficial on the land – and the same applies to water, but only in moderation. Plant and fish life both thrive from the nutrients present in animal waste,

Today the river is a playground - especially for anglers who travel from all over the country to sample the sport it offers.

but it's a delicate balancing act, and too much tips the scales irretrievably towards disaster. It's all down to the bacteria that break it down – they breed fast to cope with whatever is thrown at them, but if they multiply too rapidly they rob the water of dissolved oxygen, and every other living creature dies.

This pollution problem was compounded by the shoe factories that stood back to back in towns like Northampton, Wellingborough, Kettering, Rushden and Higham Ferrers. Deadly poisons like cyanide were used in the leather industry and some, inevitably, seeped into the river. Until 40 years ago heavy cyanide pollutions often swept down the river, with millions of water creatures perishing. For weeks afterwards the valley would be filled with the stench of bloated, decomposing fish.

After a century of abuse, in the 1950s the Nene was at an all-time low. But, remarkably, it was about to stage a recovery. The post-war years saw British heavy industry begin to decline and anti-pollution measures begin to improve. Slowly – ever so slowly – the ailing patient got better.

Today there are strict guidelines on effluent

Flooded gravel pits along the valley are now home to countless thousands of wildfowl.

discharges into rivers and stiff penalties for polluters. The Nene is cleaner – not perfect, but adequate – and getting cleaner all the time. The fish life makes it an angler's paradise, and herons and kingfishers are common sights along its banks. Even otters have returned to some of the wilder, lonely backwaters.

A haven for wildlife

Many of the flooded gravel workings between Northampton and Peterborough are now nature reserves of national importance where bird-watchers literally flock to train their binoculars and telephoto lenses on the latest rare arrivals. The Nene valley today is picturesque and alive with wildlife.

The 43 watermills that once ground grain along its banks are all now redundant, and commercial barges no longer use the Nene to ply their trades. The river is, to all intents and purposes, a playground. We sail and fish in her waters, we enjoy pints of ale and honest-to-goodness meals in the many fine pubs and restaurants that line her banks. Some of us just like to walk beside her on a sunny afternoon and simply enjoy being close to this wonderful river. This book is for all of you.

Everybody from the elderly grandparent to the toddling child is drawn like a magnet to the water.

Unlike our hunter-gatherer ancestors, we no longer need the proximity of the river for our very survival, but deep within our genes there still exists a little scrap of DNA that compels us to dip our toes in the margins all the same.

Although this book will guide you along the banks of the Nene, it is not a typical guide book. While it will certainly tell you how to sail on the river, catch fish to avoid the need for exaggeration, and be amply fed, watered and entertained, we aim to achieve much more than that.

The River Nene is a bright ribbon threading itself through the colourful tapestry of an historic part of England. It is our sincere hope that through this book you will come to appreciate the Nene, both past and present, and be encouraged to support those dedicated to securing its future for generations yet to come.

It's time now to join us as we bring the river, its people and their settlements to life. Climb aboard as we embark on a fascinating journey from source to sea, stopping off at all the celebrated places – as well as the special, hidden little nooks – along the way. Bon voyage!

Left The preserved Nene Valley Railway is the only surviving remnant of the railway that once ran alongside the river from Northampton to Peterborough. This angler at Splash Lane, Castor, is concentrating too hard to notice the steam train in the background.

Inset far left The Nene is a popular waterway for pleasure boaters, with more than 1,000 registered by the Environment Agency as well as many more visiting from the Midlands canal system.

Inset left The River Nene and its wildlife are for all to enjoy, as this young man feeding Denford's famous duck population would testify.

Right The Nene is always full of surprises. Who would expect to find such a pleasant, leafy view within walking distance of Northampton town centre?

The brook at Stoke Doyle is usually little more than a damp crease in the meadow, but summer storms can see it swell into a raging torrent, as it was when the second photograph was taken, in 1992.

1
The sources

The brook seemed purling sweeter by
As freshened from the cooling light
And on its breast the morning sky
Smiles beautiful and bright
The pool's still depth as night was by
Warmed as to life in curling rings
Stirred by the touch of water flye
Or zephyr's gentle wings

John Clare

Search for the source

There must be something special in the water that bubbles out the porous limestone hills in the uplands of south and west Northamptonshire. Is there some elusive ingredient that has weaned and nourished world statesmen, great writers, legendary heroes and industrialists? Perhaps it is time to bottle this magical elixir. Shakespeare's Avon, Oxford's Cherwell, Stamford's Welland and tributaries of Cromwell's Ouse all trickle into life from this great watershed, which is actually a continuation of the limestone ridge known further south and west as the Mendips and Cotswolds, and to the north-east as the Lincolnshire Wolds.

These same hills are also birthplace and cradle of the River Nene and its major tributary, the Ise. In fact, the Nene can boast *two* sources. One is close to Naseby, site of the great Civil War battle, where the Avon, Welland and northern branch of the Nene all emerge from the same hillside. So too does the River Ise, which is reunited with its parent at Wellingborough.

The southern branch emerges beneath the shadow of a great Iron Age hill fort, more than a mile west of Badby. Arbury Hill, at 734 feet, is the highest point in Northamptonshire, and from it – below a wild crab apple tree – bubbles the young River Nene. This branch is accepted by modern cartographers as the true

The source of the western branch of the Nene beneath a crab apple tree on a lonely hillside near Badby, Northamptonshire.

Arbury Hill, at 734 feet above sea level, is the highest point in Northamptonshire. Once a great Iron Age hill fort, it remains today the source of the western branch of the Nene.

Nene, although older maps and books often opted for the northern route. There is no point in arguing about something so academic: the lie of the land dictates that there are two separate Nenes until Northampton, where they unite to continue their journey to the sea as one.

My partner, Michelle Conway, joined me in my quest to locate and photograph the sources – the actual points where the infant twins emerge, burbling and blinking into the sunshine. The blazing hot summer of 1996 made the task arduous in every sense; trekking miles across country with the burden of heavy camera equipment is an overrated pastime when the temperature is pushing 90 degrees in the shade! It is all the more frustrating when shoulder-high jungles of stinging nettles and near-impenetrable barriers of bramble hedges have to be negotiated. But we were at least half-successful.

After a fortifying pint at the Maltsters Arms in Badby, we headed west across country, seeing the southern branch of the river diminish in stature at

Damp patches in the hillside were all that remained of the source of the northern branch of the river, near Naseby, in the long, hot summer of 1996.

every meadow. At times it disappeared altogether beneath tunnels of hawthorn and was in places swamped in muddy cattle drinks or choked by overgrown beds of rampant water mint. Dark green spikes of bog grass in a damp patch of field potholed by paddling cattle seemed a likely candidate, but again we found a trickle of water above it, yet further up Arbury Hill.

This unrivalled vantage point was the centre of a large royal estate in Saxon times, when the summit of the hill was occupied by an impressive fort, known as Badden burh – from which, much later, the village of Badby got its name. And it was here that we finally found what we were looking for.

Born beneath a crab tree

We were delighted that the Nene did not emerge in some nondescript, sodden bog. The point of emergence was plain to see as water trickled through a fissure in the rock, stained orange from some underground seam of ironstone. It was not merely visible, but audible too; a quiet, seeping chatter. The source was dappled in shade by an impressive wild crab apple growing directly above it. Excitedly, Michelle and I knelt down in turn to cup our hands and toast our endeavours with a taste of the pure Nenehead. It had a distinct mineral tang, which the warring Saxon kings of Arbury Hill must have known well more than 2,000 years before. The fort has long gone, but this jewel in a forgotten royal crown remains constant.

It was difficult to avoid feeling rather insignificant as we paused to reflect upon the history of mankind that had ebbed and flowed past this spot, while all the time the source before us had endured. Passing columns of Roman legionnaires must have paused here to slake their thirsts as they marched on to their garrisons on nearby Borough Hill; and, thousands of years further back into the mists of time, long-extinct animals like mammoth and sabre-toothed tiger probably used it as a watering hole. Packs of wolves would have loped down this hillside, while a little downstream a family of beavers probably endeavoured to construct a dam.

On a more personal note, I thought back to my own childhood. The turbid, tidal waters of the lower Nene was the very first river I ever knew when my mother took me on her weekly shopping trips to Wisbech. It had taken me 40 years to finally make the long pilgrimage upstream to the very beginning of that same river – and what a contrast! The mud-stained, polluted Nene at Wisbech cannot be compared to the pure spring born on a Badby hillside, yet they are one and the same.

Our quest for the northern source was frustrated

by the same blazing summer that turned the southern search into a sweat-soaked endurance test. The drought of 1996 that parched our countryside saw the Naseby source dry up completely and we found just an arid stream bed, interspersed with occasional damp patches. My hunch is that its source is close to the ugly embankment of the new A14 dual carriageway, but only a return in the wet season will prove that one way or the other. The Nene at this northern outpost is less appreciated than its illustrious neighbour the Warwickshire Avon, which emerges in the middle of the village in the landscaped garden of Manor Farm, no less, and whose birthplace is marked by a large, conical iron jug. Beneath the spout is inscribed the legend: 'Source of the Avon, 1822'. Every villager in Naseby knows the exact place where the famed Avon rises, but nobody in Northamptonshire seems to bother a jot that the humble Nene also starts in these parts. It remains largely ignored and, of course, underrated. It is my intention in this book to earn some well-deserved appreciation for my favourite river, but never to raise its status to the same giddy elevation of its neighbour. The Nene retains its wild, unknown places, and long may it do so.

A change in nature

It is above Northampton where the river is most unspoilt, generally rushing crystal-clear over a clean gravel and clay bottom. But even in these upper reaches Man has wrought subtle changes. Although the water is not yet polluted by sewage or industry, it is already beginning to be faintly tainted by chemical fertilisers that wash off the surrounding arable farmland and encourage excess weed growth. Dredging and drainage of the old flood meadows have also changed the nature of the river. The rich, waterlogged meadows used to act as a giant sponge, gradually releasing water to ensure a steady, even flow in the river. But today heavy rainfall is quickly evacuated into the Nene, causing it to become spate-like in character with flash floods, which equally rapidly subside. The issue is further complicated by the damming of many of the Nene's upland brooks to build great reservoirs; Pitsford, Ravensthorpe, Sywell, Daventry and Hollowell reservoirs all hold back water destined for the river.

As both upper courses progress downstream, falling 300 feet in the few miles down to the county town, the two infant rivers enter broad, flat valleys originally shaped by the grinding action of glaciers in the last Ice Age before finally merging at Northampton, the largest settlement they encounter before reaching the sea.

The Nene Way

Before they get there, let's look at some of the fascinating places they touch on the way. Starting on the southern course, we can begin at the village of **Badby**, famous for its nearby wood, which in May is ablaze with bluebells. It is also the start of the Nene Way, an ambitious cross-country footpath that follows the river for the next 67 miles. It was built by Northamptonshire County Council and ends at Wansford, on the Cambridgeshire border. It would be nice to see Cambridgeshire, Norfolk and Lincolnshire County Councils demonstrate the same enterprising spirit and continue this excellent facility all the way to the river mouth.

But the estuary is still well over 100 miles away. The next port of call for us is **Newnham**, which was in existence well before William the Conqueror landed on our shores. The Church of St Michael has a 15th century tower standing on three arches and in bygone days the bellringers were exposed to the elements as

Insignificant, but growing in stature: the infant Nene a mile below its source at Badby village.

they pulled on the ropes threaded through holes in the roof above their heads. The village was also the birthplace of the Elizabethan poet Thomas Randolph, and today boasts one of the few remaining hazelnut orchards in the country.

The next port of call, **Little Everdon**, is a tiny hamlet living in the shadow its big brother, **Great Everdon**. The pleasant rolling countryside of these parts was well known to the poet Thomas Gray, and may have been in the back of his mind when he wrote his immortal *Elegy*. His uncle, William Antrobus, was vicar of Everdon and a former Eton tutor who took the impressionable Gray under his wing as a youth.

The first settlement of substance is 2½ miles downstream, at **Weedon Bec**. The stripling Nene, growing now in size, is, however, dwarfed by more modern means of communication. The natural gap in the uplands here was first exploited by the Romans, who built their Watling Street (now the A5) through it. They were followed in the 18th century by the navigators who excavated the Grand Union Canal and built an aqueduct to carry it over the river, then the Victorians, who threw up great embankments to support the main railway line from London to Birmingham, and later on to Manchester and Glasgow; we know it today as the West Coast Main Line. Bisecting all three, and running parallel to the river, is another trunk road, the A45, which was once frequented by the infamous highwayman, Dick Turpin.

Weedon means 'Hill with a holy place', while the Bec part of the name refers not to the beck-sized upper Nene but to the Abbey of Bec Hellonin, who once owned the lands in these parts. There was a royal residence or monastery in Weedon in the 7th century. Once part of the Saxon kingdom of Mercia, legend has it that the locals had a great problem with wild geese eating the young corn crops in their fields until St Werburgh, a daughter of King Wulfhere, reproached them by performing a miracle and bringing a dead goose back to life. Since that time, it has been claimed, no wild goose has ever been seen grazing on young crops around the parish. These goosey goings-on are commemorated at St Peter's Church by a goose-shaped weather vane, while St Werburgh is depicted in a stained glass window.

Like Meriden and several other places in the heart of England, Weedon stakes a claim to be further from the sea than any other point in the British Isles. That claim was taken seriously in the Napoleonic Wars, when a Royal Military Depot was constructed in the village, just off the newly completed canal. The site was chosen by King George III as a bolt hole for when the expected invasion by the French began. The king's royal pavilion has since been demolished, but other military buildings remain, including a gatehouse with portcullis facing the canal.

Not much has changed at St Peter's Church, Weedon, since Edwardian times. The graveyard trees have grown and the old elm has gone, most likely a victim of Dutch Elm Disease, which has dramatically altered the familiar face of the English countryside in the last 20 years.

Before moving downstream, it is worth a 1-mile detour south along the Roman Watling Street to **Stowe Nine Churches**, a parish once visited, it is said, by the Devil. The village – which comprises Upper Stowe and Church Stowe – is named after an event more than 1,000 years ago, when the local residents decided to build a church at the foot of the hill. They tried eight times, but on each occasion their efforts were flattened mysteriously in the dead of night. Eventually they decided to keep watch and, one moonlit night, watched in terror as a fiendish creature the size of a wild boar used its superhuman strength to demolish the thick stone walls. Sensibly, the villagers abandoned the cursed building site and opted instead to make their ninth – and successful – attempt on the top of the hill, where it still stands to this day. Much of the Church of St Michael has been rebuilt, but the rugged Saxon tower remains – and is said to be leaning.

One village – two Presidents

The rival northern branch of the Nene can stake a claim on the ancestry of the first and most famous American President, George Washington. But close to the southern branch is the picturesque village of **Flore**, which can claim both the second and sixth Presidents, as well as the first of 43 watermills on the river.

Like the Nene itself, Flore has seen many name changes over the centuries. In the Domesday Book it was noted as Flora and other variations have included Floor and even Flower. Today it remains a fragrant place, especially in summer, when the pretty cottage gardens are in full bloom.

Two of those thatched cottages were, from 1662 and 1781, used as a Quakers' meeting house and the front gardens used as a burial ground. Of the 35 Quakers registered in the 700-year-old village church of All Saints, 21 were named Adams – including John Adams (1737) and Sarah Adams (1732), the parents of John Adams, second US President, and grandparents of John Quincey Adams, who followed his father to the Presidency 30 years later. The former is the best remembered, for he was the acknowledged giant in the great debate on the Declaration of Independence.

It is here also that we see early evidence of the Nene's tendency to flood. The field at the bottom of Flore Park, close to the church, isn't known as The Lakes for nothing. The village school is also worth a visit, for it has been the centre of the village's traditional May Day celebrations for more than a century. Each year the parish elects a May Queen, and the names of all of them, stretching back to 1890, are displayed on a board in the school.

Does every village on the Nene have a special claim to fame? You'll probably be forgiven for thinking so by the end of this journey. The next stopping-off point, a couple of miles downstream, is **Nether Heyford**. This lovely village boasts one of the biggest village greens in the country, at just over 2 hectares. It is bordered by lime trees and, until 1924, its grazing rights were let by 'sale of candle'. A pin was stuck into a lighted candle and bidding continued until the pin toppled.

The Church of St Peter & St Paul contains the tomb of Sir Walter Mauntell and his wife, holding hands. Sir Walter died in 1467, but the engraving on the brass is so clear that we can see every detail of the armour worn by the knight in the Wars of the Roses. His family had acquired the manor of Heyford a year earlier, but his fortunes were ruined by his son, who murdered a gamekeeper when he was caught hunting the king's deer in Sussex. The estate was later sold to Francis Morgan, whose monument is in painted alabaster on the south aisle of the church. The scarlet robes show that he was a judge of the King's Bench and he is said to have pronounced the death sentence on the unfortunate Lady Jane Grey. The manor house was later destroyed by Cromwell's troops during the Civil War due to the Morgan's Royalist sympathies, but was rebuilt in the early 18th century.

A futuristic fishery

For angling historians, the village is best known for the Heyford Fishery, a masterpiece devised by Daventry and Northampton tackle-dealer Ken Silverlock. As a custom-built competition venue it was the first of its kind in the country and has been imitated by many others in the decade since.

Ken realised that many match fishermen preferred to stage major competitions on canals because of the inherent fairness of these featureless waterways where fish tended to be spread evenly due to the lack of special holding features. But although canals were undeniably fair, their paucity of fish stocks hardly endeared them to anglers who wanted to catch a lot of fish.

His answer was to excavate landlocked canals of his own, artificially boosted with carp and other species of fish in numbers unheard of on an ordinary waterway. At the time of its opening, conservative anglers scoffed at the idea of a Canal to Nowhere, but Ken's vision has silenced his critics and today his futuristic fishery is the venue for many major national competitions.

Ken has planted 15,000 trees on the site to create an amenity to be enjoyed by all villagers. He also stages regular charity fishing matches to raise funds for a local children's hospice, which in 1996 benefited to the tune of over £700.

Right The Nene is already a substantial stream by the time it reaches this fine stone bridge at Kislingbury.

A milling tradition

The M1 motorway strides across the juvenile Nene valley below Heyford, but before we reach it we stumble across one of the few working water mills in the county. Well, almost.

Heygate's Mill – or rather the site on which it stands – was first mentioned in the Domesday Book, when it was forced to pay the third-highest rates in the county. Originally powered by water, it now relies upon electricity to produce flour. In 1969 it was the largest independent miller in the country and is still a major employer in the area.

Another mill follows a mile downstream at **Kislingbury**, a village that has grown in stature in recent years to serve as a dormitory village for the expanding urban sprawl of ever-encroaching Northampton. A fine stone bridge crosses the river at the approach to the village from the A45. Oliver Cromwell knew this place well, for his New Model Army, under General Fairfax, established its headquarters here prior to the Battle of Naseby before moving on to Guilsborough on the eve of that decisive turning point in the English Civil War. It was here that Cromwell's cavalry joined the foot soldiers.

We are getting close to Northampton now, but there is still time to visit the deserted parish of **Upton**. Today, humps and bumps in the surrounding fields are all that remains of a settlement that was record in the Domesday Book as Optone. Upton Hall, which dates back to the 17th century, is said to be haunted by the White Lady of Upton and, in 1611, was the birthplace of James Harrington, who embarked on a grand tour of Europe where, in Italy, he escaped with his life despite refusing to kiss the Pope's toe.

Harrington returned to England with republican convictions, yet accompanied Charles Stuart to Scotland and became gentleman-in-waiting to the beleaguered monarch when he was imprisoned in Holdenby House. Later he became famous for writing *Oceana*, an idealistic book in which he expounded his scheme for a commonwealth in which no one man held undue control. It should have appealed to Cromwell, but the Lord Protector was suspicious of Harrington's former royal connections and had him imprisoned in the Tower of London, where he went mad. He died in Plymouth in 1677, aged 66.

With the unmistakeable landmark of Northampton's Express Lift test tower in clear view, it is time now to adjourn a few miles north and trace the northern branch of the river.

The Battle of Naseby

Close to the source of the northern branch of the Nene in the village of Naseby stand two great monuments to

The Battle of Naseby was fought in 1645 close to the source of the northern branch of the Nene. The Cleopatra-esque needle erected in

one of the greatest battles ever fought on British soil. The Battle of Naseby on 14 June 1645 was the turning point in the English Civil War, where Oliver Cromwell's Roundheads achieved an historic victory over the Royalists, which spelled the end of the reign of King Charles I and determined the right of English people to run their own country.

Over 20,000 soldiers took part in that battle, about a mile outside the village. Yet, amazingly, its historical significance was not appreciated until 1823 when well-meaning Victorians erected a 60-feet-high stone monument, which, for some reason known only to the architect, was shaped like an Egyptian needle. Worse still, the bungling builders somehow contrived to erect in it the wrong place – more than a mile from the actual battlefield.

In 1936 aggrieved historians compensated for the earlier error by erecting a more modest monument on the spot from where Cromwell is believed to have led his momentous cavalry charge. Standing at the same elevated

1823 to mark the spot (left) was a mile away from the true location, marked by an equally improbable stone monument (right).

vantage point, you can share the panoramic view across the fields that Oliver himself scanned anxiously, minutes before that bloody battle. Some historians insist that even the second monument is wrong, and that it should have been erected a quarter of a mile away. Perhaps we may yet see a third Naseby monument.

Either way, local legend has it that the true marker of the exact spot lies buried 9 feet below the ground. It is said that Cromwell's dying wish was that he should be buried at the scene of his finest hour, and his body was duly smuggled out of London by his loyal supporters to be laid to rest at Naseby, where it remains to this day.

Cromwell country

Oliver Cromwell was born a mere dozen miles from the Nene at Huntingdon, in 1599. The son of a wealthy landowner, he attended Cambridge University, but left in 1617 upon the death of his father to manage the family estate. He also became involved in politics.

They were troubled times. In 1628 Parliament refused to approve new taxes requested by the extravagant King Charles I, who duly dismissed them. Cromwell sat in that parliament, as well as the new one called in 1640 by an increasingly desperate king. He was an outspoken opponent of the dictatorial monarch.

War broke out in 1642 and Cromwell returned to East Anglia to recruit an army – his famous Ironsides – who went on to victory at Naseby. The defeated Charles fled to Scotland, but was handed back to the English and imprisoned on the Isle of Wight. Cromwell at first tried to reach agreement with the king, but when it was discovered in 1649 that the latter had been plotting another civil war, the Lord Protector signed the former monarch's death warrant.

When Oliver died in 1658, he was succeeded as Protector by his son, Richard (1626-1712). But he was no match for his late father and was forced by the army to resign, allowing Charles II to regain the throne in 1662, thus ending the only period of republican government in England.

Washington's Old World

The stars and stripes that spangle the flag of the United States of America are perhaps the most potent symbols of power in the 20th century. But that imposing emblem of the biggest, brashest country of the Western World can boast its earliest origins in a secluded Northamptonshire village.

In a county renowned for its soaring spires, the humble, hunch-backed Church of St Mary the Virgin at **Great Brington** does not – from the outside, at least – merit a second glance. Its squat, functional tower never boasted a graceful, tapering finger of stone pointing heavenward. Yet step beyond its plain stone porch and you are transported to a place of worship that simply has no peers. This church has witnessed sermons, silent prayers and confessions that have shaped the world.

It was here that the hapless King Charles I took his final communion before he rode on to Naseby and lost his kingdom, as well as his life, to the Roundheads. It was also here that Lawrence Washington – ancestor of George Washington, first President of the United States of America – was buried in 1616. His memorial stone lies beneath the chancel of the church, bearing the family coat of arms that included the stars and stripes, which his great-great-great-grandson would later incorporate into his new nation's flag.

It is therefore no surprise that Great Brington is better known in America than it is in Britain. For its Washington connections don't stop there.

George Washington, arguably the most influential world figure of the last 200 years, died childless in 1799

The Washington family's coat of arms, pictured in St Mary's Church, Great Brington, later became the basis of the 'Stars and Stripes'.

at the age of 67. Countless academics have since attempted to trace his illustrious lineage, but it is only comparatively recently that the significance of Great Brington has come to light. Native Indians still had the North American prairies to themselves in 1532 when the first Washington of note – an earlier Lawrence – became Mayor of Northampton (an honour he was also to receive in 1545). At that stage the family's ancestral home was Sulgrave Manor, in the south of the county, but after his death in 1583 the Washington's wealth all but disappeared and his grandsons, Lawrence and Robert, were forced to flee to the twin villages of Great and Little Brington, where they were supported by their cousin and local landowner, the 1st Lord Spencer, who lived at nearby Althorp House.

Lawrence, who was appointed agent to manage his cousin's vast estate, was in 1606 installed in a newly built stone farmhouse in Little Brington. Here he and his wife Margaret raised 17 children. The fifth son, named after his father, died three years before his own eldest son, John Washington, emigrated to Virginia in

1656. As a confirmed Royalist, he was desperate to escape Cromwell's rule.

John – a colonel – founded a military dynasty that saw his son, Lawrence, and grandson, Augustine, both become army captains in their new country. And it was Augustine's son, General George Washington, who fought the greatest battle of all in winning independence from Britain in the bloody Civil War and founding the USA, becoming first President in the process.

By that time, of course, the once loyal Washingtons had abandoned their Royalist sympathies. But one Brington lad hadn't. His name was Peter Ridgeway and he fought as a redcoat against Washington's troops at the Battle of Bunker Hill. He too is buried in the village churchyard.

So much for American history. The historical significance of the Bringtons does not end there – far from it, for a future King of England can claim even closer ties to the village. The Spencer family that sponsored the Washingtons' move to the Bringtons 400 years ago had themselves arrived here almost 100 years earlier in 1508, when John Spencer bought the Althorp estate. Within seven years he had rebuilt the church at Great Brington and established the family shrine within it where he and his successors over the centuries now rest.

The Spencers went on to become one of the wealthiest titled families in the land, but their national

Right The lonely, church-less tower at Little Brington was saved from demolition after a plea from the RAF, whose pilots used it as a landmark.

fame reached new heights in 1981 when the late Earl Spencer's daughter, Lady Diana Spencer, wed HRH Prince Charles to become Princess of Wales. That glittering marriage sadly ended in divorce, and in August 1997 Diana died tragically in Paris following a horrific motor accident. She was just 36 years old and the country virtually ground to a halt in the extraordinary week of mourning that followed.

Diana was to have been buried beside her beloved father and 20 previous generations of Spencers in the family crypt at Great Brington church, but concern that her grave would become a tourist attraction as popular as Elvis Presley's at Graceland, Memphis, led to a change of plan by Charles, Diana's brother and the present Earl Spencer, who arranged for a lake in the grounds of Althorp Park to be consecrated by the Bishop of Peterborough. On Saturday 6 September 1997, following a funeral service at Westminster Abbey and unprecedented scenes of public grief throughout Britain and the world, Diana was finally laid to rest on an island in the centre of the ornamental lake, known as The Oval, and a favourite playground in those carefree days before she became a member of the Royal Family.

The death of the princess - Britain's 'Golden Child', according to the reworked words of 'Candle in the Wind', performed by Elton John at the funeral service - had probably the biggest impact on the monarchy since Cromwell's day. What the general public perceived as an uncaring attitude by the Windsors prompted an outcry and ensured that the Royal Family became better equipped to deal with the fast-changing world nearing the second millennium.

In that respect, Diana has left an enduring legacy to her sons, William and Harry, who are respectively second and third in line to the throne. Some time in the next century history will be made when a new king is crowned who not only has Northamptonshire blood coursing through his veins, but also shares a common ancestry with George Washington.

The churchless tower

Washington's home village of **Little Brington** boasts an impressive church tower and spire – but no church! It wasn't always so. The Church of St John was built by the 4th Earl Spencer in 1856. It is said he erected it because village folk could not be bothered to attend services at nearby Great Brington and the Earl feared they might start going to chapel instead.

Unfortunately his generosity was not rewarded by

The unspoilt upper reaches of the northern branch of the Nene, pictured below Brixworth.
Trout and crayfish populations exist here, clear evidence of the excellent purity of the water.

packed congregations. Far from it – by the end of the Second World War the church became disused and demolition began. But before the work was completed, the Royal Air Force asked for the tower and spire to be preserved, as they were used as a landmark by low-flying pilots, as they still are to this day.

Brixworth's Saxon church

History moves apace. When Arthur Mee embarked on his epic journey around the country to write the comprehensive 'King's England' series in the 1940s, he described **Brixworth** as an 'old-world village with cottages clustered round the 18th-century hall'. How times have changed.

Today Brixworth is a bustling place with sizeable housing estates serving the population that has overflowed from Northampton into the surrounding villages. It has not lost the shops, pubs and schools of many of its so-called unspoilt neighbours, and so remains a vibrant place, retaining a true sense of community. Sadly, so many picture-postcard Northamptonshire villages are doomed to decline into sterility as wealthy newcomers, their child-bearing years long behind them, colonise the thatched cottages. Dormitory villages are the scourge of the English countryside. We need places like Brixworth, where a natural mix of residents live in healthy harmony. We want villages where folk welcome the sound of the cockerel crowing in the dawn rather than ringing the local council's environmental health department to demand decibel-measuring instruments. . .

Brixworth boasts a venerable Saxon church with few rivals in all England. All Saints was built between AD 670 and 680 and is older than King Alfred. It is said to be the most imposing architectural memorial of the 7th century north of the Alps. The great arches are turned with Roman tiles and only St Martin's, at Canterbury, can definitely claim to be older. It is also said to contain an important relic – a bone of St Boniface, who travelled in Europe and crowned the father of Charlemagne.

Spencer's development

The lower reaches of the river's northern branch, which can be clearly seen on the left from trains arriving at

The upper reaches of the western branch of the Nene and the Grand Union Canal run parallel as they approach the town from the A45 bypass, close to the A43 junction. The Express Lift tower dominates the skyline.

Northampton station from Rugby, remain unspoilt as they approach the town and union with the western branch. Crayfish, the essential litmus test of water quality, are present, along with specimen roach topping 2 lb and some decent chub, perch and dace. There are even trout to be found, and otters are rumoured to be making a comeback to the area. But anglers and conservationists fear that this little watery paradise could be threatened by a multi-million-pound development scheme proposed by the Althorp Estate, which wants to develop 482 acres at Kings Heath, Northampton, building 2,000 new homes, factories and a shopping complex.

Northampton Nene Angling Club has controlled fishing rights on the 1-mile stretch for at least 40 years. Club vice-president Geoff Ringer told me: 'I grew up 150 yards from this bit of river and I've fished it ever since. It has already suffered over the years like most upper rivers through abstraction and canalisation, but it still holds some big fish. I can't see this plan being approved – it is a local beauty spot with lots of wildlife. Otters have been seen here.'

At the time of writing, in January 1997, Northampton Borough Council confirmed that it had received 200 individual letters of objection as well as petitions from local residents, anglers, nature lovers and environmentalists like Friends of the Earth.

In a report to councillors, the Director of Environmental Services admitted, 'The environmental implications of this planning application are profound and extensive.' Council spokeswoman Bridget Peet added, 'The planning application has been deferred because applications of this nature require considerable consultation. It will probably take several months or even a year before a decision is reached.'

We have already noted earlier in this chapter how the Spencer family has had an enormous impact on the countryside in these parts for many centuries. Let us hope that any schemes planned by the present Earl are in keeping with the family's proud traditional of stewardship and do not threaten a stretch of the Nene that has changed little since the last Ice Age.

2
Northampton to Wellingborough

Summer morning is risen
And to even it wends
And still I'm in prison
Without any friends

John Clare

Northampton town in the middle of the 19th century was not a happy place for our poet, John Clare, who spent the last two decades of his life there, locked up in a lunatic asylum. We'll meet him again later in Chapter 5, but in the meantime we'll continue downstream and enjoy the river – and town – he knew so well.

The northern and western branches of the river finally unite in the south-west corner of the old town, a little above the South Bridge and the distinctive Carlsberg Brewery, and almost opposite the junction of the Northampton branch of the Grand Union Canal. The Nene is now navigable, connected via the canal to the Midlands waterways network, and downstream to The Wash and, ultimately, the North Sea. The absolute upstream limit of navigation on the Nene itself is a little further along the northern arm, at West Bridge.

Historic Northampton

Northampton is steeped in history, and no wonder. Archaeologists have unearthed evidence proving that people have lived here for around 5,500 years. Excavations at Briar Hill in the late 1970s found a large, circular earthwork enclosure where Neolithic farmers held tribal ceremonies. It was built around 3,500 years before the birth of Christ and abandoned about 1,500 years later. Overlooking the town is Hunsbury Hill, today a modern housing development, but occupied by Celtic tribesmen between 400 BC and AD 20. Known locally as Danes Camp, it was in fact a

thriving township long before the Danes or even the Romans arrived.

The Romans, in fact, did not arrive until a couple of decades later, when they founded a small market town where Duston stands today. They stayed until around AD 300 and all was quiet for 500 years until the Danes stormed in and made Northampton a base for their armies, which conquered the old kingdom of Mercia, of which the town was part. In AD 913 the Anglo-Saxon Chronicle reported an army riding out of 'Hamtun' to kill many men. This is the first recorded written reference to the town that was about to grow and prosper with the trade and crafts encouraged by the new invaders.

Saxon Hamtun covered 60 acres and was defended by the Nene to the south and west. After the Norman Conquest of 1066 it expanded rapidly and within 20 years there were 300 houses and 1,500 residents. During the century that followed, the expansion continued at a breakneck pace and town walls were built, enclosing an area of 245 acres, making Northampton the third largest town in England.

Through the centuries Northampton's fortunes waxed and waned. The Plague, or Black Death, struck at least twice, in 1349, when as many as half the population died, and again in 1638, when 533 people – one-seventh of the population – succumbed. In 1516 a great fire swept through the old town, destroying a large part of it, but another in 1675 was even greater, razing three-quarters of the buildings and making 700 families homeless.

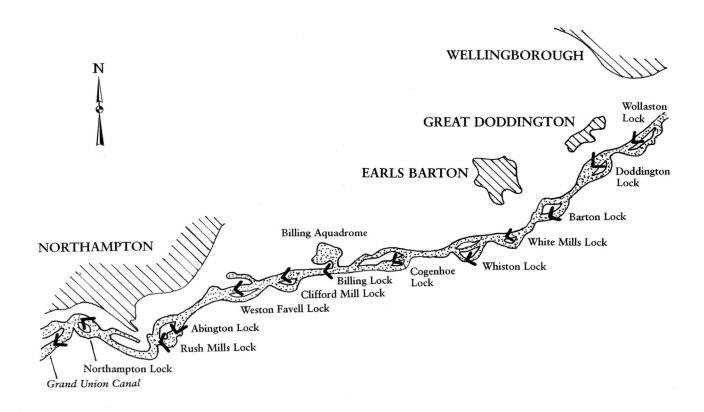

The town also knew strife. In 1264 rebellious knights from all parts of the kingdom assembled at Northampton and a large army under the command of King Henry III and Prince Edward attacked and broke down the town walls. The rebels were taken prisoner and the town pillaged for its treachery. Then, in 1460, the banks of the Nene near Midsummer Meadow were the bloody setting for the Battle of Northampton, a key engagement during the Wars of the Roses. The Earls of Warwick and March defeated Henry VI's forces and the king was taken prisoner.

Two centuries later, in 1643 at the start of the English Civil War, Northampton was attacked by Prince Rupert and an army of 2,000 men. The anti-Royalist townsfolk, however, thwarted his attempts to enter the town via the old north gates with cannon and musket fire.

These were intolerant times. In 1557, during the reign of the Catholic Queen Mary, a local shoemaker named John Kurde was burned to death for his Protestant belief and in 1612 five women and a man were executed for alleged witchcraft. As late as 1787 an estimated 10,000 people crowded into the town to witness the public execution of six members of the infamous Culworth gang of highwaymen, who had been terrorising the neighbourhood as well as the surrounding counties for more than a decade.

A few decades after that, the shoe industry began to flourish and Northampton saw a great expansion as people from the surrounding villages flooded into the town to work in the industry. Around 1800 the population stood at 7,000, but a century later it was 87,000. Population growth then slowed until the Northampton Development Corporation was formed in 1968 to expand the town and accommodate overspill from London. By the time the Corporation was wound down in 1985, Northampton had built another 20,000 homes, housing 40,000 newcomers.

First steps of industry

The urban sprawl that clutters the Nene valley between Northampton and Irthlingborough has been lambasted in the past, not least by the valley's own popular novelist, H. E. Bates, who scorned the red-brick factories and houses that sprang up and smothered the picturesque stone-built villages during those heady days when Northamptonshire was the shoemaking capital of the world. But the outside world was less judgemental and respected the county for its footwear – as it still does today.

Great armies have marched to battle in Northamptonshire boots. Today everybody from fashion-conscious Californian teenagers to toiling

Red-brick shoe factories still line many of the streets north of The Mounts area of Northampton.

Latvian labourers share an affinity for the world-famous 'Doc Marten' shoes and boots from the Nene valley. They, and other brands of footwear from the area, still maintain a global fame for quality based upon centuries of world dominance. There was a time when Northampton and its neighbouring towns literally couldn't put a foot wrong.

Nobody should be surprised that this enviable state of affairs came about. Leather was always an important product in the lush Nene valley, which yielded rich grazing for the cattle that provided the hides as well as plentiful oak forests for the tanning. The river itself produced the copious quantities of water required. Saddlers and shoemakers were already important members of the business community in Northampton by the 13th century. It was in 1213 that the first written record of the town's footwear industry was recorded, when a pair of boots were made for the infamous King John. At that time wool and cloth produced rather more prosperity for the town, but by 1401 there were sufficient shoemakers to form the first guild, and by the middle of the 16th century shoemaking was the largest craft.

The greatest boost to this industry came in the 17th century during the troubled years of the English Civil War. Northampton craftsmen received important military contracts to produce the boots for Cromwell's army. In 1642 4,600 pairs of boots and shoes were ordered for the Roundheads for a bloody tour of Ireland, and another major order followed six years later. Oliver's New Model Army was apparently happy with the end results, for orders began to flood in for armies fighting in the far-flung shores of the expanding British Empire.

In 1712 John Morton wrote: 'The principal manufacture at present is that of shoes; whereof mighty numbers are, and have been, sent to foreign plantations, and to the Army in Flanders. Northampton has for many years had the reputation of the best shoes of any place in England.'

He was echoing Northamptonshire antiquarian, Thomas Fuller, born by the Nene at Aldwincle, who in 1662 famously remarked that 'the town of Northampton may be said to stand chiefly on other mens' legs'.

During the 19th century the industry flourished as never before. The area of Northampton east of The Mounts was the centre of the trade and the red-brick factories that H. E. Bates so detested soon covered this area, as well as spreading down the valley through Earls Barton, Kettering and beyond. At the end of Queen Victoria's reign approximately 40 per cent of the adult urban population were employed in the shoe industry.

In those days warfare depended upon footwear. Armies consisted of tens of thousands of foot soldiers, who lived up to their name by marching long distances to battle. Boots were the military hardware of the day and their strength, warmth and ability to keep out water could mean the difference between victory and defeat. The troops of Napoleon and Hitler, although separated by a century, both foundered in the harsh discomfort of Russian winters – how those hapless, frostbitten armies must have longed for stout, Northampton-manufactured boots! It's a sobering thought that the Second World War might have ended on a very different note but for the Nazi army's second-rate footwear as they marched towards Moscow. That alone should have been cause to celebrate the superiority of the home-grown product, but instead of a well-deserved boom, the post-war years saw the Northamptonshire shoe industry suffer.

The austerity of the war years resulted in a dramatic

Northampton. *Abington Street*

The old view of Abington Street, Northampton, was probably taken between 1910 and 1920. But by 1996 all the buildings have either disappeared or been changed beyond recognition. Such is progress.

*The poet John Clare mused upon the steps outside All Saints' Church, Northampton, during the final decades of his troubled life,
and the scene can have changed little by the time the 'past' photograph was taken in the early years of the 20th century.
But horse-drawn carriages had been well and truly replaced by the motor car by 1996.*

mood swing by the British public. They didn't want solid, sensible footwear any more – they wanted to be frivolous. Just a few years previously Italy had been our arch-enemy, but in the post-war years flimsier, fashionable styles from the Mediterranean began to gain favour with a fickle population who were in the mood to let their hair down. So what if foreign shoes only lasted half as long? The consumer boom meant that fashions were changing long before shoes had worn out.

Cheaper, mass-produced imports began to flood in from other countries where labour costs were cheaper, and soon the Northamptonshire footwear factories fell into decline. Like so many other British industries, they couldn't compete on equal terms.

Today the bulk market has gone. But the Nene valley still produces plenty of footwear, thanks to its reputation for never compromising quality. Modern machinery has replaced the closing-rooms of the early 19th century, when whole families worked from home to hand-sew shoes and boots, but the solid reliability remains.

Even now Northampton and the Nene valley is renowned throughout the world for footwear. Shoe manufacturers Philip Manfield (1819-99) and William Barratt (1877-1939) remain familiar High Street names, and both are further recognised in their home town by a hospital and maternity home, respectively. In the middle of the pedestrianised Abington Street in Northampton town centre stands an impressive bronze sculpture called the 'Cobbler's Last', which depicts two young children skipping across the tool of the shoemaker's trade. Those youngsters are representatives of tens of millions of children worldwide who have grown up wearing Northamptonshire shoes. Meanwhile, Northampton's Central Museum & Art Gallery on Guildhall Road boasts the world's biggest boot and shoe collection.

More famous still are the fashionable 'DMs', or 'Doc Martens', which are produced in huge numbers along the Nene valley downstream to Irthlingborough. The boots go back to wartime Munich, when a Dr Klaus Maertens made himself a pair of shoes out of old tyres following a skiing accident. Later, with his old friend Dr Herbert Funck, he managed to produce a leather shoe with the trademark air-cushioned sole.

In 1959 Wollaston-based R. Griggs & Co (founded 1901) bought the rights to manufacture the shoes in Britain and the first 'Dr Martens' rolled off the production lines in 1960. They were instantly popular with postmen, policemen and other workers who were on their feet for long periods. They were later to become fashionable footwear items for teenagers, starting with the skinheads of the late 1960s, through to the brighter young things of today. The first

aristocrat ever to wear them was said to be Viscount Stansgate, later left-wing politician Tony Benn, who wore them on protest marches in the early 1960s. Other fans, apparently, include the Dalai Lama and the Pope.

Today the success of the 'DM' goes from strength to strength and the Griggs Group enjoys annual sales of £170 million. It is said that the weekly production could fill Wembley Stadium twice over.

On a lighter note, you could be forgiven for thinking that the local football club's nickname, The Cobblers, had something to do with their relentlessly disappointing performances! In fact it is a plain statement of what Northampton is famous for. Perhaps their fortunes would change if a local company started making superior football boots for them. . .

Northampton Town Football Club is trying hard to live down the dubious distinction of achieving a place in soccer history through its a free-fall from the First to the Fourth Divisions of the old Football League in consecutive seasons. More than 30 years on it is now housed in a proud new stadium at Sixfields, and counting on local support to herald in some long-awaited glory, glory days. At the time of writing, in January 1997, The Cobblers are in contention for a play-off place to Division Two.

The most famous brewery in town (probably)

The Nene valley has long been famous for its pubs as well as its breweries – and nowhere more so than in Northampton, which, even in the 18th century, could boast no fewer than 60 inns. The George, on the corner of George Row and Bridge Street, was described by the writer Daniel Defoe as 'more like a palace than an inn' with its 40 rooms and stabling for thirsty visitors' horses.

Brewing was an important art throughout the valley, with many independent, family-run breweries producing ales for all tastes. The Wisbech-based Elgoods Ales still does just that from its famous North Brink brewery, supplying pubs throughout the Fens as well as upstream to Fotheringay.

Northampton's South Bridge area has long been dominated by breweries. Earlier this century P. Phipps & Co Ltd and the Northampton Brewery Company were based in the locality, while later Watney Mann operated a large brewery on the riverfront. But all were dwarfed in 1972 by the futuristic new Carlsberg Brewery that appeared on the site. The northern branch of the Nene was actually diverted to join the western branch 100 yards further upstream in order to make way for the massive new building.

Carlsberg lager has been brewed in Denmark since 1847. It was first sold in Britain in 1868, when lagers

Left This quiet junction once buzzed with activity, for it marked the connection of the Northampton branch of the Grand Union Canal - a vital trade route to the Midlands before the railways were built in the middle of the 19th century.

Below This aerial view of the Nene at Northampton, taken in 1972, shows the massive Carlsberg Brewery under construction. The river itself, in the left foreground, was diverted to make way for this development, but the entrance to the Grand Union Canal remained unchanged (bottom right). The northern end of the South Bridge can just be seen at the extreme right-hand edge, before the river continues to Becket's Park, just beyond the top right of the picture. Carlsberg Tetley

Opposite The award-winning architecture of the futuristic Carlsberg Brewery has blended nicely into the riverside scene in the quarter-century between these two photographs, taken in the winter of 1972-73 and the autumn of 1996. Carlsberg Tetley/author

were a rarity, but they now represent more than half of the UK beer market – and Carlsberg has been instrumental in that change. The company's founder, J. C. Jacobsen, was born in 1811, the only son of an established Danish brewer, Christen Jacobsen, of Copenhagen. In 1835 Christen died, leaving his son sole heir to the business, which he systematically improved with a scientific approach to the so-called bottom fermentation of lager beers. The first Carlsberg brewery – named after his son, Carl – was built in 1847, and the company never looked back. Its success enabled Jacobsen to set up the Carlsberg Foundation in 1876, which financed a scientific laboratory and funded a museum and works of art in Denmark, including the famous Little Mermaid sculpture at the entrance to Copenhagen harbour.

The success of the Carlsberg brew in Britain through the 1960s encouraged the company to build the Northampton brewery, which stands on a 20-acre site and has a capacity of two million barrels a year. It brews only lagers – the original Carlsberg Lager, Carlsberg Export, Carlsberg Special Brew, Tuborg Gold, Carlsberg Beer and, more recently, Carlsberg Ice. It was opened on Friday 10 May 1972 by HRH Princess Benedikte of Denmark. The brewhouse, which achieved its first brew in August 1973, faces on to the river and is particularly dramatic at night, when the brewing machinery is lit up and in full view through the huge glass windows measuring 26 metres by 70 metres. It is certainly striking, and in 1975 it was selected as the 'outstanding winner' of the ninth Financial Times Industrial Architecture Award.

The Campaign for Real Ale may bemoan the loss of many of the small, local breweries, but the truth is that the pub drinker has never had it so good when it comes to choice. Most pubs along the Nene valley offer a range of real ales as well as cool, refreshing lagers. The latter may not impress the real ale aficionados, but they are certainly very welcome after a summer's day by the river! I'll leave it to the reader to decide whether he or she agrees that a certain product brewed in Northampton lives up to its claim as 'probably the best lager in the world'.

An Archbishop's escape

Moving downstream from the South Bridge we pass what was once a thriving commercial centre where barges loaded and unloaded alongside wharfs and

South Bridge, Northampton (below), and the view downstream (right). This area, once dominated by industrial premises and warehousing, could now become a picturesque riverside walk within easy reach of the town centre.

warehouses. Today the area is being redeveloped and may soon be as attractive as the next port of call, Becket's Park, which is named after the famous yet unfortunate former Archbishop of Canterbury, who was later made a saint. To find out why, we have to slip back over 800 years to a time when there was a constant power struggle between sovereign and church. The Archbishop of Canterbury, Thomas à Becket (1118-70), was fatally involved in that conflict and Northampton was the setting for one of the key episodes that eventually led to him being murdered on the altar of his own cathedral.

The son of a rich merchant, Becket was a close friend of the young King Henry II and was made Lord Chancellor in 1155 before becoming Archbishop in 1162. At this point he abandoned the extravagant trappings of court life, opting instead for a simple, religious existence. He soon found himself in conflict with his former ally, the king, when he refused to accept the sovereign's authority in church affairs. The row boiled over at the Council of Clarendon, held in Northampton in 1164. Becket realised that his life was in danger and escaped through a gate in the old town walls – which still stands at the northern corner of Becket's Park and is known to this day as Becket's Well.

Becket eventually fled to France, where he appealed to the Pope, and in 1170 Henry allowed his absentee Archbishop to return to England. He was received by rapturous crowds, appreciative of his stance against regal authority. However, instead of resuming his pious existence, Becket foolishly meddled in politics, punishing some bishops who had supported the king. The news reached exasperated Henry, who groaned: 'Will nobody rid me of this turbulent priest?' Unfortunately he was overheard by four over-zealous knights who promptly rode to Canterbury Cathedral and hacked Becket to death at the altar.

His assassination rocked the religious establishment and in 1173, three years after his murder, Pope Alexander III made him a saint. He is also commemorated in a stained glass window at the cathedral, close to the murder scene. Ironically, it depicts Becket and the king as friends. With friends like that. . .

Becket's Park was for centuries known as Cow Meadow, because freemen of the town were allowed to graze their cattle there. But by Victorian times it became a popular public park, despite the close proximity of the town's raw sewage outfall – the smell from which had to be treated in hot weather by dumping cartloads of chloride of lime into it. Incredibly, the intake for Northampton's public water supply was located nearby,

This pleasant view of Becket's Well, taken around 1920, would probably have been recognised by the troublesome Archbishop himself as he fled from the town in 1164. But by the time the modern view was photographed, in 1996, the constant stream of heavy traffic pouring into Northampton had destroyed the tranquil scene for ever.

Above and right These picturesque views of the river at Becket's Park (formerly Cow Meadow) clearly show the riverside haven that tends to be neglected by the hordes of shoppers and visitors in the town centre, just a short stroll away.

with pumps to propel water through bored elm pipes to the town centre.

The open spaces of the park were also used by pupils from a nearby girls' school for games. Local wags could not resist making unkind remarks about the young ladies of Cow Meadow, and the embarrassed headmistress was successful in getting the name changed in 1934. The former Cow Meadow Lock – the first to be encountered on the river – was renamed Northampton Lock at the same time. Interestingly this lock was the last to be constructed in 1761 when the Nene was first made navigable to Northampton, as well as the first to be replaced when the navigation was modernised in the 1930s. Today the 18-acre park remains an unspoilt green oasis within easy walking distance of the bustle of the town centre, yet is under-used by locals and visitors alike. Sadly, many thousands of people visit Northampton each year without ever knowing that the River Nene runs through it.

The masters of modern trout fishing

Some of the finest fly fishermen in the history of the sport have hailed from Northampton. This is due in no small part to an accident of geography, for nowhere in lowland England is there more abundant stillwater trout fishing.

Ravensthorpe and Hollowell reservoirs were early trout fisheries, but it was the opening of Pitsford Reservoir in 1963 and Grafham Water in 1966 that revolutionised the sport. But saying that is to take nothing away from the men on the spot who led the way in catching the fish made available.

Chief among them was Bob Church, Northampton born and bred, who was already well known as a pioneering big-fish angler, specialising in the capture of big eels from the Grand Union Canal on the outskirts of the town. Inspired by local trout experts like Cyril Inwood (nymph fishing) and Dick Shrive (deep lures), Bob turned his talents to trouting.

His creations included the famous Church Fry, Appetiser and June Fly. He also developed the boat drogue, was the first to use lead-core shooting heads and was largely responsible for the success of trout match fishing. He now runs a successful Northampton-based tackle and outdoor clothing manufacturing business.

Washlands flood prevention scheme

The Nene around Northampton has been much changed by drainage engineers, concerned by the threat of flooding to much of the building development that has been allowed – foolishly, some may say – to take place in recent decades upon the river's flood plain. A broad, deep channel was dug to bypass the inadequate old course of the river alongside the Bedford Road and a new sluice was constructed. In 1976 a reservoir was also built to hold back floodwater, which is pumped into the washlands at the Bedford Road sluice to be released later at Weston Favell Lock when the risk of inundation lower down the valley is minimised. The total storage capacity is 500 million gallons and the scheme was completed in 1979 at a cost of £3.8 million.

Billing Aquadrome

Billing Mill was among many in the Nene valley mentioned in the Domesday Book. It remained a working mill until the Second World War and today has been restored to working order as a mill museum, forming part of the Billing Aquadrome holiday complex.

The meadows in these parts were excavated from gravel in the early part of this century. When the workings became redundant, in 1928, the owner, Sam Mackeness, landscaped the area to provide an inland rival to the holiday camps being built along the coast by Billy Butlin.

The complex was closed during the Second World War, but re-opened when hostilities had finished to a true 'Hi-Di-Hi' atmosphere. Today new leisure facilities have been added to create a site-caravan village, with accommodation for touring vans as well as regular special events and vintage car rallies.

In the 1950s Billing also hit the angling headlines when its lakes began producing monster carp. These fish were of the same fast-growing Galician strain stocked into the famed Redmire Pool in Herefordshire, and were in fact were supplied by the same Surrey fish farmer, Mr Donald Leney. Until 1957 no angler had ever landed more than one carp over 20 lb in a single session, but Northampton expert Bob Reynolds achieved the unique feat of landing two – twice in the space of a week! More big carp followed, including a 42-pounder to another local, Ray Clay, in September 1966. At the time it was only the second carp over 40 lb from the British Isles.

Today big carp are still present at Billing, but the noise and activity from the thousands of visitors make serious fishing difficult, to say the least. But one or two dedicated specialists still persevere, and venerable specimens estimated at over 50 years old and weighing in excess of 30 lb have been recorded in recent years.

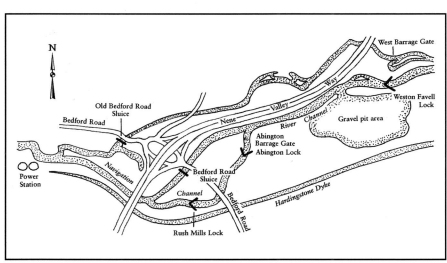

The Northampton flood prevention scheme.

Statesman supreme

And so we move on downstream, past yet more myriads of gravel workings to **Cogenhoe**, pronounced 'Cook-noe'. Its church dates back to the 13th century when the Lord of the Manor, Nicholas de Cogenhoe, commissioned the present building, which contains his effigy – a cross-legged knight – in the south aisle.

But it is on the other side of the river, at **Ecton**, where we again stumble upon a spine-tingling slice of history. In this pleasant village we know that we are treading in the footsteps of the ancestors of one of the most brilliant men the world has ever known.

Some men become great statesmen, others diplomats. Yet more become famous writers and scientists. Benjamin Franklin (1706-90) was one of that almost unique breed who became all four. One of the greatest figures of American history, Franklin's achievements included helping to write the Declaration of Independence and the first United States Constitution.

The 15th of 17 children, he was born in Boston, Massachusetts, where he became a printer and earned enough money to buy his first newspaper, the *Pennsylvania Gazette*, in 1728. At the same time he founded a university, one of the earliest fire brigades, and became postmaster. In 1752 he proved that lightning was caused by electricity by flying a kite in the middle of a thunderstorm. He duly invented the lightning conductor. He is even credited with the invention of bifocal spectacles and the rocking chair.

Unlike Washington, Franklin returned to his ancestral home at Ecton on the River Nene and felt a warm affection for the old country. He came across as a diplomat in 1764 to try to solve the disputes between Britain and America, which was then still a colony. While here he could not resist paying a pilgrimage to Ecton and the grave of his uncle, Thomas Franklin, who had been the village blacksmith until his death in 1702.

Although a staunch supporter of American independence, Franklin favoured conciliation instead of the bloody War of Independence that followed. Following the conclusion of that epic struggle, he was made ambassador to France, returning to the USA in 1785 to be made Governor of the state of Pennsylvania.

Another Saxon monument

In the last chapter we visited Brixworth and its celebrated Saxon church. Now, at **Earls Barton**, we witness yet another piece of Saxon church architecture that acted as a landmark in this area a hundred years before William the Conqueror's Norman troops landed at Hastings. The exceptional west tower of All Saints Church is decorated with raised vertical strips and is believed to have been a look-out tower for the community in the days when water-borne invaders were an ever-present threat.

When the church was built the village was known simply as Barton. It did not acquire the 'Earls' suffix until the 12th century, when the manor was owned by David, Earl of Huntingdon. In those days the tanning of animal hides was the chief industry in the village, and it continued until 1984. No tanneries exist today, but of course the leather and shoe industry is as important as ever.

A mile downstream, at **Great Doddington**, is Hardwater Mill. It is here that Thomas à Becket is believed to have fled after escaping from Northampton. At that time the mill was owned by the nuns of Delapre Abbey in Northampton, and they are said to have offered him shelter before he secretly slipped off to Great Doddington manor house to plan his exile to France.

Wellingborough's poor son

As it approaches **Wellingborough** the Nene flows around yet more gravel pits, and a major nature reserve, dividing into two channels to negotiate Upper Wellingborough Lock, and disappearing beneath the A45 flyover before emerging at Whitworth's famous Victorian mill, built by J. B. Whitworth in 1866 after his previous premises on the Great Ouse at Turvey had been gutted by fire. The site for the new mill was chosen because of the superiority of the Nene's navigation, with its connection upstream at Northampton to the Midlands canal system. The newly built Blisworth-Peterborough railway (at which we'll look in more detail in Chapter 5) also offered much-improved communications. Road transport, of course, began to play an ever-increasing role in the 20th century, but river barges still loaded and unloaded at the mill until the 1960s. Like most towns along the flood-prone Nene, the centre of Wellingborough is situated a full mile from the river. But the embankment, known locally as The Walks, is still a very attractive public place and is famous for its flocks of semi-tame mute swans always eager to be fed. It is interesting to note that around 1320, when most of the town was owned by Crowland Abbey, the enterprising abbot founded a swan farm in this area.

The town itself is well worth a visit. Its famous public school was founded in the reign of Richard II and retains some of its fine old buildings. But one of Wellingborough's most famous sons did not receive the benefit of expensive schooling. He was John Askham, a poor cobbler's son born in 1825, who went to work at the tender age of 10, yet who later wrote poetry surpassed only by that of his hero, John Clare. Despite hardships and physical handicap, he published five volumes of verse and, in recognition of his work, received a grant of £50 from the Queen's Bounty. He named his home Clare Cottage and died there in 1894, aged 69.

In times past Wellingborough was also famous for its wells and springs, which is how it is supposed to have got its name. The most famous of the wells were the Red Well and the White Well, the former so named because of its water's ironstone content that was supposed to boast health-giving properties. In the 17th century it even looked likely that the town would become a fashionable spa, but this never amounted to much. A little over a century ago a local brewery tapped into the Red Well and advertised its iron-rich brews as possessing stimulating medicinal qualities. The subsequent disappearance of both the brewery and its products indicates that the drinking public were less than enthusiastic.

It was no easy task standing in the same spot as this early 1960s view of Sheep Street, Wellingborough, as the vantage point today is in the middle of a very busy one-way system. The pace of life has changed, but most of the old buildings remain intact.

3
Irchester to Thrapston

The sun looks down in such a mellow light
I cannot help but ponder in delight
To see the meadows so divinely lye
Beneath the quiet of the evening sky

John Clare

Iron Age Irchester

On the outskirts of Wellingborough, and close to **Irchester**, the Nene's biggest tributary, the lovely River Ise, joins the parent stream. This important meeting place has also been a gathering point for humans over the centuries. Iron Age traces have been unearthed here by archaeologists, and an important walled Roman town stood here in the 4th century, close to the river and a little north of the present site of Irchester.

The most impressive modern monument to Man's architectural prowess is the imposing Wellingborough viaduct, which strides across the valley carrying the main railway from Sheffield, Nottingham and Leicester to London, stopping at Kettering and Wellingborough en route. It was originally opened as the Leicester & Hitchin extension of the Midland Railway on Thursday 7 May 1857, then later, in 1868, the MR built its own line from Bedford to its own terminus in London at St Pancras. Today's High Speed Trains are operated by the privatised Midland Mainline company.

Returning to the Nene, we now move on to **Ditchford**, where a bridge has crossed the river since at least 1292. The Domesday Book also mentions a mill on the river here, which would have stood where the animal waste products processing plant now stands. Despite the rather offensive smells that waft across the river here – especially in high summer – the fish do not seem to mind and the fast-flowing backwater close to the factory is a noted hot-spot for roach, bream and

Anglers from all over the country travel to the Nene to enjoy superlative fishing. Pictured here is Graham Eden, whose 4 lb 8 oz bream and wide grin combine to demonstrate that his long journey from Mansfield to Ditchford was considered worthwhile.

Almost 90 years separate these two views of Higham Ferrers Market Place, taken in 1907 and 1996. The famous chestnut trees that feature in the writings of local author H. E. Bates can hardly be seen for parked traffic in the modern shot.

chub; the latter can be clearly seen around the sanctuary of the overhanging tree above the road bridge.

Earlier this century the area was nicknamed Ditchford-on-Sea, thanks to the vast numbers of holidaymakers who swarmed to the area courtesy of the Blisworth-Peterborough railway. Passenger services on the line were withdrawn in May 1964 by the infamous axeman, Dr Richard Beeching, although Ditchford station itself was closed to passengers as early as 1924.

Simply perfick!

Nostalgia is a central – and very worthy – theme of this book. We all rightly yearn for a past, which so often seems better and more secure than the present. The so-called 'feel-good factor', which proves so elusive to modern politicians, resolutely insists upon coming home to roost in those decades that have slipped by, yet are still within memory's easy recall.

The millions of eager television viewers who boosted

The Darling Buds of May to the top of the ratings charts did so because they loved to wallow in a warm, comforting bath of nostalgia. The fictional Larkin family provided a rose-tinted tonic with which we could all identify. And no wonder. The series was based upon a trilogy of books by the Rushden-born author H. E. Bates – a prolific writer whose ability to express Englishness was peerless.

Herbert Ernest Bates was born on 16 May 1905 in Rushden, a town that was to later feature in his books, thinly disguised as 'Evensford'. He spent much of his childhood on his maternal grandfather's farm on the outskirts of nearby **Higham Ferrers**, and loved to walk along the Nene valley with his father, from whom he inherited his love of the countryside.

Young H. E. was fortunate to win a scholarship to Kettering Grammar School, where, in 1919, he was taught English by Edmund Kirby, an infantry officer who had been wounded in the First World War. The young master recognised and encouraged H. E.'s budding talent – which Bates in turn readily acknowledged in later life by dedicating two of his books to him. But all that was in the future. In the meantime the budding author's first printed work was a poem in the school magazine about Armistice Day, November 1920.

Bates left school at 16 to work as a junior reporter with the *Northampton Chronicle & Echo* in its Wellingborough office. Initially he was thrilled at the prospect of being paid to write, but the dream soured when he realised that life on the bottom rung of the journalistic ladder offered little opportunity for expressive writing. A cub reporter like the teenage Bates was more likely to have to cycle miles to stand outside

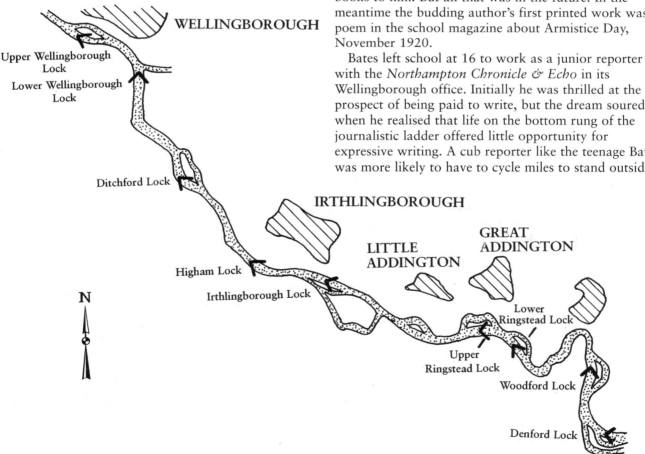

a church and collect the names of funeral mourners. It was a dull, dreary job made worse by the fact that he had formed an intense dislike for his boss.

Disillusioned, Bates resigned and went to work instead as a warehouse clerk for a leather merchant in Rushden. His new job was no more challenging than the first, but it left him with plenty of spare time on his hands – time that he put to good use by writing his first novel, *The Two Sisters*. The manuscript was rejected by nine publishers before it was published by Jonathan Cape in 1926, when Bates was just 21.

Bates married his wife, Madge, at Rushden in 1931. They later moved to Kent, but in the succession of novels and short stories that poured from his pen in subsequent years, the Nene valley featured strongly. *The Poacher* (1935) was based upon a rascally Rushden friend, Sam Smith, while his much-loved 'Uncle Silas' stories were influenced by his great-uncle, Joseph Betts.

The outbreak of the Second World War in September 1939 marked the beginning of a difficult time for writers. Drastic paper shortages and the blitzing of many of the London-based publishing houses meant many authors were only too pleased to be called up and work for the Ministry of Information, where their talents were turned to writing bland propaganda pamphlets.

Bates was luckier, and the customised role created for him by the Intelligence branch of the Air Ministry was unique. Given the pseudonym 'Flying Officer X', he was given a free rein to visit all Royal Air Force stations to research and write about the war in the air. His first journalistic essay was published in the *News Chronicle* on 2 February 1942, and further stories followed at weekly intervals. They were later assembled into a best-selling volume for which Bates, as a Crown Servant, did not receive a penny in royalties. In 1944 the official story of the Allied air forces from the occupied countries, entitled *There's Freedom in the Air*, was published by HMSO. Soon afterwards Bates wrote *Fair Stood the Wind for France*, which sold 87,286 copies and which was regarded by many reviewers as his greatest work.

However, two of H.E.'s wartime manuscripts were suppressed by the powers that be. *The Night Battle of Britain* and *The Battle of the Flying Bomb* were both suppressed and remain, unpublished, in the Public Record Office.

By the end of the war Bates had been promoted to Squadron Leader and his fact-finding tours took him to India and Burma to witness the war against Japan. His experiences in the Far East were later to prove the inspiration for three best-selling novels, *The Purple Plain*, *The Jacaranda Tree* and *The Scarlet Sword*.

The horrors of war had a profound effect upon his generation and Bates was no exception. He sensed the passing of a more innocent world and set about the task of both mourning and resurrecting it in his writings. Memories of his beloved Nene valley returned time and again. In *The Country Heart*, published in 1949, he wrote of Fotheringay Church 'standing like a small lost cathedral over the graves of kings', and Lilford, which he said had 'a stone humpbacked bridge over the Nene that is not equalled anywhere in England'.

The Feast of July (1954), a tale of love, jealousy and murder among a shoemaking family, is set entirely upon the Nene at the end of the 19th century. The central character, Bella Ford, leaves her imaginary seaside home at the mouth of the river and proceeds inland – in the exact opposite direction to this book – by heading upstream to 'Nenweald' (probably Irchester). 'Evensford' (Rushden), Nenborough (Wellingborough), Northampton and Addington all feature, or are mentioned, in this passionate plot.

At that time Bates, his wife and four children, Ann, Judith, Richard and Jonathan, were happily ensconced in the family home at Little Chard, where the author had turned a wilderness into a fine garden. His enthusiasm for his favourite pastime was reflected in four books – *The Seasons and The Gardener*, dedicated to his offspring, *The Country Heart*, *A Love of Flowers* and, finally, *A Fountain of Flowers*, published posthumously in 1974, a year after his death.

To describe fate as fickle is a cliché, yet true. If Bates had not won a scholarship to Kettering Grammar School and English master Edmund Kirby had not been invalided out of the army, the impressionable youngster would not have met his mentor and would probably have instead become a gardener or, possibly, a professional footballer. He had been a promising player in his youth and he never lost his love for the game. After the 1958 Munich air disaster in which many of the great Manchester United 'Busby Babes' perished, no written tribute was more genuinely moving than the one Bates penned for the Football Association.

A living literary legend, acclaimed on both sides of the Atlantic, Bates never forgot his Northamptonshire roots. Rushden was the backdrop for the *Love for Lydia* (1953), while the picturesque, chestnut-lined market square in Higham Ferrers featured in *The Sleepless Moon* (1956). There is no doubt, too, that the earthy humour of the Nene valley characters he knew in his youth rubbed off on to the page when he wrote the 'Larkin' trilogy *The Darling Buds of May* (1958), *A Breath of French Air* (1959) and *When the Green Woods Laugh* (1960). The breezy nature of the books did not win accolades from stuffy critics, but Bates himself defended them by saying 'the books are as English as pubs, steak and kidney pudding and the *Canterbury Tales* of Chaucer'. Bates's son, Richard, produced the highly successful television spin-off, just as he had in 1976 with *Love for Lydia*.

Bates was also a poet and it is no surprise that he was an admirer of John Clare, about whom he first wrote in his school magazine. Like Clare, he was a lover of the countryside who succeeded in preserving its atmosphere in words for future generations to enjoy. 'Perfick', as Pop Larkin would say.

Bates died in 1973 after being troubled by illness since 1966. An obituary in *The Times* declared: 'He was without an equal in England in the kind of story he had made his own, and stood in the direct line of succession of fiction writers of the English countryside that includes George Eliot, Hardy and D. H. Lawrence.'

Today most of his writings remain in print, and Rushden library – built at the time Bates was born – boasts a collection of books and magazine articles by him, as well as a comprehensive file of cuttings about him. It is well worth a visit.

Henry of Higham Ferrers

Another famous son of this neighbourhood was Henry Chichele, born the son of a farmer in Higham Ferrers in 1362. As a boy he worked for a local baker, but a wealthy benefactor, William of Wykeham, noticed his intelligence and sponsored his education at Winchester and Oxford. Chichele later became Archbishop of Canterbury, from 1414 until his death in 1443. But he never forgot his lowly place of birth and used his wealth and influence to found a grammar school, the Bede House and a college. His statue looks down from the town's famous church tower, with a spire that soars 170 feet to act as a landmark for miles around.

Irthlingborough's two bridges

On the opposite side of the river stands **Irthlingborough**, which is connected to Higham on the south bank by two bridges. One – a 14th-century stone bridge – has the cross-keys of Peterborough Abbey carved on a stone on the upstream wall, suggesting that it was originally built by the monks of that city. Its ten ribbed arches – cursed by many generations of navigators – are all different. Grooves worn in the stonework by the tow-ropes of the old bargemen can be clearly seen. The bridge was superceded in 1936 by the more workmanlike viaduct, which stands 26 feet above the flood meadows and carries the busy A6 trunk road.

Irthlingborough's most famous son was John Pyel, a

The fine old stone bridge at Irthlingborough, viewed here from the later A6 viaduct, has been a landmark - and hazard - to generations of boaters.

The tendency of the Nene to flood across its broad valley caused our prudent ancestors to build their towns on higher ground. In this case, Irthlingborough seems determined to keep a respectable distance from the river.

merchant who was Lord Mayor of London in 1373. He built the unusual tower of St Peter's Church, which stands 40 feet from the nave and was connected by domestic buildings John had planned as priests' dwellings. He died before the work was complete, but his widow, Joan, oversaw the completion of the project.

In 1913 a silent movie of the Battle of Waterloo was filmed in and around the town, the Duke of Wellington having earlier remarked upon the similarity between the Nene valley and the original battlefield. It cost £6,000 to film and provided temporary employment for locals as extras.

Stanwick's vantage point

Downstream, the village of **Stanwick** boasts a commanding view across the valley. Its lofty position was first exploited by the Romans, who built a villa, temple, farms and other houses here – in contrast to the earlier Saxon hill fort at Crow Hill, on the opposite side of the valley.

The son of a 16th-century rector of Stanwick, John Dolben was born here and brought distinction to the village by becoming Archbishop of York.

Ringstead dates back at least to Saxon times – its name means 'circular place' – and once boasted two mills. The lower mill was demolished when the Blisworth-Peterborough railway was built in 1845, but the upper mill – known locally as Willy Watt Mill – still stands and was once used for paper making. It still contains two water wheels, one of which is visible from the outside.

Britain's biggest carp

Follow the Nene downstream of the mill and after a quarter of a mile or so you will see on your left a gravel pit, almost encircled by a sweeping loop in the river that is known to locals as Ringstead Shallows.

The gravel pit – which is known to carp enthusiasts everywhere as the Mid-Northants Fishery – is too new and barren to be considered picturesque. Mother Nature has not yet completed her task of reclaiming it and healing the scars torn in the meadows when the minerals were extracted. But although this lake is not – yet – a beauty spot, it holds a special place in the angling record books, for this is the water that

The Nene at Lower Ringstead Lock, September 1992 and September 1996, showing what a difference torrential rain can make. On the first occasion floodwater was pouring over the banks of the river into the adjacent Ringstead Grange trout fishery (left).

Left Springtime means trout fishing to many anglers - among them John Sharpe, of Northampton, who was successful with this 11 lb 13 oz rainbow from Ringstead Grange when the daffodils were in flower in 1993.

produced Britain's biggest carp twice in a matter of weeks.

Early in June 1995 a young Leicester lad named Roddy Porter landed a 53 lb 15 oz mirror carp there that shattered the previous record of 51 lb 8 oz, which had stood for 15 years.

But Roddy's reign as a record holder was short-lived. In fact it lasted barely a fortnight before his fish was beaten by a 55 lb 4 oz specimen from the same venue. The captor this time was Alex White.

The truth is that both records were one and the same fish – an oft-caught female carp that was so well known to previous captors that she had actually acquired a nickname. Regulars at the exclusive syndicate water named her Scaley on account of her distinctive scale pattern. Scaley's history was well-documented. She was first landed in 1976 as a tiddler from a local farm pond by Higham Ferrers carp enthusiast Duncan Kay, who brought her home in a bucket. He later released her in a local gravel pit that he was developing as a carp fishery. At that stage she weighed all of 2 oz.

Below Gravel workings, like these near Stanwick, are a distinctive feature of the mineral-rich Nene valley.

But she grew fast in her new environment. Around 1990, when gravel extraction recommenced at the pit, she weighed about 30 lb and had already been landed and gently returned by a number of grateful captors. They were all concerned about her welfare when it was time to remove the pit's stocks to their new home at Ringstead, but they need not have worried. Scaley again flourished and was soon topping the 40 lb mark.

It came as a great surprise to all when she finally appeared at over 50 lb in the early summer of 1995, but her new bulk hid a tragedy. Scaley was spawnbound, having failed to shed the tens of thousands of eggs trapped inside her body, and was slowly dying. Sure enough, the grand old lady was found washed up dead a couple of weeks after her final, record-breaking appearance.

Scaley – or rather Alex White – held the British record until the autumn of 1996, when it was beaten by a 55 lb 13 oz monster from a gravel pit at Wraysbury, in the Colne valley, close to Heathrow Airport. That fish was also well-known and had acquired the nickname Mary. Non-angling readers may at this point be puzzled why some carp fanatics insist upon 'christening' their fish with nicknames. I'm afraid to admit that although I'm a keen carp angler myself, I can't enlighten you. The world of the obsessed carp angler is a mystery to outsiders, who cannot understand why a human should purposefully live like a hermit on the bankside for weeks on end in pursuit of a single fish. But I digress.

Returning to the Nene valley, it is doubtful whether the lake contains any further huge carp to threaten the status of either Scaley or Mary, although there are rumours of fast-growing fish nudging 40 lb. There must be some potential, however, as the syndicate, which costs several hundred pounds a year to join, is fully subscribed.

Perhaps one of those carp – maybe even one of Scaley's offspring – will produce a new British record in the future. But fishing is full of surprises and such a fish is just as likely to come from one of the many neglected gravel pits along the Nene valley controlled by angling clubs that anybody can join for £20 or so a year.

Health checks for fish

Before new fish can be stocked into the Nene or its lakes – or indeed any river in this country – the batch has to be checked by the Environment Agency to prevent diseases being spread. To a handful of unthinking angling club officials and unscrupulous fishery owners, these rules are purely bureaucratic red tape. But the sobering truth is that they prevent our fisheries from being wiped out by a host of contagious diseases. Fish that look fine to the untrained eye often carry killer diseases – deadly parasites and viruses that can spread like a plague through every fish in the water, killing the lot.

In the Agency's pioneering Fish Health Laboratories at Brampton, near Huntingdon, 14 scientists work at the cutting edge of the highly technical fight against these threats. They have even discovered a few parasites previously unknown to man. The Agency's lab work also includes studying an incredible 50,000 fish scales every year. Routine surveys are constantly carried out on rivers nationwide. During each survey, sample fish have a few scales carefully removed and sent to Brampton, where fishery scientists 'read' them as avidly as any best-selling book. Each scale has a ring pattern like the rings inside a tree. Every year, as it grows, the scale gets bigger. During the best feeding periods in the summer, the growth rings are spaced widely apart, but as the fish slow down in winter the rings are set closer and appear darker under the microscope. By counting the dark winter rings – known as annual checks – the scientists can tell how old the fish is. And by comparing its age to its length and weight, they can tell whether it is healthy and thriving.

A grisly find

Below Ringstead the Nene sweeps through a broad expanse of meadows before arriving at **Woodford**, a large village that has been inhabited since Saxon times. There is a pleasant village green and some pubs to enjoy here, but if you prefer to shiver in the chill of history at its most macabre, a visit to the Church of St Mary the Virgin is a must.

In the spring of 1867 workmen restoring the stone arches in the nave uncovered a mummified human heart, wrapped in a piece of coarse cloth and placed inside a small, round box. But to whom did the heart belong? Local opinion is divided. Many locals believe it is the heart of Sir Walter Trailly, a former lord of the manor, who died while on a Crusade to the Holy Land around 1290. As was the custom in those days, his body would have been buried abroad and his heart embalmed for transportation back home, so that it could rest among his ancestors. This theory is given some substance by the fact that effigies of Sir Walter and his wife, Eleanor, stand at the top of the north aisle. He wears his helmet and a sword, while Eleanor, who died in 1316, wears a hooded gown. Their hands are clasped in prayer.

But did Sir Walter rest in peace? The church is famous for being haunted by the ghostly figure of a knight, who has been seen kneeling at prayer at the altar. On one occasion the apparition was photographed and published in the press; scientific tests failed to cast any doubt over the picture's authenticity!

A lone angler concentrates on his fishing, unaware of the grisly goings-on to which the ancient church in Woodford bore witness.

Another theory about the heart is that it belonged to another local man, Roger de Kirkton, who died and was buried in Norfolk, or a thieving vicar of the parish who fled with some of the church's treasure only to be apprehended and dealt summary justice by a local pursuer. Either way, the heart has been placed in a glass-fronted case which is set in the same recess where it was originally found.

Denford's ducks

The next settlement, **Denford,** is situated on the slope of a hill that sweeps down to the fertile river and its flood plain. Two mills once stood here, but today the river splits into a number of streams and there is a syphonic sluice gate installed to keep the water level high for navigation.

The approach to the village by road from Thrapston has little changed over the centuries, with one channel of the river running alongside, dotted with gnarled old pollarded willows and ablaze with bright yellow water lilies in high summer. This stretch of water is noted for its semi-tame ducks, which flock eagerly to visitors with a few crumbs of comfort. The best spot to enjoy the ducks – and the view – is from the village war memorial.

More Washington connections

Like most small towns, **Thrapston** once prospered from the shoe and steel industries. Older residents will also recall the days when it boasted two railway stations. All these elements have now gone, but Thrapston retains its vibrant sense of identity thanks to the industry upon which it was founded – agriculture. It was granted its status of market town by King John in 1205, reinforced in 1871 by an Act of Parliament – the Thrapston Market Act – which placed the weekly cattle market slap-bang in the middle of the town. It is still the most important weekly livestock market for miles around.

The town also receives its share of American visitors, attracted to yet another Washington connection. On the west wall of the nave of St James's Church is a stone tablet depicting the family crest of stars and stripes that we have already encountered way upstream at Brington. There is no inscription, but it is assumed that they are the arms of Sir John Washington, lord of the manor of Thrapston, who died here in 1668. Sir John, who is buried somewhere in the churchyard, was knighted by Charles Stuart and was the brother of Laurence Washington, whose son John emigrated to America and became the great-grandfather of the first President.

The churchyard at Denford, pictured in the 1920s and 1996, is now a nature reserve.

*Above Pollarded willows line this backwater of the Nene, which runs alongside the Denford-Thrapston road.
In the background the new A14 sweeps across the valley.*

*Below The stone bridge that crosses the river and divides Thrapston from Islip is also the point
at which the pronunciation of the river's name changes from 'Nenn' to 'Neen'.*

Mill Road, Thrapston

These houses were newly built when this photograph was taken at Mill Road, Thrapston, in 1927. Seventy years on, it has been renamed Oakleas Rise, presumably by a well-meaning local council believing the historic name to be somehow lacking in romanticism. . .

Again, 70 years separate these shots of Huntingdon Road, Thrapston, in 1927 and 1997.

Huntingdon Road, Thrapston

4
Islip to Fotheringay

Sauntering at ease I often love to lean
O'er old bridge walls and mark the flood below
Whose ripples through the weeds of oily green
Like happy travellers mutter as they go
And mark the sunshine dancing on the arch
Time keeping to the merry waves beneath
And on the banks see drooping blossoms parch
Thirsting for water in the day's hot breath

John Clare

What's in a name?

A fine, nine-arch stone bridge divides the market town of Thrapston from its smaller neighbour, **Islip**. Of medieval origin, five arches were rebuilt following a devastating flood in 1795. And it is at this point that the Nene changes its name – or, rather, its pronunciation.

From the source to Thrapston the river is pronounced 'Nenn', but from Islip downstream it is called 'Neen'. The reason for this is lost in the mists of time, but a glance at maps from Tudor times onwards reveals that the old cartographers even varied the spelling, marking it down variously as Nene, Nen, Nenne, Niene and Neen. Call it what you will, but be prepared for a rebuke if you mispronounce it in the wrong company. Northampton folk will abruptly correct any Fenlander foolish enough to speak of the 'Neen', while a true Fen Tiger who has never prowled far from Wisbech's North Brink will feign ignorance of any river known as the 'Nenn'.

The demarcation point at Islip is one of the few places along this river where any old pronunciation will do. Perhaps the linguistic tolerance rubbed off on its former inhabitants, for on the south wall of the chancel of the 15th-century Church of St Nicholas is a wall tablet in memory of Mary Washington, yet another ancestor of the first President of the United States. George Washington, it can be universally agreed, was not a man to quibble over such regional trivia.

Notable buildings in the village include Islip House, which was once the home of Thomas Squire, one of the leaders of the bid to make the river navigable between Peterborough and Thrapston in 1737. Two and a half centuries later, in 1987, Water Board workers building a new sewer stumbled upon a secret passage between the house and the Woolpack Inn, which stands close to the wooden wharfs and warehouses built beside the river during the heyday of the commercial navigation age. That time is, of course, now long gone, and it is hard to believe that this shabby area was once a bustling waterfront, but a few rotting wooden stages and long-demolished buildings offer crumbling evidence of the river's former status.

A little downstream is yet more evidence of the commercial importance of the river to the population in the not-so-distant past. Impressive Islip Mill was still grinding corn until 22 August 1960. In its heyday in the late 19th century it boasted two water wheels and also incorporated a built-in eel trap, from whence the rich harvest was dispatched to London to serve the East Enders' appetite for jellied eels.

The biggest gravel pit

Below the mill the river skirts Thrapston Lagoon, at 210 acres the biggest gravel pit in the valley and said to be one of the largest in the country. From the high ridge along the road from Aldwincle to Lowick it looks for

Opposite Seventy years separate these views of Islip School in 1927 and 1997, and although the buildings remain much the same, what was once a vibrant educational establishment is now boarded up and the local children are taken elsewhere by bus for their education. Another pillar of the local community has thus been toppled.

The School, Islip

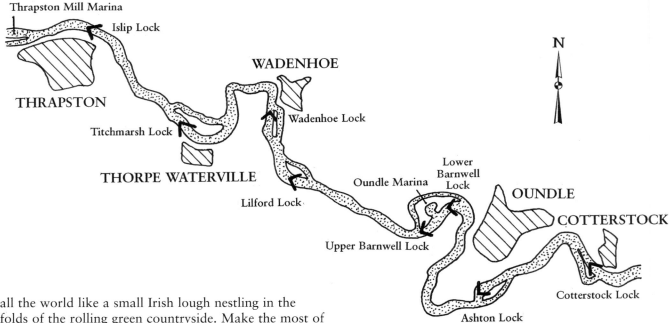

all the world like a small Irish lough nestling in the folds of the rolling green countryside. Make the most of these hills, for they become much scarcer as the river snakes through its broad flood plain towards the flat fenlands below Peterborough.

The nature of the plain makes the next few miles of the Nene as picturesque as any and, certainly, very important for wildlife. Below Thrapston Lagoon is the **Titchmarsh** Local Nature Reserve, owned by the Northamptonshire Wildlife Trust and covering 150 acres of flooded gravel pits, meadows and woodland. It incorporates one of the biggest heronries in the country in the wood adjacent to the former duck decoy, built by Lord Lilford in 1885. We'll meet that famous ornithologist again a little further downstream at the hamlet of his title, but for now, as we wander within this species-rich nature reserve, it is easy to imagine the joy he would have had at recording the 130 species of birds that have visited here in recent years. Rare warblers, grebes and the mysterious bittern have all stopped off here, along with magnificent birds of prey like the osprey and marsh harrier. An annual visitor is the nightingale, whose incomparable song can be heard from the impenetrable thickets after dark on warm June evenings.

Below the reserve the navigable Nene continues to Titchmarsh Mill – now the headquarters of the Middle Nene Cruising Club – while the run-off roars over a weir to form Brancey Brook and to rendezvous with Harper's Brook at the corner of yet another large gravel pit. This attractive sheet of water has been flooded barely a decade, yet it already holds large coarse fish as well as flourishing beds of freshwater mussels, which in turn attract large numbers of oyster-catchers.

The navigable main river skirts the village of **Thorpe Waterville** and the remains of its Norman castle before being reunited with the combined Brancey and Harper's brooks half a mile or so downstream. The river now broadens and deepens before dividing around a small, wooded island, which was formed by navigation engineers excavating a short-cut across a sharp bend in the course. The backwater behind the river is now overgrown with lilies and a popular summer meeting place for large shoals of tench, which average close to 4 lb.

Waterside perfection

Beyond the island, on the right-hand bank, extends one of the wonders of the Nene valley. It is Achurch meadow (also known locally as Wadenhoe meadow), which is the largest area of riparian wetland in the county as well as a Site of Special Scientific Interest (SSSI). Over 100 flowering plant species have been recorded in this vast flood meadow, situated on the inside of a huge, sweeping bend in the river. Like most of the fields along the Nene in this area, it remains unspoilt thanks to the Countryside Stewardship Scheme, in which farmers are awarded grants for maintaining traditional grazing and hay harvesting. Spring is the best time to visit, when the meadows are studded with

Titchmarsh Mill is now the headquarters of the Middle Nene Cruising Club.

cowslips, and hares prance across the wide-open spaces. Former courses of the river can be traced across the meadows as either muddy, snaking ditches or full-blown oxbow lakes. These and the wet meadows provide suitable breeding and feeding for redshank, snipe and lapwing, while the eerie, liquid call of the curlew is often heard. If you are lucky you may even see this elusive bird using its distinctive, curved beak to extract worms and insects from the mud.

Opposite the meadow on the far bank of the river is a very different landscape, as a ridge of limestone abruptly descends down to the brink. This ridge, covered by an old alder wood and fringed by overgrown pollarded willows, is the origin of several mini-brooks that bubble out of the limestone as small springs, each tumbling just a hundred yards or so down to the boggy margins of the river. Alder woods were once common along the banks of the Nene, prior to so-called improvements for agriculture, drainage and navigation. This area is also an SSSI and is known as Wadenhoe Marsh, providing a rare example of an undrained riverside marsh. Unusual plants, including the southern marsh orchid, can be found here.

Behind the ridge is the pleasant village of **Aldwincle**, whose name probably originates from the bend in the river we have just visited. It was recorded in the Normans' Domesday Book as Eldewincle, the final two syllables coming from the earlier Saxon word 'wincel', meaning bend or corner.

The long, rambling village has a church at either end – and the rectories of both were birthplaces of famous literary figures. The poet and playwright John Dryden – regarded in the last quarter of the 17th century as England's best living poet – was born at the rectory of All Saints Church in 1631. He went on to become Poet Laureate and Histographer Royal in 1670. His death 30 years later was marked by public mourning, and a procession of 100 carriages followed his funeral cortège to Westminster Abbey.

At the other end of the village the former rectory of St Peter's Church was, in 1608, the birthplace of Thomas Fuller, author of *The Worthies of England*, and chaplain to King Charles II. He died in 1661 at Cranford, in Middlesex, where he was buried.

Despite its size Aldwincle does not have a pub. It does, however, boast a family-run village store and post office that recently won a national award for its old-fashioned standards of service. Trevor Watts and his family provide all the supplies needed for hungry

Aldwincle village in the 1920s was a sleepy place - just as it remains in 1996, when the modern view was photographed.

The family-run post office and stores at Aldwincle won a national award for its first-class service in 1996, here held by the proud owner, Trevor Watts.

families on boating holidays, fishing trips and hikes along the nearby Nene Way. Thankfully, in such a shamefully dry parish, it is also an off-licence.

Wonderful Wadenhoe

To enjoy a decent pint of draught ale you have to travel downstream a mile or so to the King's Head at **Wadenhoe**. But that is no hardship, since this village is regarded as one of the most picturesque in the valley – and the aforementioned pub certainly enjoys the best riverside setting along the entire Nene.

But, for once, the best way to view this village and its unspoilt surroundings is not from the river but from the high knoll on which the Church of St Michael & All Angels stands, slightly removed from the village, and commanding a panoramic view of much of what we have described so far in this chapter. The Norman tower is topped by a saddleback roof and contains six bells that are said to produce the most musical peal in

the county. If you want to hear them, turn up on a Wednesday evening when the local campanologists are putting them through the paces. Around 9 pm you can even reward bell-ringers Ken and Connie and their pals with a well-deserved pint when they decamp for the King's Head and a relaxing game of skittles.

Returning to the church, you will find inside a memorial tablet that commemorates the tragic deaths of the local squire, Thomas Hunt, and his new bride, Caroline Isham, daughter of the rector of nearby Polebrook, who had travelled to Italy for their honeymoon in 1824 only to be attacked by bandits, who robbed and murdered them.

The estate was later inherited by the Rt Hon George Ward-Hunt, who became Chancellor of the Exchequer in Disraeli's Government in 1868. Thanks to this gentleman's influence, Wadenhoe became the first village to have a postal telegraph office, installed to keep him in touch with the affairs of state. It is still in business today – complete with the original 'Postal Telegraph Office' sign in black letters on a white enamel background. A year later Ward-Hunt also built his own gasworks, which served the local stone-built cottages as well as illuminating the quiet village streets. Today those same streets are unlit . . . so much for progress!

Huffing and puffing back up the hill to the church again, look around you at the strange humps and bumps all around. Their origins are unclear, although many locals believe they are the earthworks of a long-forgotten castle. Others say they are all that remains of the original village, deserted more than 300 years ago after the plague. Archaeologists agree it is probably a defended site and add that it could date back to the Iron Age. Wadenhoe means 'Wada's spur of land' and is a Saxon name.

After all this strenuous exercise, climbing up and down that hill, it is time to return to the King's Head. In the balmy days of summer, dozens flock here to sit on the willow-shaded paddock and watch the world – and the River Nene – go by. There can be nothing more relaxing than seeing the semi-tame ducks squabble in the margins while the cruisers and narrowboats queue up to use the locks.

The paddock also marks the finishing line of the annual charity raft race, staged every summer, in which local teams launch their home-made craft at Thorpe Waterville for the perilous 2-mile voyage downstream. All too often their efforts prove hopelessly optimistic – 'shipwrecks' and duckings galore are assured – but it's fun to watch all the same. The current champions (1996) were skippered by one Peter Townsend, the buccaneering publisher of this book, but bankside rumour insisted that there were some piratical goings-on involved and the sooner we draw a veil over that episode the better. . .

The dilapidated shack previously used as a village hall has been replaced by a modern building, but otherwise these views of Wadenhoe and the Nene from the vantage point of Church Hill remain little changed in almost 70 years. The spire of St John the Baptist, Achurch, can be seen above the distant trees.

These remarkable photographs show the same person at Wadenhoe millstream in 1929 and 1997. Peter Hall is the baby in the arms of an unknown neighbour in the first photograph. Recently retired as secretary of the Wadenhoe Trust, Peter still lives in the village and kindly agreed to return to the same spot, more than 68 years later. Peter Hall/author

Wadenhoe Mill was very much a working enterprise in the 1920s, when the first photograph was taken. Corn was ground, eels were trapped from the mill race and residents bought their milk and butter there. Today the building has been renovated to become a luxury private residence. *Peter Hall/author*

Northamptonshire skittles

In winter the King's Head paddock is deserted and, after heavy rain, often flooded. But since the publishers and author of this book are based in this pleasant village (and all too often known to adjourn to the said hostelry) the reader can be excused for doing exactly what *they* do – linger a while longer at the bar and indulge in the unique local version of skittles.

Traditional Northamptonshire skittles is most definitely not a quaint rural anachronism. In these parts it is taken deadly seriously, with thousands of pub-based players competing in fiercely contested leagues and knock-out cup finals. The King's Head team are in the local First Division and, with their attacking flair, could be compared to soccer's Newcastle United. Local hero Tony Harrison is a striker comparable only to Alan Shearer, while Irish-born skipper Michael Hamill supplies the unpredictable foreign skills of Tino Asprilla.

Unlike football, however, skittles is not a macho Saturday game played between the lads. The gentle sex often provide a few surprises and Ireland's Michelle Conway – another foreign import – gave Harrison his toughest test in the recent King's Head Christmas Knock-Out (Wadenhoe's equivalent of the FA Cup).

If you are visiting this area for the first time, it is imperative that you have at least one visit to the skittles table. For one thing, it is very therapeutic knocking seven shades of stuffing out of nine boxwood skittles with three missiles (called 'cheeses'). You could even become hooked and spread the gospel elsewhere. Believe it or not, the author recently spoke to a French hotelier who has imported Northamptonshire skittles to Bordeaux and has set up a local league with a distinctive Gallic flavour. Who knows – it could soon have its own international slot on Sky Sports!

The rebel preacher

Reluctantly tearing ourselves away from our favourite village, we head downstream to **Achurch**. Also known as Thorpe Achurch, the village is again of Saxon origin and the Church of St John the Baptist was built around 1300 in the shape of a cross by the Knight Asceline de Waterville in gratitude for his safe return from the Crusades.

The most famous rector of this church was Robert Browne. He preached here for 40 years, but was the first man to separate from the church after the Reformation and was the founder of the Brownists sect. A true rebel, he took to preaching in the open air in defiance of his superiors. Backed by eager disciples, he wrote and printed books that men were hanged for circulating. Browne escaped with his life but was thrown into prison dozens of time, being eventually excommunicated by the church. He was ridiculed at the time, but his new movement sowed the seed from which the whole body of Nonconformists sprouted to life. His son Edward was one of the founders of the American state of Maryland, and many Americans boast of descent from his grandsons.

Also from Achurch were the ancestors of Joshua Quincey, President of Harvard University. They were said to have sailed to the New World with Sir Walter Raleigh during the reign of Queen Elizabeth I and went on to become mayors of Boston, entering into the tea business that caused so much upset on that fledgling continent! They then founded the town of Quincy, Massachusetts, which was the home of the second President of the United States, John Adams, and after which the sixth President, Quincy Adams, was named.

Left Northamptonshire skittles action at the King's Head, Wadenhoe. Michael Hamill prepares to let fly with a wooden cheese, watched by Paul Turner and a pensive Tony Harrison (right).

Opposite Despite the millions of pounds spent on flood prevention schemes since the Second World War, the River Nene is still subject to flash floods. These photographs are taken from the same vantage point - Lilford looking upstream towards Achurch - during a late summer flood in September 1992 and the dry spring of 1996.

Another aspect of the excitement of being close to a river is witnessing it in all seasons, in all its moods. The author shot these three very different photographs of Pilton bridge and backwater in January 1991, February 1992 and September 1996.

Above right The Jacobean architecture of Lilford Hall stands impressively on the east bank of the river, opposite Pilton village.

Right The summer sunshine pours through the trees in Lilford Park, once home to a leading ornithologist.

A little owl for Lilford

Thomas Littleton Powys, 4th Baron Lilford, was buried in Achurch churchyard in 1896, after passing away at the age of 66. He was one of Britain's most celebrated ornithologists and his seat at **Lilford Hall**, which commands a superb view over the River Nene below Pilton, half a mile downstream, became a shrine to his passion. The best viewpoint of the house is from the opposite bank of the river and the best time is in spring, when the parkland sloping down to the Nene is ablaze with tens of thousands of yellow daffodils.

The fine Jacobean house, completed around 1635, is notable for its unique double chimney stacks, 13 in all and linked by arches. It was originally built for William Elmes, whose family lived there for 200 years until it passed to Sir Thomas Powys, the Attorney General. His grandson, the first Lord Lilford, demolished the Saxon village of Lilford – including its church – to create a 240-acre parkland estate.

Between 1860 and 1890 the 4th Baron created his aviaries in the park, building upon a sound knowledge of the natural world, which had interested him since boyhood. Although an early conservationist, Lilford was also a keen shot and in 1886 killed a rare night heron that had strayed to Titchmarsh. Probably out of remorse, he set about trying to introduce the species to the locality, without success.

He had much greater success with the little owl, which at that time was not present in Britain. He purchased many live specimens from the continent and set about releasing them into the wild. In July 1888 he gave 40 their freedom. They soon bred and thrived in the mixed woodland and farmland of the area, much to the consternation of gamekeepers who erroneously blamed them for predation upon game bird chicks. Today it is known that little owls prey mainly upon beetles, insects and small mammals and cause little damage, but in retrospect Lilford's actions were irresponsible, to say the least. Thankfully, the 1981 Wildlife & Countryside Act now prevents arrogant mavericks from introducing alien species to the wild.

Nevertheless, it is difficult to be too harsh on Lilford and his whims. He never enjoyed robust health and in his later years had to be wheeled to the House of Lords to record his vote. Despite that considerable handicap, he still managed to write two volumes on the birds of the county – *The Birds of Northamptonshire*, published in 1895 and based upon articles penned for the *Journal of the Northamptonshire Natural History Society*. Although unfinished at the time of his untimely demise from gout, they are today true collector's pieces and fetch exorbitant prices among modern bird lovers.

Below and right Lilford's Saxon church was demolished to create the present landscaped park around the hall. Materials from the old church were used by Lord Lilford to build a folly in the wooded area known as the Lynches, on the east bank of the river between Achurch and Lilford. This neglected structure has become overgrown between this sketch, believed to date back to the turn of the century, and the photograph, taken in 1996.

Lilford Hall was commandeered during the Second World War as a field hospital for the American forces, who had many bases in the area. Even today the park is marked by many strange oblongs of crumbling concrete, which turn out to be the foundations of the dozens of wartime Nissen huts that once stood around the house. In the post-war years the park was used as a country club and a wildlife theme park, neither of which ventures appeared to have been financially successful. Recently the estate has been bought privately and is being restored to its former glory as a private family home.

A snack fit for an Earl

Between Lilford and **Pilton** the Nene splits into two and runs through a delightful wooded area known as the Lynches, which stands on the Nene Way footpath and is a popular beauty spot for visitors. Below, the valley is no less picturesque as it continues to snake between timeless water meadows and countless contentedly grazing sheep and cattle. Some are owned by Howe Hill Farm, at **Stoke Doyle**, a 590-acre enterprise run by the conservation-conscious Gent family, which includes 250 acres of grass for beef and sheep. For the last 30 years the Gents have improved wildlife habitats on their farm, while still running it as a successful commercial business. They have retained hedges and planted small areas of tree cover in field corners, on steep slopes and upon unproductive, heavy soil. Old ponds have been restored and new ones created. In 1984 the Gents deservedly won a national Country Life Farming & Wildlife Award for their endeavours.

This land borders the Nene through a lonely stretch of the valley between Pilton and Barnwell. The meadows are unspoilt in these parts and provide rich grazing for flocks of sheep and cattle. With just those beasts for company as I fished from the opposite bank one recent summer's day, I watched two hen harriers soaring high on the thermals above the meadows. With rare birds such as these present, or attracted to visit, the success of such nature-friendly farming is evident.

The next parish we meet is **Barnwell**, until recently home to the Queen's cousins, the Duke and Duchess and Gloucester, who lived in the manor bought by the Duke's father in 1938. The manor gardens include the ruins of a 13th-century castle, once occupied by the Le Moine family. The ruins are said to be haunted by a monk brandishing a whip – coincidentally, the family crest incorporated a monk and a whip. Spooky, eh?

But Barnwell's most famous family is the Montagus, after which the village pub (the Montagu Arms) is

Opposite At first glance, little has changed in the six short years between those two photographs of picturesque Stoke Doyle, taken in 1990 and 1996. Flocks of sheep are still driven along this narrow valley lane, but the traditional red telephone box, such an emblem of old England, has in the meantime been replaced by its less sympathetic modern counterpart.

Above The navigation of the River Nene in the last two centuries has left many dead arms and truncated stretches of old course which, although redundant to boat traffic, are rich havens for fish escaping winter floods. This backwater near Barnwell, which was once a twisting section of the original waterway, is now a floodwater haven for pike, carp and tench.

named. They were better known as the Earls of Sandwich, and notable members of the clan over the years included the Earl who invented *the* sandwich, as well as the 4th Earl, the most incompetent naval supremo that Britain has ever known. His neglect of the fleet during his spell in charge led to 800 men perishing in 1782 when rotten timbers led to the warship *Royal George* sinking. Known as 'Jeremy Twitcher' to his many foes, he, along with more deserving members of his family, are commemorated in the remains of Barnwell's All Saints Church, which was partly demolished in 1825. Today the village is served by the 13th-century St Andrew's Church.

Turn off the main A605 Peterborough-Northampton road at Barnwell, head towards Oundle and after half a mile on the left you will come to Barnwell Mill, which is probably the oldest on the river. The present building – constructed from local limestone – dates back around 300 years, but there has been a mill on the site since at least 875 AD, when it was first mentioned in the *Anglo-Saxon Chronicle* during the reign of King Canute. Today the mill has been converted into a restaurant and is a popular haunt for boaters and motorists alike. Anglers might also be interested to know that the race of turbulent water below the mill holds a lot of medium-sized pike as well as some huge eels.

Immediately downstream of the mill is Barnwell Country Park, a 37-acre area of woodland, lakes and grassland that were once old gravel workings. Owned by Northamptonshire County Council, they are popular with anglers, birdwatchers and folk who simply enjoy a stroll through pleasant surroundings. Besides the obligatory, cosmopolitan collection of semi-tame ducks eager to be fed, there are some feathered rarities to be found skulking in the willows, alders and sedges. At least 32 species of birds have been recorded breeding here, and the spring and autumn migrations witness a few rare visitors. The park is also home to the rare noctule bat, the largest in Britain and the size of a swift; the tree-lined flooded pits provide it with its ideal

Barnwell Mill has been converted into a restaurant and is a popular spot in summer.

habitat. In recent years the resident rangers have also scraped out an amphibian pond where rare and threatened species of newts are thriving.

The country park is also a popular outdoor classroom for local schools, and the visitor centre, run by the helpful rangers, contains thoughtful displays that explain the diversity of nature all around. Such a pre-packaged parcel of countryside is not to everyone's taste – the well-worn paths and trails will never lead the visitor to wilderness – but the superb facilities succeed brilliantly in opening up the countryside to the very young, old, infirm and physically disabled.

Father of the nature conservation movement

Below Barnwell Mill the Nene is within splashing distance of the market town of Oundle, but just as it gets close it seems to change its mind and veer away again through the flood meadows, passing Oundle Marina on the left and yet another old, flooded gravel pit on the right before it loops toward Polebrook, then **Ashton**, which is a very special place to anybody interested in nature conservation.

Charles Rothschild (1877-1923) of Ashton created the Society for the Promotion of Nature Reserves in 1912. This later became the Royal Society for Nature Conservation, which now encompasses as an umbrella body the many wildlife trusts and groups nationwide. His daughter, Dr Miriam Rothschild, still lives at Ashton Wold and is an eminent entomologist. In a memoir on her father she wrote:

'It has been said with an element of truth that he invented conservation, since, years ahead of his day, he realised the importance of protecting and preserving the habitat and special biotopes rather than the individual rare species threatened with extinction, and the necessity of obtaining government support and massive publicity.'

Rothschild certainly led by example. He set aside part of his Ashton estate as a nature reserve – the first of its kind in the country. Ashton Wold, close to the old USAF base at Polebrook, contains many old oaks, some of which are more than 250 years old and are, therefore, among the oldest in the county.

Right Many parts of the middle Nene have a timeless quality about them. This section at Polebrook, looking downstream towards Oundle, has changed little in hundreds of years.

Ashton village itself is also owned by the Rothschild family. Entering it from the Polebrook road, close to Ashton Mill, is like being transported back in time to Merrie Olde England. The picturesque village green is surrounded first by sturdy horse chestnut trees, then by thatched cottages. At the far end of the green is a matching pub. It is a scene you expect to see on one of those old, flat boxes of chocolates you used to give your gran for Christmas. You could be forgiven for thinking that this timeless rural idyll has remained virtually unchanged for hundreds of years, but in fact Ashton village was planned and built around the turn of the century by the Rothschild family, whose admirable views on conservation obviously extended beyond nature.

The village pub, the Chequered Skipper, is at the time of writing being rebuilt following a disastrous fire that started in the thatch and spread quickly to raze the fine building to the ground. It is named after a rare butterfly that once thrived in the dappled sunlight of the grassy rides through Ashton Wold, but which became extinct in the 1960s due, it is thought, to a deadly cloud of insecticide wafting in from neighbouring farmland.

The tranquil peace of sleepy Ashton is disturbed one day every year – on the second Sunday in October, to be exact – when it becomes the bizarre setting for the World Conker Championship. Every year thousands of entrants arrive from all over the world to contest a nutty game that most of us abandoned in childhood. It all began in the autumn of 1965 when a group of disgruntled anglers sought solace in the Chequered Skipper after their fishing match on the nearby Nene was cancelled due to stormy weather. Seeing the fallen chestnuts lying around the village green, they decided that a game of conkers would make an ideal substitute.

In the years that followed the event was first repeated, then expanded. Today it resembles a medieval jousting tournament, with a central arena and a host of country crafts, stalls and other games going on. Women and children also join in the fun, although it has to be said that it is grown men that take it most seriously. Despite the fancy dress and the fact that the whole event is staged to raise money for charity, they go there to win! It is a fun event that is well worth a visit by spectators and would-be participants alike.

Old town, old school

After Ashton Mill the Nene strides purposefully towards **Oundle**, yet, once again, it seems to change its mind at the last moment and veer away. The historic market town is virtually encircled by the Nene and its many backwaters, but because of its position on a low hill it is never threatened by the winter floodwater – although the bridges that lead out of the town and

across the wide riverside meadows have not fared so well. The North Bridge over the river had 30 arches until it was destroyed by a great flood in 1570 and rebuilt the following year. A stone tablet in the centre of the bridge records this piece of history, but it was lost until the first half of the 19th century when building workers carrying out repairs found it buried beneath the walls. When the bridge was widened in 1914 to accommodate the ever-increasing volume of traffic along the main road, it was recut and set in the parapet.

That main road from Peterborough to Northampton, known today as the A605, finally bypassed the town in the mid-1980s, with the new road following the trackbed of the former railway line between the two towns. It has greatly believed the burden of heavy traffic that was threatening to shake to pieces many of the town's fine stone buildings.

The finest of them all is the Talbot Hotel, with its charming grey stone front that is almost 400 years old. It is said that the materials for its construction were brought from the ruins of Fotheringay Castle by William Whitwell, whose initials and the date 1626 are in the gable of a house nearby. Within the hotel is a grand staircase, supposed to be the very same one that Mary Queen of Scots walked down to her execution at Fotheringay.

Situated to the rear of the hotel is Drummingwell Lane, so called because local legend has it that a ghostly drumming noise emanated from a well behind the hotel whenever a momentous event was about to take place in England. The Great Fire of London of 1666 was said to have been predicted by Oundle's spooky well which, unfortunately, went mute some time in the 18th century and was thus filled in.

The poet John Clare knew the town well, for he was billeted at the Rose & Crown on the Market Place when he served briefly in the militia. He must have often gazed up at the elegant spire of St Peter's Church, which soars high above the slate rooftops of the town to over 200 feet and is a landmark for many miles around.

Although that 17th-century spire dominates the skyline, the town itself its dominated by its famous public school. Oundle School had its origins in the 14th century, as a small grammar school attached to the Guild of Our

Right This view from the tower of Stoke Doyle church has changed little in centuries. The spire of St Peter's Church, Oundle, still dominates the valley, which remains green with rich meadows, thanks to the tendency of the river to flood.

Inset A pike angler tackles up early on a winter's morning at Oundle Wharf, a short canal off the Nene once used by barges delivering barley to the town's maltings. Today the maltings are long gone and the only activity is from fishermen or from passers-by on the town bridge, which runs parallel to the wharf.

Lady of Oundle. After the dissolution its fortunes declined until a famous former pupil, Sir William Laxton, a London grocer during the reign of Henry VIII, rescued it with cash and ambitious new plans in 1556, two years after he became Lord Mayor of London.

Old Laxton School, rebuilt in 1852, is sandwiched between the Market Place and the graveyard of St Peter's Church. But it is in the later buildings that the reputation of the school spread worldwide. The man who earned the distinction of achieving this was the school's most famous headmaster, Frederick Sanderson, who devoted three decades (from 1892 to 1922) to halt the decline of the old school and achieve a milestone in the development of modern education.

Sanderson refused to believe there was such a thing as a bad boy; he insisted that it was always possible to find some subject that would stimulate the child's imagination and convert him to a discipline of learning. To achieve that aim he build workshops, laboratories and great libraries. The famous memorial chapel he commissioned to commemorate those who died in the 1914-18 war was consecrated in 1923. Its stained windows were designed by John Piper, who was also responsible for the world-famous window in the new Coventry Cathedral, built after the old cathedral was destroyed by the Luftwaffe in the Second World War.

Sanderson, the great educationalist, was proved right; his vision can be measured today by the thriving success of the modern school, which is scattered all about the town and includes an indoor sports complex as well as fine playing fields, dormitories and yet more modern science blocks. The school even has its own observatory, which includes a telescope made in 1736 by the celebrated astronomer James Short – the first man to mount an equatorial telescope with any success.

Famous old boys include Sir Peter Scott, the great conservationist and son of the ill-fated Scott of Antarctica. Young Peter was the subject of the bronze statue of a young boy outside the school's memorial chapel, sculpted by his mother, Lady Scott. He was later to know the lower reaches of the Nene well when he lived by his beloved salt marshes in a converted lighthouse near the estuary of the river below Sutton Bridge.

A broadcast pioneer

Even in his wildest dreams, Sanderson could never have imagined the amazing, adventure-packed life achieved by one of his pupils. Cecil Lewis, who was born in 1898, ran away from Oundle School at the age of 16. His masters probably regarded him as an academic failure, but failure was a word Lewis never understood.

After fleeing Oundle he lied about his age and joined the fledgling Royal Flying Corps (later RAF), flying over the Western Front during the First World War and winning the MC for bravery. After the war he was invited to Peking to teach the Chinese to fly. While there he met his first wife, the daughter of a Russian general. They returned to Britain in 1922, when he was appointed programme manager for the new BBC and was in charge of the small team that made the first-ever public broadcast, on 18 October of that year. Among the celebrities Lewis met during his five-year stint at the BBC was the playwright George Bernard Shaw, who encouraged him to take up writing when he eventually went freelance in 1926. Lewis obliged and, within a decade, he had decamped to Hollywood where he won an Oscar for his screenplay of *Pygmalion*.

When the Second World War dawned, Lewis rejoined the RAF, teaching hundreds of young pilots to fly. In 1947 he briefly tried his hand at farming in South Africa, before returning to England where he dabbled in the new commercial television before joining the *Daily Mail* as a journalist, in 1956. After retirement a decade later, he moved to Corfu, where he wrote novels, his autobiography and a series of travel books. He died on 27 January 1997 aged 98.

Today Oundle School attracts both boys and girls, boarders and scholarship day pupils. At breaks between lessons the town swarms with uniformed youngsters as they rush between the scattered school buildings to their next classes. The modern prosperity of the town owes much to the school; it is Oundle's biggest employer and the income generated by thousands of visitors each year gives the local economy a much-needed boost. While many small towns of a similar size seem shabby and caught in the spiral of economic decline, Oundle appears to flourish.

Returning to the North Bridge, and peering over the stone parapet along the west side, Oundle Wharf can be seen. This short canal of 400 yards or so was dug when a local brewery built its maltings on the edge of the town, just a few vital feet above the treacherous flood plain. The maltings, brewery and the barges that once delivered barley are all long gone, but the canal still exists and has proven to be an unlikely anglers' paradise. In summer it is a veritable hot-spot for tench, which love to browse under the shade of the dense lily pads, while in winter its placid waters provide a refuge for fishes escaping from the spate-like floodwaters of the main river. I have enjoyed some fabulous pike fishing here, while the Nene itself, just yards away, has been an unfishable, swirling torrent. The very mouth of the canal, opposite the school boathouses, is probably the best-known hot-spot on the entire river for carp. Huge specimen common carp to 30 lb inhabit this area and are even caught in the depths of winter.

Oundle itself is steeped in history, having been a human settlement since at least the Iron Age, and was once a monastery founded by Saint Wilfred, who died in AD 709. But being removed from the river, the town is best explored on foot. For now we are rejoining the Nene and heading downstream as the main water course, growing ever larger in stature, sweeps majestically across the rich meadows below the town.

The next port of call, **Cotterstock**, is a quiet village these days, but was once a Roman settlement. The Romans may even have built the first mill here on the site of the present building, which is, of course, now redundant and a private residence. The Aldwincle-born writer John Dryden often stayed at Cotterstock Hall, which was built in 1658, and would have enjoyed the view of the village church from the river, which we now pass on the left as we move on downstream to Perio Mill and the remarkable gravel pits that lie in the loop of the river just before Fotheringay.

The lair of a monster

In Chapter 9 we take a more detailed look at the Neneside lake with a reputation for breeding the biggest pike in Britain. It is part of the chain of flooded former gravel quarries at Bluebell Lakes, which can be reached easily from the river at Perio Lock or by road from the A605 at Warmington. To get there, turn right at the roundabout before the Little Chef services and after half a mile turn left at the T-junction. The fishery entrance is signposted on the right after 200 yards.

Besides being home to Britain's biggest known pike, seven-acre Kingfisher Lake holds carp to well over 30 lb, grass carp of more than 20 lb, catfish weighing almost 30 lb and chub over 6 lb.

Like so many of the gravel pits that line the Nene valley from Northampton downstream, the three lakes in the Bluebell complex provide a rich environment for fish and other wildlife. Anglers pay £5 per day for the privilege to fish there, but owner Tony Bridgefoot allows birdwatchers and country lovers to roam the picturesque setting free of charge.

Above An angler tries his hand from a precarious position above the swirling mill race at Cotterstock.

Below A couple of trees have disappeared, but otherwise these views of Cotterstock Church, taken around 1920 and 1996, remain little changed.

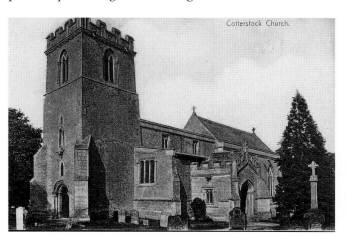

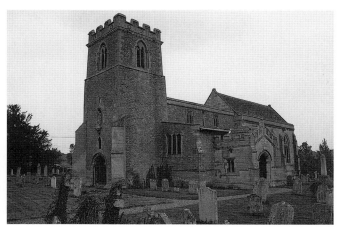

The mill stream at Perio, a mile upstream of Fotheringay, is an artificially stocked trout fishery. The main river is a winter hot-spot for pike and roach, while big tench and carp can be expected in summer.

Local residents are vociferous in their complaints when mineral companies apply for planning permission to extract gravel deposits from river valleys, but their inconvenience is only temporary. Once the bulldozers and diggers have finally departed, nature soon heals the scars to the landscape. Alders and willows spring up, apparently from nowhere, followed by reeds and sedges.

Landscaping and ambitious tree-planting schemes by the retreating gravel companies accelerate the naturalisation process, and within a short time what were once considered blots on the landscape become beauty spots. Meanwhile the water in the flooded pits has cleared and weeds become established, along with the underwater food chain that provides nourishment for all species of fish and fowl. It is true that unique water meadows have been destroyed in the past by gravel workings, but it should not be forgotten that the newly formed pools themselves are replacing the wetlands lost by the relentless canalisation of the river over the last two centuries.

5
Fotheringay to Peterborough

The flag-top quivers in the breeze
That sighs among the willow trees
In gentle waves the river heaves
That sways like boats the lily-leaves.

John Clare

Tragic Fotheringay

We are now entering Clare Country; the famous peasant poet of Northamptonshire knew these reaches of the river well. We'll return to his unhappy life later in this chapter, but let's start by exploring our first extraordinary port of call – historic **Fotheringay**.

The landscape around us begins to change as we arrive at the village and its classic humped stone bridge over the Nene. The rolling countryside characteristic of the upper and middle reaches of the river has all but gone as we get ever closer to the Fens. The houses are still built of stone, but from their upstairs windows the villagers can enjoy a panoramic view over the flat meadows.

The level landscape around Fotheringay is dominated

One of the most famous Nene views of all, and certainly one of the most impressive. Fotheringay's famous church, with its lantern tower and flying buttresses, and the nearby stone bridge over the river, have changed little since Mary Queen of Scots looked over them from her bleak cell within the former Fotheringay Castle.

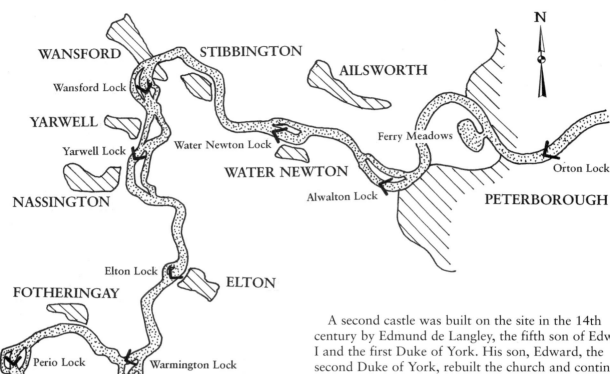

by the magnificent village church with its famous lantern tower, but a less dramatic riverside landmark nevertheless played a more dramatic role on the stage of British history – Fotheringay Castle. Its history stretches back to Norman times, for it was built in 1100 by Simon de St Lys, husband of William the Conqueror's great-niece, Maud, who also founded a nunnery. When Simon died, Maud married David, King of Scotland.

Earlier Maud's mother, Judith, had been granted over 500 acres of forest in these parts by her indulgent uncle. But it was not long before Fotheringay got its first taste of aristocratic blood. Earl Waltheof, Judith's husband, was sentenced to death for over-ambition. His punishment seems a little harsh for an era when ambition, greed and treachery would have appeared on the curriculum vitae of any self-respecting English earl, but unlucky Waltheof was beheaded all the same – reluctantly making history by becoming the first Englishman known to have been executed in such a manner. But a more notorious head was yet to be severed on the block at Fotheringay.

Left This wonderful view of Fotheringay church, taken from below the stone bridge over the Nene, remains as picturesque in 1996 as it was in the 'past' photograph, dating from 1935. Shame about the telegraph wires, though.

A second castle was built on the site in the 14th century by Edmund de Langley, the fifth son of Edward I and the first Duke of York. His son, Edward, the second Duke of York, rebuilt the church and continued building work on it until his death at the Battle of Agincourt in 1415. This was an unhappy place for the House of York; in 1462 Edward IV sadly returned to his castle with the remains of his father, Richard Duke of York, who had been killed at Wakefield, Yorkshire, two years earlier, and a brother, Edmund Duke of Rutland, who had been murdered. Edward's brother, Richard III, was born at Fotheringay in 1452. The family crest of the House of York can be seen on the golden weather vane atop the octagonal lantern tower of the church.

Today little remains of Fotheringay Castle – just a raised mound, the remnants of a moat and a few crumbling blocks of masonry mark the spot where Mary Queen of Scots was executed on 8 February 1587. But search around those dusty earthworks in high summer and you may experience a cold shiver down your spine as you stumble upon true Scottish thistles growing on the very spot where the unfortunate Queen lost her head – and where her heart was secretly buried. Her story was one of contrasting fortunes that turned eventually to tragedy.

The daughter of King James V of Scotland, Mary Stuart was born in 1542 as her father laid on his deathbed, and became Queen at just a few days old. Her mother, the devoutly Catholic Mary of Guise, was afraid of the growing influence of Protestantism north of the border, and sent the young Queen far south to be educated in France. There she eventually married the future King Francis II, who died after just one year on the French throne.

A narrowboat moored beside the mound that is all that remains of historic Fotheringay Castle.

The widowed Mary returned sadly to Scotland, where as Queen she wisely showed religious tolerance, continuing to worship as a Catholic while at the same time allowing the more numerous Protestants the freedom to worship as they chose. She seemed a popular Queen.

Her fall from grace began in 1565 when she married the scheming Lord Darnley. Hungry for power, within a year he had murdered Mary's chief advisor. He paid the ultimate price soon afterwards when he himself was killed – by a bomb explosion, plotted by yet another over-ambitious aristocrat, the Earl of Bothwell.

When Mary married Bothwell just three months later, her subjects were outraged. In June 1567 she was forced to abdicate in favour of her son, James VI of Scotland, and fled south to England, where she hoped that her Protestant cousin, Queen Elizabeth I, would welcome her and offer a safe refuge. Good Queen Bess, however, would have none of it. She was aware of Mary's murky past and suspicious of her future intentions, knowing that her very presence in the country could spark unrest from discontented Catholics.

Mary was duly incarcerated in the formidable medieval fortress of Fotheringay Castle, from where she gazed across the green Nene valley for the next two decades. She might have ended her days there peacefully, but inevitably she did indeed become the figurehead of the disillusioned English Catholics plotting Elizabeth's downfall, and hoping to install Mary on the throne instead. One such plot – the so-called Babington Conspiracy – was, when uncovered, shown to have had Mary's approval. She was duly tried and convicted of treason, and Elizabeth, who had been reluctant to execute her cousin, finally allowed her Privy Council to sign the death warrant.

The medieval chronicler Froude described the execution of Mary Queen of Scots in gory detail. He said she descended the staircase to the great hall where the scaffold was draped in black cloth. On the black block was a black cushion and, a short distance away, a black chair. The two masked executioners were, no doubt, also dressed in black. She walked to the block without expression, pausing only to recite a psalm.

The chief executioner was an accomplished headsman from the Tower of London, but somehow he failed to strike the right spot and barely broke the skin. The second blow, however, severed the head, which, according to Froude, immediately changed from that of a beautiful queen to a wizened old woman.

An eye-witness description – probably from the Earl of Kent – also described her final minutes, showing that Mary protested her innocence until the very last moment:

'After blubbering a while, she sayd yf ever I made any suche devise agaynst the Queene, my sister, I praye God I never see the face of God . . . then laye she downe verye quietlye stretchinge out her bodye & layinge her necke over the blocke, cryed, *In manus tuas domine*. One of her executioners held downe her hande, the other did with two strokes of the axe cut of her head, whiche fallinge of her attire appeared verye graye & near powled [bald].'

After the execution the Queen's blood-stained clothes and the executioner's block were burned.

Between the execution on 8 February and burial at Peterborough Cathedral on 31 July, Mary's body was embalmed and placed in a lead coffin under guard in the castle. But her heart was removed and buried secretly by the county sheriff somewhere in the castle grounds.

Mary's execution was a turning point in British history, and led to the attempted invasion of these shores by the Spanish Armada. Even today, more than 400 years later, the dramatic episode still creates enormous interest. In December 1996 the Church of England paid almost £100,000 for the original death warrant (which had been sold at Sotherby's 50 years earlier for just £230!). It had once been in the possession of John Selden, a 17th-century lawyer and politician, who had stolen it in 1641 from Lambeth Palace, the London home of the Archbishop of Canterbury, as Archbishop William Laud was dragged to the Tower of London for his own execution.

A Roman connection

The pleasant village of **Warmington** is a quiet place these days, thanks to the completion in 1996 of the long-awaited bypass which diverts the heavy traffic of the A605 away, closer to the river. Warmington is but a short stroll across the pleasant flood meadows from Fotheringay, but huge sweeping bends in the Nene mean that Warmington is 6 miles by river from

The oak tree near the gate had received a severe pruning when the original photograph was taken, around 1930, but had recovered enough to dominate the front view of Warmington Church in 1996.

Ashton, compared to less than 2 miles as the crow flies. This considerable inconvenience was too much for the impatient Romans, who built a road between the two villages, the remains of which are still present today, and form part of the Nene Way long-distance footpath.

Warmington and its rich farming lands belonged to the Abbey of Peterborough in Saxon times and in the Middle Ages was a prosperous agricultural community. The wealth generated helped pay for the village church of St Mary the Virgin, completed in 1290 and noted for its distinctive broach spire.

Closer to the river, the adjacent village of **Eaglethorpe** has been around since Danish invaders sailed up the river from the North Sea and founded a settlement there. It thrived until the 16th century, when the grounds of nearby Elton Hall were enlarged and little Eaglethorpe depopulated. A redundant watermill, built in 1880 and closed just a decade later, remains, along with a fine 17th-century dovecote, with nesting boxes for almost 800 birds. The latter is a Scheduled Ancient Monument, and is just visible from that very new monument to modern society, the A605 bypass.

The derelict Elton Mill, pictured in June 1991.

Tales of the riverbank

Until recent times a mink coat was considered a touch of class to which most women aspired. Today the slaughter of mammals for the whims of fashion is considered offensive, but the popularity of mink pelts earlier this century saw fur farms set up all over the country. Unfortunately, many of the mink escaped and flourished in the wild, where their fierce predatory habits wreaked havoc along the riverbank. These cuddly looking creatures, which originate from North America, are actually blood-thirsty killers with little fear: they will even attack humans if cornered.

On the Nene the worst victim has been the gentle water rat – the harmless rodent immortalised by the character of Ratty in Kenneth Grahame's *The Wind In The Willows*. Numbers of water rats have fallen by 70 per cent this century – all innocent victims of the mink. In the summer of 1996 the Environment Agency funded a two-year £130,000 research project by Oxford University to halt Ratty's decline. Scientists have even fitted water rats with collars containing electronic tracking devices so that their movements can be traced and their strongholds protected from their deadliest enemy.

Appropriately enough the River Nene is believed to

have been the inspiration behind *The Wind In The Willows*. Author Kenneth Grahame spent his summers with friends at **Elton Hall**, the seat of the Proby family, built in the 15th century and rebuilt in the 17th, with more additions following in subsequent years. Here Grahame liked to relax in a summerhouse beside the river. In fact one of the islands in the river in this area is known to this day as Ratty Island.

It does not take much imagination to picture the peaceful, willow-lined Nene of old as the setting for the tales that have delighted generations of youngsters and adults alike.

Sadly, there were more willows along the Nene in Grahame's day than there are today. In the past they were a valuable countryman's crop and were duly harvested. Regularly cutting back the pliant young shoots – a process known as pollarding – yielded material for basket-making, fencing, thatching and firewood. Pollarded willows still remain as an important feature of the Nene valley, but to save them from decline the Nene Valley Project has funded grants for landowners to pollard the trees, and has also offered free saplings for conservation-minded parishes along the river. It is hoped that imaginative projects like this will ensure that the scenery so beloved of Ratty, Mole and friends will live for ever.

An alien exterminated

When fur coats were all the rage, a cheaper alternative to mink was nutria, a fur produced from a rodent known as the coypu. This water-loving South American native was also farmed and, inevitably, some escaped. Its greatest stronghold was the Norfolk Broads, although it eventually spread westward to the Fens and, eventually, the Nene valley.

Unlike the voracious mink, the coypu was an endearing vegetarian that caused no harm to other wildlife. But it committed the cardinal sin of nibbling at farmers' crops, and the Ministry of Agriculture decided to wage war on the unfortunate creature. Once commonplace in East Anglia, the coypu is now extinct in this country, the very last specimen being trapped and shot on the banks of the River Nene near Peterborough more than ten years ago. The coypu had a sweet tooth and, sadly, its taste for a little sugar beet cost it its life. The mink commits murder and mayhem every day . . . but gets away with it.

Whose county is it anyway?

It is at Elton that the River Nene, having flowed the length of Northamptonshire, finally meets another county – officially Cambridgeshire, but morally Huntingdonshire. Prime Minister Edward Heath's unpopular attempts at Local Government reorganisation annexed Cromwell's county in 1974 – appropriately enough, on All Fools' Day – just as nearby Rutland was tacked on to Leicestershire. The indignant residents of Rutland, Britain's smallest county, never accepted the ignominy of extinction, and their relentless battle against bureaucracy has finally led to the return of their birthright. Perhaps it is time that the yeomen of Huntingdonshire performed similar protests – along with the folk of the Isle of Ely, which was similarly swallowed up by Cambridgeshire a decade earlier; in 1965 Huntingdonshire stole the Soke of Peterborough from Northamptonshire, in whose tender care it had been since the beginning of the 10th century, when King Alfred's son, Edward the Elder, created the shires. Huntingdon's tenure was much shorter, of course – just nine years before it was in turn engulfed by Cambridgeshire. In the late 1960s there was even a proposal to surrender the east bank of the Nene below Wisbech, thus shunting West Walton and surrounding areas of Norfolk into the great marshalling yard known as Cambridgeshire. Fierce local opposition put paid to the plan, but the pertinent question remains: is there a more voracious county in these islands than Cambridgeshire?

The truth is that it's not actually Cambridgeshire's fault. Not enough politicians from parish to Brussels care for the rich tapestry of our history. The fact that shire and parish boundaries have existed for thousands of years seemingly makes little difference to such people.

At present the Nene is the dividing line between Northamptonshire and Cambridgeshire for the next 4 miles, through **Nassington** and **Yarwell**, until it finally leaves the county of its birth altogether. The river in these parts has played an important part in the lives of local inhabitants since Roman times. The Romans built a village and excavated ironstone at Nassington, while quarries at Yarwell have, over the centuries, supplied limestone for building, clay for brick-making and, in more recent times, tons of gravel for new roads. Throughout this time the river was used for transporting these materials throughout the region.

Barnabee's misadventure

We take leave of Northamptonshire at **Wansford**, which is also known as Wansford-in-England. It is here too that the Nene, after tracking in a north-easterly direction from Northampton, suddenly sweeps around to flow eastward and on towards the sea.

The Great North Road used to pass through the centre of the village on its way from London to York, and once crossed the river via the old stone bridge; today, however, the picturesque village is spared the

Wansford Bridge, pictured around 1930 and in 1996. This is where the unfortunate Barnabee ended up after falling asleep on a haycock and being swept downstream in a flood.

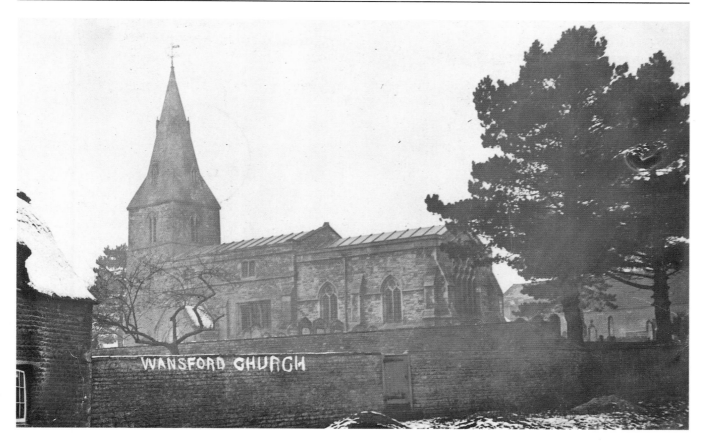

*New buildings and mature trees in 1996 prevented the author from enjoying the same view of
Wansford Church as the 1909 photographer achieved.*

intolerable noise of the traffic on the A1 by a newer bridge constructed a couple of hundred yards downstream in 1959. The original bridge was built of wood, to be replaced by a stone structure in the 13th century. It has 13 arches and was partly rebuilt in 1796 following severe flood damage.

The name Wansford-in-England comes from an old story, which has since been immortalised in picture and song, about a traveller named Barnabee who, in the reign of King George III, arrived in the parish while fleeing from the plague. Afraid to sleep in any of the local inns, he instead settled down for the night upon the top of a haystack in a meadow beside the river. During the night the river rose on account of a storm further upstream and the haystack duly floated off down the Nene before wedging itself firmly against the buttresses of the stone bridge.

Barnabee somehow slept through this chain of events, but was woken the next morning by an excited crowd of onlookers gathered on the bridge above him. In a state of shock he asked where he was. On being informed that he was in Wansford, and convinced that the raging river must have carried him much further, confused Barnabee is said to have replied, 'What, Wansford in England?'

The story's substance is backed up by the adjacent Haycock Inn, known today as the Haycock Hotel, built in 1632 and named after the celebrated incident. The inn sign splendidly depicts Barnabee's unwanted river voyage. The Haycock's strategic position, on the Great North Road and close to the thriving wharf on the river, must have made it a bustling place in the 18th and 19th centuries. It is said that the infamous highwayman, Dick Turpin, was among its visitors around 1737.

Quarried limestone and timber felled from the nearby remnants of Rockingham Forest were the main cargoes loaded at Wansford, while grain and coal brought upriver accounted for most of the goods unloaded. A little downstream of the bridge, in the grounds of Stibbington House, were situated the Wansford paper mills, which once supplied newsprint to *The Times* in London.

The Nene Valley Railway

On the opposite side of the A1 to Wansford stands the village of **Stibbington**, home of the Nene Valley Railway. This preserved line runs to Peterborough from the village station, which despite its location is known at Wansford. Mind you, it wasn't always so – when the station first opened in 1845 it was named Sibson, after another nearby village. The station building itself, incidentally, is said to be haunted by an elderly lady.

The Nene Valley Railway opened on 1 June 1977.

A trip on it is a splendid way of enjoying the adjacent river right through to Peterborough, and we'll shortly climb aboard for the next stage of our journey downstream to the Nene's only cathedral city. But in the meantime, while the train stands at the platform, let's take another trip . . . down Memory Lane to the lost and lamented days when the whole Nene valley from Northampton echoed to the sound of steam.

It all began on 17 September 1838 when the London & Birmingham Railway Company opened its 112-mile main line between the two cities. To the considerable annoyance of dignitaries in Northampton, it bypassed the county town by a full 5 miles, just as the Grand Union Canal had at the end of the previous century. The great Victorian railway engineer, Robert Stephenson, had, like the canal engineers before him, balked at the prospect of connecting with Northampton, due to the ridge of high ground south of the town. Blisworth, the point where the railway ran closest to Northampton, was a full 120 feet higher than the low valley in which the town was situated. When a canal connection had been finally excavated in 1815, that precipitous fall had required a full 17 locks, including ten in one flight.

Stephenson, whose with his father George had in 1829 built the world-famous *Rocket* locomotive, was concerned that the early steam locomotives would be incapable of tackling gradients much steeper than 1 in 330. 'It would be easy to get trains into Northampton, but very difficult to get them out again!' he said at the time.

But relentless pressure from industrialists in Northampton, concerned that the town was in danger of becoming a backwater on account of being bypassed by the most important form of modern transport, mounted a successful campaign to get connected and, within seven years, the Nene Valley branch line from Blisworth to Peterborough was opened, bringing the railway to Northampton as well as other major towns along the route, including Wellingborough, Irthlingborough, Thrapston and Oundle. Stations were also built in villages along the valley – namely Billing, Castle Ashby, Ditchford, Ringstead, Thorpe Waterville, Barnwell, Elton, Castor and Orton.

The line was built despite considerable opposition from powerful landowners along its route, including Lord Lilford of Lilford Park, and Earl Fitzwilliam of Milton Park, near Peterborough. The latter was the biggest thorn in the side of the railway engineers and

Right An autumn sunset over Castor backwater, once the haunt of thousands of Roman soldiers and potters, but now the home of recently re-introduced barbel.

Inset The mysterious pool below Water Newton Mill looks an inviting prospect for any angler.

Alwalton Lynch, across the river from Castor, remains a beauty spot in 1996, but it is not quite as leafy as it was in the 1930s, due to the felling of the old alders that once stood on the far bank.

did everything he could to make their lives as difficult as possible. No doubt it had a lot to do with the fact that he was the backer of a rival proposal to build the Northern & Eastern railway from London north via Cambridge and Peterborough.

The awkward earl did indeed have vested interests, but happily his spurious complaints that the railway's construction would cause flooding and damage to mills and other properties along the Nene were brushed aside in the general euphoria. Local people wanted the railway and the selfish views of one or two landed gentry were sensibly ignored. He certainly benefited financially from the line, pocketing £1,195 in compensation for land lost to the railway (out of a total of £10,000 paid to landowners along the route).

The 48-mile line opened on Monday 2 June 1845, with thousands of spectators and would-be passengers flooding to stations along the route. It is estimated that as many as 5,000 people travelled to Peterborough by stage coach from as far afield as Lincoln and King's Lynn. Most of the city's population of 7,000 also thronged to the new station to see the miracle of modern technology arrive and depart, and there were ugly scenes as passengers clamoured for the very limited number of seats available. Some even sat on the roofs of the carriages – a precarious position that meant having to remember to duck when the train went under low bridges!

The railway changed the tranquil course of the Nene, and it was reported that livestock bolted in terror at the approach of the iron monster. Near Milton three horses broke free from a wagon and galloped for 2 miles over hedges and ditches, dragging the broken harness.

The line between Northampton and Peterborough followed the easy, level route of the Nene valley and only one tunnel was required, at Wansford (617 yards). It cost just £429,409 against an estimated £500,000. Its engineer was Robert Stephenson, who had earlier hesitated to connect Northampton. The engineers, contractors and surveyors shared payments of £10,000. The hundreds of workers employed fared less well, with navvies and labourers receiving 3s 3d per day, bricklayers 5 shillings, carpenters 4s 6d and blacksmiths 5s 6d. Wages were paid fortnightly and the area saw rambling shanty towns built by the workers to house themselves in primitive conditions. Some were built from scraps of stone and timber, others from clods of earth! By July 1844 an estimated 1,000 men were employed at Wansford alone.

Ironically, the building of the line created the greatest commercial boat traffic ever seen on the River Nene, as thousands of tons of steel rails and wooden sleepers were delivered by barge, with traffic upstream from Wisbech docks being particularly busy. Between April and July 1844, 170 barges carrying 1,800 tons of

materials for the railway were logged at the junction with the Grand Union Canal at Northampton. Much more was delivered in the opposite direction, from the sea. All that was to change drastically after the opening of the line, which of course eventually killed off the river as a commercial highway.

Freight services followed and the popularity of the new railway was so great that a second track was installed. It was thought that this would improve the line's safety record, which had been marred by a series of accidents, but in fact the very worst accident in the line's history occurred on 18 October 1877, following the derailment of a goods train at Castle Ashby. With one line closed, all trains were diverted on to the other, and a railway inspector inadvertently allowed two trains on to the same section at once. They collided head-on and four people, including three police officers returning from court in Northampton, perished.

Following the Second World War competition from motor vehicles increased and signalled the end of the Peterborough-Northampton line, as well as many other branch lines throughout the country. Despite fierce opposition and imaginative protests in towns throughout the valley, the infamous Dr Richard Beeching, Chairman of the British Transport Commission, announced that the line would close on 9 September 1963, although in fact the final through passenger train ran on Saturday 2 May 1964. Freight services continued to run for a while, and special trains were laid on for pupils at Oundle School until 1972, but the very last train on the branch was chartered by the Peterborough Railway Society and ran on 4 November 1972.

It seemed that British Rail was keen to dash any hopes of future reopening as it set about demolition and track removal at an indecent haste. However, with the help of Peterborough Development Corporation the railway society succeeded in securing the last 7 miles of the line, which is today the Nene Valley Railway. The railway attracts tens of thousands of visitors every year, including enthusiasts who come to see British and continental locomotives and rolling-stock at work on the same system. The railway has also been the setting for many film and television sequences, including the James Bond movies *Octopussy* and *Goldeneye*.

In the author's opinion there is no better view of the lush Nene valley – and arguably no better way of enjoying it – than from a sedate steam train travelling from Wansford to Peterborough (or vice versa, of course). It is a crying shame that the line does not exist in its entirety and I have no doubt that many readers will share my contempt for Beeching and the short-sighted politicians who murdered it. Thirty years on it would have made a wonderful tourist attraction as well as relieving pressure upon our overloaded roads.

I sincerely hope the rumour I have recently heard of plans to extend the line with the help of National Lottery grants is true.

Little Italy by the Nene

It is a long way from the Mediterranean, but there must have been something special about the Nene valley that the Romans couldn't resist. Perhaps the fertile valley and, maybe, a slightly warmer climate allowed them to plant vineyards? The image of toga-clad Latin types sipping the fruits of their labours by a sun-kissed River Nene is hard to resist as one puffs by on the train from Wansford, but whatever the truth we are certainly travelling through what was once a Roman city.

The original, arrow-straight course of the Romans' Ermine Street, which the modern A1 largely follows, crosses the fields, railway and river here between **Castor** and Water Newton. Beside it, a mile or so from Alwalton, is the remains of what was known to the Romans as Durobrivae.

It was first excavated by Edmund Artis, steward to Earl Fitzwilliam of Milton Hall, when a new road was being built on the estate early in the 19th century. Ornate pavements and the foundations of villas, baths, temples and forums were uncovered, measured, sketched and covered up again – except for the finest of the pavements, which Earl Fitzwilliam ordered to be relaid in the dairy at Milton Hall!

But it was not until 1930 that the full significance of the Roman remains was discovered by the famous antiquarian, Mr O. G. S. Crawford, then director of the Ordnance Survey, as he flew over the area in a light aircraft. Revealed below him in the growing corn of the fields close to the river was the clear outline of the town, as well as a huge garrison.

Later excavations discovered pottery kilns and valuable hoards of coins and silver. Local clay was used to produce what is now known as 'Castorware', which was exported throughout the Roman empire – some has even been traced to Turkey. It is also certain that materials from the buildings of the lost city were used in subsequent centuries for new structures, including red tiles and parts of white columns that helped build the village church in nearby Castor (which, incidentally, comes from the Latin word for 'fort'). The Saxon church was founded in the 7th century and dedicated to St Kyneburga, a daughter of Penda, King of Mercia. The church was largely rebuilt by the Normans, an inscription above the priest's doorway indicating that is was re-consecrated on 17 April 1124.

In more recent times the most dramatic event to occur at Castor was in January 1945 when a German V1 'Doodlebug' rocket landed close to the railway line near Castor station. Nobody was hurt and, apart from a few slates dislodged from the station buildings, no damage was caused . . . except for a huge crater marking the site of the missile. Despite the near-miss, it is doubtful whether Hitler was actually aiming at the station, which was of little or no strategic importance. It is more likely that the missile was intended for Peterborough and, fortunately, missed.

Ferry Meadows

Just 2 miles further down both the railway and the Nene is **Ferry Meadows** station, which serves the 2,500-acre Nene Valley Country Park. Just 25 years ago its 120 acres of landscaped lakes were gravel workings supplying aggregate for the building boom that signalled the peak of Peterborough's expansion. The Nene skirts this modern pleasure park and, close to Milton Hall, is crossed by the stone Milton Ferry bridge, built in 1716. As its name suggests, there was a ferry across the river at this point before the bridge was built.

Just as tens of thousands of visitors flock to Ferry Meadows to relax in the countryside, so did their predecessors a hundred years and more earlier. In Victorian and Edwardian days Ferry Meadows station was known as Overton (the old name for Orton) and was a popular destination for families visiting the local beauty spot known as Alwalton Lynch. The wooded riverside Lynches, easily accessed from Alwalton village, are just as pleasant today – and a lot less crowded than in their heyday.

The countryside in these parts has changed a lot over the centuries, but it was well known and appreciated by a local peasant who, against all odds, became a great poet. It is now time to leave the railway and follow in the footsteps of a great man.

The Peasant Poet

He loved the brook's soft sound
The swallow swimming by
He loved the daisy-covered ground
The cloud-bedappled sky
To him the dismal storm appeared
The very voice of God
And when the Evening rock was reared
Stood Moses with his rod
And every thing his eyes surveyed
The insects i' the brake
Were creatures God almighty made
He loved them for his sake
A silent man in life's affairs
A thinker from a boy
A Peasant in his daily cares -
The Poet in his joy.

Man's love for woman has provoked wars, and founded then destroyed great empires. It has also inspired men to poetry – and none more poignantly than John Clare. The peasant poet's unrequited love for his childhood sweetheart endured beyond her life and to the last dying breath of his own. It still lives as vividly today, two centuries later, through his remarkable verse.

More than that, John Clare's eccentric life story is hopelessly entwined with the erratic, meandering course of the River Nene. Indeed, through his poems we are privileged to step back two centuries to experience the richness of this valley and the people who lived there before the Industrial Revolution. It is a unique insight into a tangible paradise lost to the poet as well as ourselves. It's so earthy you can taste the soil.

Today the village of Helpston is within sight and

These views of - and from - Milton Ferry bridge are every bit as pleasant in 1996 as they were earlier this century.

The Ferry Bridge, Milton, Peterborough.
J. W. B. Series.

sound of the urban sprawl of Greater Peterborough. Its picture-postcard cottages of weather-worn limestone are usually described by estate agents as 'prestige properties', sometimes 'picturesque'. Simple John Clare would have scratched his puzzled red head at the sharp-suited babblespeak we all seem destined to endure in the closing years of the 20th century. When he and his twin sister were born over 200 years ago in Helpston, the village was within the old county boundary of Northamptonshire and his family's cottage was no desirable residence. It was a plain hovel in which country folk like the Clares endured their hard struggle against grinding poverty and shocking infant mortality. Indeed, Clare's twin – although seemingly stronger than her brother – died after only a few weeks.

Back in 1793 Helpston was situated on the edge of Peterborough Great Fen and a full 6 miles from the old cathedral city. His parents – a farm labourer and his illiterate wife – could hardly have dreamt that their baby son would ever grow up to become anyone other than another labourer.

Sure enough, the youthful John Clare was soon working in the fields, employed in turn as ploughboy, reaper, thresher, gardener and lime-burner. But from his father – a recounter of folk verse in the oral tradition – young John inherited his love of words. Amazingly he taught himself to read and write, and began to write verse at the age of 13.

Soon afterwards the young dreamer met and fell in love with Mary Joyce, a local farmer's daughter. But her stern father disapproved of her relationship with a lowly ploughboy and forbade her to see him again. The relationship ended in 1816, but Clare never forgot her:

> Fate and fortune, long contrary
> Grant but one request to me
> Bless me in the charms of Mary
> Nothing more I ask of thee

In 1820 his first book, *Poems Descriptive of Rural Life*, was published. A minor sensation ensued. Poets were supposed to come from privileged backgrounds and Clare had broken the established mould. He wrote about the rural scene through fresh, innocent eyes – through which his affected, and sometimes precious, poetic contemporaries were never privileged to see. Perhaps he didn't have access to appropriate quantities of opium. . . Clare's unlikely success sent tremors through a world that was still essentially feudal.

That same year he married Patty (Martha) Turner, and the following year his second collection of poems, *The Village Minstrel*, appeared. He then began writing on his epic work, *The Shepherd's Calendar*, which subsequently appeared in 1827, albeit savagely edited.

Around that time Clare's mental health began to deteriorate, with frequent bouts of melancholia and depression providing the first signs of the tragic years that were to follow. He had already travelled to London and met the literary giants of the time; imagine the contrast he felt when he returned to his rustic existence in Helpston where his illiterate neighbours distrusted him. He had tasted both worlds, but belonged to neither.

His status as a minor celebrity attracted well-meaning patrons, who believed that his squalid existence was the cause of his problems. In 1832 they arranged for him to be rehoused in a larger cottage in neighbouring Northborough, but his departure from his native village deepened his paranoia.

Clare had a wife and six children to feed. Then, as now, a career as a poet was not exactly profitable and he was forced to seek work on the land to make ends meet and put food on the table. As if that was not enough, the rustic life into which he had been born in the closing years of the 18th century was passing. He had previously felt secure describing the commons, heaths, pastures, woods and undrained fens of his youth. But the red-hot furnace of the Victorian economy was blasting away his beloved countryside as landowners took advantage of new enclosure laws and parcelled it up neatly for themselves. Angry and frustrated, Clare wrote at the time:

> There was a time my bit of ground
> Made freemen of the slave
> The ass no pindar'd dare to pound
> When I his supper gave
> The gipsy's camp was not afraid
> I made his dwelling free
> Till vile enclosure came and made
> A parish slave of me

Woods were torn up, commons and heaths put to the plough and fens drained. Babbling brooks were diverted and canalised and the wildlife with which he identified so closely all but fled the scene.

Yet he continued to write of the world he had loved. *The Rural Muse* was published in 1835 to considerable acclaim, but in June 1837 Clare was admitted to a lunatic asylum in Epping, Essex. He escaped in 1841 and walked home to Northborough, convinced he would be reunited with his childhood sweetheart, Mary. He was convinced he was married to her, whereas she had actually died a spinster at the age of 41, in 1838. When told, Clare stubbornly refused to believe it.

The reunion was, understandably, a disaster. Martha tired of her husband's confusion and longing for a lost love. After five tempestuous months back within the family fold, she agreed to have him committed to Northampton General Lunatic Asylum.

The cottage in Helpston where John Clare grew up, and his grave in the village churchyard.

There he could easily have lived out his twilight years in the unspeakable horrors of Bedlam. Instead, tormented John Clare penned the finest verse of his career, still lamenting the lost love for Mary that burned at his very soul:

To Mary

I sleep with thee and wake with thee
And yet thou art not there
I fill my arms with thoughts of thee
And press the common air
Thy eyes are gazing upon mine
When thou art out of sight
My lips are always touching thine
At morning noon and night

I think and speak of other things
To keep my mind at rest
But still to thee my memory clings
Like love in woman's breast
I hide it from the world's wide eye
And think and speak contrary
But soft the wind comes from the sky
And whispers tales of Mary

The night wind whispers in my ear
The moon shines in my face
A burden still of chilling fear
I find in every place
The breeze in whispering in the bush
And the dew fall from the tree
All sighing on and will not hush
Some pleasant tales of thee

John Clare passed away on 20 May 1864 and was buried at Helpston four days later. But his reputation lives on. Famous in his heyday as a curiosity, Clare and his gentle, thoughtful poetry were largely forgotten in the years following his death. Happily the iron-clad critics of Victorian society were followed by more appreciative souls and his reputation was first revived, and later enhanced, through the 20th century.

Today he has gained his rightful status as one of our greatest writers. It took a long time, but on 13 June 1989 a memorial to Clare was finally unveiled in Poet's Corner at Westminster Abbey. God bless his tortured soul.

The memorial to Clare, the Peasant Poet, at Helpston.

I am

I am – yet what I am, none cares or knows
My friends forsake me like a memory lost
I am the self-consumer of my woes
They rise and vanish in oblivion's host
Like shadows in love-frenzied stifled throes
And yet I am and live – like vapours tost

Into the nothingness of scorn and noise
Into the living sea of waking dreams
Where there is neither sense of life or joys
But the vast shipwreck of my life's esteems
Even the dearest that I love the best
Are strange – nay, rather, stranger than the rest

I long for scenes where man hath never trod
A place where woman never smiled or wept
There to abide with my Creator, God
And sleep as I in childhood sweetly slept
Untroubling and untroubled where I lie
The grass below – above, the vaulted sky

Of saints and sinners

Clare's fame and the attention it drew to him were not always welcomed by the awkward poet. In the 1820s Mrs Marsh, elderly and bored wife of the Rt Rev Dr Herbert Marsh, Bishop of Peterborough, had taken an interest in Clare and offered several invitations for him to visit her at the Bishop's Palace.

He was taken to a room, supplied with paper, pens and ink and expected to write a masterpiece there and then! Mortified, he fled through the cathedral gardens and into the sanctuary of the Red Lion pub on the Market Place. Several pints of strong ale soon revived his spirit as he slowly acquired the Dutch courage necessary to return to the formidable Mrs Marsh. By then he was clearly drunk, but happily the Bishop's wife wrongly attributed his condition to 'high poetic musings'.

Peterborough is the only cathedral city on the banks of the Nene. Traces of Roman settlements have been found here, but were dwarfed into insignificance by the thriving industrial area to the west known as Durobrivae. Situated on the Nene and close to the Fens with their rich stocks of fish and fowl as well as plentiful reed for thatching, Peterborough was bound to become a popular place to dwell.

But in its earliest recorded incarnation, its name was Medeshamstede ('meadow homestead'), founded in 655 when a great abbey was built. In Saxon times it was one of the most important religious centres in the country, and a town duly grew around it.

But that town was utterly destroyed by raiding Danes

The embankment of the Nene at Peterborough has changed a lot between these two photographs dating from the 1950s and 1990s, but the magnificent Norman cathedral still dominates the scene.

around 870, who according to the *Anglo-Saxon Chronicle* left the abbey a smoking ruin, littered with the bodies of the slain. Medeshamstede seemed all but finished – and only saintly intervention resurrected it.

That saintly figure was St Aethelwold. One day God appeared to him in a vision and instructed him to go to the land of the Middle Angles and rebuild a monastery dedicated to St Peter. Aethelwold followed his orders, but mistakenly turned up at Oundle, where he proceeded to commence building work. It was necessary for God to appear to Aethelwold a second time with more detailed instructions, ordering him to proceed downstream along the banks of the River Nene until he arrived at the walls of a ruined monastery.

It took him just a day to arrive at the remains of Medeshamstede, where he built a new church. A wall was built around the new settlement and in 972 the new church was dedicated to St Peter and the town became St Peter's Burh (the latter word meaning a

defended settlement). Over the centuries the name has evolved to the present Peterborough.

Spoil-sport historians over the years have poured cold water on this tale and insisted that the 'Burh' part of the name was wrong because the old town was not a defended settlement. Happily, proof of the latter came in 1982 when a trench dug close to the present cathedral precinct uncovered the foundations of the old wall. It is of course impossible to prove that Aethelwold's saintly doings were indeed done . . . just as it is impossible to prove they were not.

Two Queens buried

The magnificent cathedral we see today was built by the Normans, with work commencing in 1172, but it did not become a cathedral until the 16th century when King Henry VIII dissolved the monasteries and made the abbot, John Chambers, the first Bishop of

At the turn of the century the area immediately downstream of Peterborough's Town bridge was a commercial area where lighters loaded and unloaded goods. Today it is part of the Town Embankment and boasts a floating Chinese restaurant. Beyond the modern bridge, and out of shot, is a matching floating pub with a vast array of real ales.

Peterborough's modern Cathedral Square was known as the Market Place when the earlier photograph was taken, around 1910.

Peterborough. Buried inside the cathedral is Henry's pathetic first wife, Catherine of Aragon, whom he divorced after she failed to produce the required son and heir. It was that divorce that changed the course of English history and, ironically, caused the abbey to become a cathedral.

Catherine's body lies beneath a marble stone placed there in 1895 by the Catherines of England, Ireland, Scotland and America. Henry's daughter, Elizabeth I, was responsible for the burial of the only other Queen to be buried at the cathedral, Mary Queen of Scots, who, as we saw earlier in this chapter, was executed at Fotheringay Castle on 8 February 1587. After embalming, her remains were buried at the cathedral in July, where they remained until 1612, when her son, James I, had them removed to Westminster Abbey. There is a certain irony in the fact that she is now buried a few feet from Elizabeth.

Both Queens were buried by the cathedral's famous verger, Robert Scarlett (1496-1594), who claimed that he had buried the entire population of Peterborough twice over. This colourful character, known as Old Scarlett, is depicted on a curious painting from 1747 that hangs in the nave, where he is pictured holding a spade, pickaxe, keys and a whip.

Today the cathedral is best known for its famous – and glorious – West Front. But there is much more to Peterborough than its most famous building.

Despite its long history, it was a small town for many centuries. In 1801 the population was less than 4,000, although that had doubled by the middle of the century as the Industrial Revolution and agricultural depression brought families from the countryside to the towns. But there is no doubt that Peterborough was a very backward place – the last sedan chair for public hire in England was in use on the streets here in the 1860s. Although major companies like the Perkins Group, Hotpoint and Peter Brotherhood opened factories, Peterborough never seemed to keep pace with the rest of the world.

That stagnation ended in 1968, when the Peterborough Development Corporation was formed and the city received New Town designation. Since then the population has almost doubled and is expected to reach 180,000 by the year 2001. It is Europe's fastest-growing city.

But while Peterborough has flourished and changed out of all recognition, there are still places to enjoy by the River Nene, which was first bridged by Godfrey of Croyland (Crowland) in 1308. That structure was made of wood and cost £13. It survived until 1872, when it was replaced with an iron span that cost all of £5,500. In 1934 the present stone viaduct, a full 442 feet long, was built in five spans to stride across the river and the adjacent railway line. Beside the bridge stands the classical Custom House with its lantern roof.

Below the bridge on the north bank is the tree-lined embankment, while the opposite south bank is currently the subject of a multi-million-pound redevelopment scheme that entails demolishing scruffy old warehouses and factories to create 200 new homes and a leisure park. The scheme has already been approved by Peterborough City Council planners and is expected to go ahead before the end of the century.

❧6❧
Down to the sea

Brown are the flags and fading sedge
And tanned the meadow plains
Bright yellow is the osier hedge
Beside the brimming drains

John Clare

A man-made river

Leaving Peterborough behind us, we embark on the final stage of our journey to the mouth of the river and the sea. It is a voyage the poet Clare knew well, for as a lad in 1807 he took a seat on a passenger boat from Peterborough to Wisbech for a job interview. Councillor Bellamy, a solicitor in the town, was seeking an apprentice. Clare's chance came courtesy of his uncle, Morris Stimson, who was footman to the Councillor. Happily for the future of English poetry, the rustic rough edges of the young Clare were deemed unsuitable for such a distinguished career, and John – probably secretly relieved – climbed back aboard the passenger lighter and returned back to Peterborough and the countryside he loved so much. 'Wisbeach was a foreign land to me for I had never been above eight miles from home in my life,' he later wrote, adding that the 21-mile journey cost 18d.

The North Bank of the Nene, looking upstream towards Peterborough from near the tidal sluice.

It is immediately below Peterborough that the real Nene ends, so to speak. For as we leave the city behind and cruise along the modern, straight channel towards the tidal sluice, we pass on our starboard side the entrance to Stanground Lock. It is at this point that the Nene used to turn sharp right and follow an entirely different route. We'll be tracing the course – or rather courses – of former incarnations of the River Nene in the next chapter, but for now we'll follow the present course, which was entirely engineered by man.

We are entering the true Fens now – low-lying land that was once a vast, malaria-plagued wetland before it was drained to become the finest agricultural land in the country. We'll also look more closely at the drainage of the flatlands in the next chapter, but in passing this area we should spare a thought for the Bronze Age farmers and warriors who settled in this difficult terrain around 3,000 years ago. Archaeologists are currently unearthing the evidence left by these fascinating people at Flag Fen.

The broad, lily-fringed river, a reach known as the North Bank, is very different from what we have experienced so far. But very soon the nature of the river changes even more dramatically as we meet the tides from the Wash.

Until the 1930s and the formation of the Nene Catchment Board, high spring tides actually surged upstream and lapped on Peterborough's doorstep, but a new sluice erected in 1938 at Dog-in-a-Doublet, 3 miles downstream of the city, created a new tidal barrier. It is here, adjacent to the inn of the same name, that we get our first taste of salt – the tangible test that the sea is getting closer. In 1995 a £50,000 fish pass was installed at the sluice to assist young eels in their upstream migration; the elvers couldn't negotiate the powerful flow beneath the sluice gates and were left stranded in the tidal river. But the high-technology fish pass – which counts every fish that swims through – has changed all that.

'We've counted as many as 2,000 eels pass through in a single day, as well as good roach, chub, dace, bream and pike,' says the Environment Agency's local fisheries officer, Chris Reeds.

Other finned visitors through the fish pass have included big carp, zander and even a stray sea trout. The pass also acts as a safe haven for these fish during low oxygen levels in the tidal river, which sadly suffers from sewage pollution.

This imposing steel structure is Dog-in-a-Doublet sluice, built in the 1930s to halt the upstream march of high tides.

Above This beautifully marked pike weighed a little over 15 lb and was landed by Wisbech angler Steve Hicks from the tidal Nene a few yards below Dog-in-a-Doublet sluice in February 1983.

Below The tidal Nene between Thorney and Guyhirn is skirted to the south (right) by the rich meadows of the Nene Washlands, which when flooded in winter provide a valuable feeding ground for wildfowl.

A brickyard town

The tidal sluice stands a mile and a half from the town of Whittlesey. Parallel to the river lies Morton's Leam, one of the earliest attempts at draining the Fens, and between it and Whittlesey lie the Washlands – rich areas of pasture that are allowed to flood in winter and provide a valuable habitat for rare water fowl. During the exceptionally hard winters that we so seldom get these days, but which were commonplace in Victorian times, thousands of skaters flocked here to skim across the ice on the shallows.

Whittlesey was a town well-known for its skaters, but even better renowned for its brickworks. The collapse of the construction industry in recent years has been mirrored by a decline in the local brickworks, but the towering chimneys of the local kilns are still landmarks for miles around.

The secret of the town's success in brick-making literally lies under its feet in the form of blue-black Oxford clay containing a high proportion of bituminous material. This makes the bricks self-firing at high temperatures, and therefore very cheap to produce. It is said that you can tell which part of the country bricks come from by their finished colour: Whittlesey bricks turn a blushing pink after their sojourn in the kilns.

The landscape of the area is scarred with huge clay

Thorney Abbey has seen momentous changes in its turbulent history, but these views taken in the 1920s and 1990s are remarkably similar.

quarries that have yielded the raw material over the years. The excavations have also revealed some stunning fossils of long-lost marine creatures from the days when this area was part of a tropical prehistoric sea; in September 1987 the complete skeleton of a massive swimming reptile known as a plesiosaur was unearthed. Estimated at 160 million years old, the fossil is now housed at Peterborough Museum. Other finds have included marine crocodiles and whale-sized fishes.

The countryside along the south bank of the Nene below Whittlesey may appear flat and monotonous, but don't let appearances deceive you. Just 4 miles below the town, at Poplar House Farm, the river effects a remarkable invisible transformation as it flows from the western hemisphere to the eastern hemisphere. It is at this point that the Greenwich Meridian (longitude 0 degrees) bisects the river – and the world. Isn't it a shame that nobody has ever erected a suitable pillar or obelisk to mark the very spot?

Also in this area is a buried Roman Causeway between Goosetree and Eldernell. **Eldernell** today is populated mainly by a thriving heron population, but in 1055 it was an early Christian shrine and site of miracle healing. In that year Robert Whyt of Whittlesey was dying, and so weak that he was unable to get out of bed; he could also hardly speak. But one night he received a vision of the Blessed Lady of Eldernell who promised to preserve and comfort him if he would tell the vicar of Whittlesey to preach a sermon condemning parishioners for swearing and blasphemy. Suitably encouraged, Robert managed to rise from his death bed, get dressed and stagger barefoot 3 miles across the frosty fens to Our Lady of Eldernell . . . followed inevitably by a throng of inquisitive neighbours, plus the doubtful vicar.

When he arrived he instantly fell to his knees and was struck dumb for 15 minutes before he eventually cried out: 'Lady, help!' At this point tears flowed from the eyes of the statue and Robert was healed to live to a ripe old age. It is not known whether the townsfolk of Whittlesey heeded the vicar's subsequent warnings of bad language.

Thorney's abbey

The straight drain heading due north from the Dog-in-a-Doublet sluice is the canalised section of the old Thorney River, which runs for 2½ miles to the village of **Thorney**. Here stands Thorney Abbey, originally founded in 662 by Sexwolf, Abbot of Peterborough, who asked to 'build there a Minster to the Glory of St Mary, so that they who would lead the life of peace and rest may dwell therein'. His priory was razed to the ground in 870 by Danish invaders, rebuilt in 972 and demolished a century later by the Normans, who constructed the magnificent Benedictine Abbey, the west front of which still stands as part of the present parish church.

A harmless scapegoat

Farmers have, inexplicably, failed to recognise the virtues of the humble mole. In its favoured home on pastureland its underground endeavours aerate compacted ground and its insatiable hunger helps rid the soil of unwanted pests like leatherjackets, yet for centuries the mole has been persecuted – nowhere more so than on the Nene below Peterborough, where it was believed that the mole's burrowing could weaken flood defences and cause river banks to burst and inundate

Lancashire-based pike fishing expert Gord Burton is a regular visitor to the Nene valley. Here he is pictured pitting his wits against the big predators that prowl the Thorney Toll Drain, which empties into the tidal Nene 5 miles above Guyhirn.

low-lying land. It was nonsense, of course, but hardly surprising. Superstitious drainage commissioners of earlier centuries buried so-called witches alive in breached banks as insurance against future floods. In the light of such old wives' tales, the case against the unfortunate mole seemed almost rational.

Perhaps it is wrong to be too harsh on our ancestors. The Fens, with their makeshift drainage schemes of years gone by, were a dangerous place to live. The inhabitants had every reason to be nervous, because they lived out every day in the knowledge that their livelihoods – and indeed lives – could be swept away in a moment if the banks burst . . . which they did, with alarming frequency.

Moles lived below ground, so were easy to blame. The fact that they restricted their burrowing to the surface layers was missed, perhaps deliberately, by the drainage chiefs who did not like to admit that the banks had an inherent fault – they were mainly built up from the soft, unstable silt and peat from the adjacent land and were, therefore, fatally flawed. They were weak and burst from the bottom under intense water pressure; the moles' surface workings were merely superficial and didn't make a blind bit of difference.

Drainage engineers eventually woke up to reality and replaced the banks with clay, reinforced by willow bundles and even stone – yet poor old mole still didn't earn a reprieve. His wholesale slaughter was still sanctioned well into the present century, with armies of professional mole-catchers patrolling every vulnerable bank where traps were set and poisoned bait (earthworms laced with strychnine) laid to kill the harmless creatures.

The locals did not complain. Mole-catching was a doddle compared to the arduous slog of farm labouring, and the fur of the little victims were valuable, in season. At the turn of the century, when fur coats were essential fashion accessories for women, the pathetic velvety black pelts of moles fetched as much as 3s 6d each, which was a substantial sum of money in those days. In spring, when the moles were moulting and their little coats therefore valueless to the fashion industry, mole-catchers advertised their proficiency by stringing their victims together and displaying them along fences and hedgerows in gory gibbets.

Their mummified little front feet were, meanwhile, carried in the pocket of many countrymen as a cure for rheumatism, just as other people still carry a rabbit's foot as a good luck charm.

Professional mole-catchers still plied their trade as little as 20 years ago. Today they have all but died out, although some old-timer no doubt still brings his traps out of retirement on demand when some local farmer complains that moles are disturbing the roots of his young sugar beet crop.

Those who lament nostalgically the passing of the colourful characters of yesteryear should remember that not all country crafts and activities were rustic recreations whose demise is a great loss. Mole-catching, like badger-baiting and otter-hunting, was a barbaric anachronism which, thankfully, is no more.

Guyhirn

Newcomers to the Fens are struck immediately by the absence of trees in this flat landscape. The horizons are endless and the wide skyscapes, with their associated winter sunsets, sublime.

Curves do not exist in this part of the world. The Nene cut from Whittlesey and the A47 trunk road from Thorney both converge arrow-straight on the Neneside village of **Guyhirn**. All the fields are perfect rectangles, and if you look at the neatly tended gardens of the lonely, windswept cottages, you'll see that local horticulturalists mirror the same geometric lines. Borders are straight and the rows of plants orderly; rare indeed is the cluttered floral chaos of a typical cottage garden in less bleak parts of the country. The wild abandonment of nature plays no part in the lives of folk living on the dangerous edge of land and water, where Mother Nature herself has for generations been seen as an adversary. At Guyhirn the A47 runs parallel to the river, which itself is contained within banks high above the fields, providing obvious proof of the danger of living below sea level.

Guyhirn itself lies skulking beneath the far bank of the river, perched on the divide between the peat soil of the Fens and the silt soil of the marshland. Floods have come from freshwater and saltwater incursions, and for centuries locals have prayed to God for deliverance from the waters.

The village's Puritan Chapel, also known as the Guyhirn Chapel of Ease, was built in 1660 – ironically the very same year that England ceased to be a Commonwealth and Charles II ascended to the throne following the death of Oliver Cromwell. It is believed to have been built from stone salvaged from the ruins of Thorney Abbey, augmented by plain, local brick. It has a stark, bare interior and hard wooden pews purposefully placed close together to prevent 'Papist kneeling'. The last service was held here on 5 November 1960, since when it has been maintained by the Redundant Churches Fund.

Capital of the Fens

Whether by river or by the adjacent A47, our approach to **Wisbech** is greeted by the unspoilt spectacle of the fine Georgian architecture of the town's famous North Brink. First port of call on the left is the grand facade of Elgoods

The North Brink and Bridge, Wisbech

The absence of road traffic in the 'past' photograph (taken in approximately 1930) contrasts with the much busier modern view, from 1996. But the famous architecture of the North (left) and South Brinks remains little changed. Note that the fences that once stood at the top of the banks have been replaced by flood defence walls following disastrous high tides in 1947, 1953 and 1978.

Freedom Bridge in Wisbech is the last fixed bridge over the river. This is the view downstream, towards the port.

brewery, a family-run concern that has produced fine real ales for generations, and which owns a large number of no-nonsense tied houses throughout the area. It is said that Elgoods draught bitter (known nowadays as Cambridge Ale) is best served by the pubs that line the banks of the Nene, as the river cools their deep cellars and keeps the ales in pristine condition. While it is true that beer from these pubs tastes wonderful, in my experience it is equally certain that beer from hostelries miles distant tastes just as good. But then, I can possibly be accused of bias since I was born in this neck of the woods and practically weaned on the stuff! In my subjective opinion, you won't find a better bitter in the kingdom.

But before 'refuelling' at any of these pubs, don't rush past the town's other historic buildings. Unlike most towns along the Nene, Wisbech is built around the river as opposed to slightly above it. That is not surprising since Wisbech has been an important port for centuries. It claims to be the first place to have imported port into England – once deemed essential in these parts to 'cure' the ague, or malaria, which was such a curse before the Fens were drained. Not for nothing is Wisbech known as the Capital of the Fens.

Founder of The National Trust

On the South Brink at Wisbech a blue plaque commemorates the birthplace of Miss Octavia Hill, born in 1838, who became a great philanthropist and reformer of living conditions for the poor. She is remembered mainly for co-founding The National Trust in 1895 with Canon H. D. Rawnsley and Sir Robert Hunter, but was earlier – in 1856 – secretary to the Educational Classes for Women at the Working Men's College, Great Ormond Street, London, and later formed a school where girls were trained in home management.

The National Trust's main treasure in Wisbech is Peckover House, on the opposite side of the river along North Brink. It was built by the Southwell family in 1722, who sold it to Jonathan Peckover, a banker, who, appropriately enough, named it Bank House. Eventually, late in the 19th century, it passed to his nephew Alexander, who was later made a peer and became Lord Peckover of Wisbech. He was a keen collector of books, fine furniture and paintings, which today's visitors flock there to see.

The fight against slavery

It was a full 150 years after his death before Wisbech-born Thomas Clarkson received the national recognition he deserved for his unstinting fight against slavery. The son of the cleric-headmaster of the town's grammar school, Clarkson was born in 1760. He too was expected to become a clergyman, but at the age of 25 his life took a dramatic change of direction when he entered a Cambridge University essay competition. The set topic was 'Is it right to enslave men against their will?', and Clarkson recoiled at the unsavoury results of his own research.

For the rest of his life he travelled the length and breadth of the country in his campaign for the abolition of slavery. He collected testimonies from 20,000 sailors who had worked on slave ships and had seen the appalling overcrowded conditions in which the shackled negroes were transported to the New World.

His public lectures gained support from the great thinkers of the day, including the poet Coleridge, who described him as 'a moral steam engine'. Wordsworth, in turn, wrote a sonnet to him. Meanwhile, Clarkson's efforts attracted the attention of the Prime Minister, William Pitt, who was himself an abolitionist. This did not go unnoticed by the ambitious MP William Wilberforce, who was keen to find political favour and thus zealously attached himself to Clarkson's cause.

It was 48 years later, in 1833, before public opinion finally overcame commercial greed and 800,000 slaves across the British Empire were freed. Wilberforce died the same year and was buried amid worldwide acclaim in Westminster Abbey. Yet Clarkson, who died 13 years later, was overlooked except by the proud inhabitants of his home town, who in 1881 raised just over £2,000 to build a fine statue commemorating their most celebrated son. Designed by Sir Gilbert Scott and standing 68 feet high, the gothic structure still stands today, overlooking the town bridge across the Nene and the fine, Dutch-influenced architecture of the equally famous North Brink.

Thus the self-seeking Wilberforce got all the credit, while the publicity-shy Clarkson was largely forgotten. His cause was not helped by the mischievous but influential sons of Wilberforce – a bishop and an archdeacon – who instigated a campaign of character assassination against the one man who could take some of the shine off their father's self-polished reputation.

Yet history never quite forgot the modest Thomas Clarkson. *The Dictionary of National Biography* (1888) says: 'It is almost impossible to overrate the effect of Clarkson's unceasing perseverance in the cause. Before he entered on the crusade slave-holding was considered – except by a chosen few – as a necessary part of social economy. It was largely due to Clarkson's exertions that long before his death it had come to be regarded as a crime.'

Of course, the proud Fen Tigers of Wisbech were never inclined to allow a local hero's feats to be lost in the mists of time. Besides that imposing statue, they exhibited Clarkson's few remaining artefacts in the town's museum. It was there that Wisbech resident Margaret Cave was inspired by his unique achievements and formed the Clarkson Anniversary Committee, which itself faced an uphill struggle – this time against bureaucracy – to get its hero suitably honoured. And on 26 September 1996 – exactly 150 years after his death – a plaque to his memory was finally unveiled, close to Wilberforce's tomb, at Westminster Abbey. Already honoured where his efforts were most appreciated – in

Thomas Clarkson's contribution to the anti-slavery campaign is marked in Wisbech by this impressive memorial to the town's most famous son.

The pedestrianisation of Wisbech Market Place has created a pleasant, open square, but the demolition of the fine old buildings on north side (right) to make way for a 1980s shopping arcade was questionable. Two fine pubs, The George and The Angel, were among the buildings that had been lost to the bulldozer by the time the second photograph was taken more than 70 years later, in 1996.

Africa, the Caribbean and by American negroes – Thomas Clarkson's achievements have finally been rewarded by an all too often ungrateful nation.

Riot for a dead doctor

In 1913 a riot broke out in Wisbech following the introduction of Lloyd George's new national insurance plan. The trouble started when only two of the town's doctors agreed to take on the ailing poor, known as 'panel' patients. The Isle of Ely Insurance Committee therefore sent down a third, Dr Dimock, to help cope with the growing number of sick people entitled to treatment.

Although considered a hero among the poor who had never been able to afford medical care in the past, Dr Dimock was less popular with the local doctors who had opposed the scheme, and they attempted to discredit him by accusing him of sending libellous letters about them. The worried young doctor hastened to London to seek advice from the British Medical Association and, on his return, committed suicide with an overdose of drugs.

There was an uproar in Wisbech when the tragic news broke. A crowd several thousands strong spontaneously gathered in the Market Place to sing hymns and listen to eloquent speeches in praise of Dr Dimock. Then the mood changed and the crowd began rioting, stoning the houses of the dead doctors' accusers and resisting all attempts by constables to restrain them. Eventually the Mayor was called to read the Riot Act and the constables used their truncheons indiscriminately to disperse them. Violence broke out again in the days that followed, and extra police were drafted in for the day of the funeral, when sympathisers, including students from Cambridge University, travelled in by train and swelled the crowd. It was a full week before calm was restored to the capital of the Fens.

Great floods

From bank to bank the water roars
Like thunder in a storm
A sea in sight of both shores
Creating no alarm
The water-birds above the flood
Fly o'er the foam and spray
And nature wears a gloomy hood
On this October day

John Clare

At the time of the Domesday Book, Wisbech was situated just 4½ miles from the mouth of the Nene, but reclamation of the marshes over the centuries has seen

that distance increase to a dozen miles or so. Throughout that time the sea has always threatened to claim back what has been so hard won by Man.

The Nene at Wisbech has an average tidal difference of 17 feet, but freak weather conditions can see huge flood tides pouring down the North Sea, into the bottleneck known as the Wash, and spilling over into the marshland. This was last suffered in 1978, when a fifth of the town was flooded and even the North Cambridgeshire Hospital had to be evacuated.

Floodings have been a regular nightmare for local folk. Records show that in 1236 a flood caused hundreds of sheep and cows to be lost, while an even greater one in 1260 destroyed most of the town, including the old castle. Just 25 years later Wisbech and the surrounding villages of Elm, Tydd and Leverington were drowned. It has been the same ever since. In 1570 the historian Holinshed recorded that, 'There chanced a terrible tempest of winde and raine, the sea break in betwixt Wisbech, Walton, Walsoken, drowning Tilnie and old Lin.'

In more recent times deep snow that fell during the hard winter of 1947 melted on 16/17 March and flooded 700,000 acres of fenland, while on 31 January 1953 a depression passing from the Atlantic Ocean to the North Sea sent hurricane-force winds to 175 mph south to the Wash and again flooded the low-lying areas around Wisbech. On that fateful night my father had been stoking the coke-fired boilers at some greenhouses 2 miles from home. Hearing the steel frame start to groan in the gathering storm, and the glass lights start to shatter, he abandoned his task and made a dash for home on his bicycle.

'I had a back wind and I reckon I must have broken the world speed record,' he recalls. 'I didn't need to pedal – I had the brakes full on to slow me down, but I still got home in 5 minutes flat. The next morning when I looked at the brake pads they had burnt away to nothing.'

The adventures of Mr Bream

Living on the banks of the Nene at Wisbech is an angler who has become a legend in his own lifetime as the greatest exponent of catching bream. The deep-bellied bream is a ponderous fish that likes the easy life and is generally found in slow-flowing rivers. For Sid Meads they have been a lifetime's obsession.

He first made his name as a bream angler in the 1960s, when the Nene and the drains around Wisbech were famous for vast shoals of the fish. Even when stocks declined in the 1980s, he kept in touch with his favourite fish by travelling to Ireland and Denmark, where even bigger shoals of bream are to be found.

Sid uses a leger rig and for bite indication relies upon a swingtip, a hinged attachment at the tip of his rod that clearly shows when a crafty bream has taken an interest in his bait – which will most likely be a worm, red-dyed maggot or a caster.

For newcomers to fenland bream fishing, Sid advises looking for a quiet spot, well away from bridges, and fishing close to reed beds, lilies or other banks of weed that the shoals prefer for cover. Places to fish for bream include two man-made tributaries that join the Nene downstream of Wisbech. The North Level Main Drain, whose pumping station dominates the west bank of the Nene near Tydd Gote, and the South Holland Main Drain, 2 miles nearer the estuary, both contain huge shoals and catches to over 100 lb have been recorded when the bigger bream, which often go to 7 lb apiece, get their heads down to feed.

With such rich feed available, it is no surprise that both drains have also produced pike over 30 lb in the past, the best being a 34 lb 4 oz specimen landed from the North Level in October 1981. To the best of my knowledge that is the biggest pike ever landed from any Fen drain in this country and, believe it or not, I was there when it was caught. The captor was my old fishing partner, Martin Geraghty, and the successful bait was a crucian carp, fished about 6 feet away from my own offering, a sardine. While delighted with Martin's outrageous stroke of luck, I couldn't help feeling disappointed over its choice of food.

To add insult to injury, six years later I was fishing on the South Holland with Nige Williams when I spotted a very big pike cruising just below surface. It swam straight past my baits before arriving in Nige's swim, where it promptly decided to feed. That one weighed 27 lb 12 oz!

This superb 27 lb 12 oz pike was taken from the South Holland Drain by Nige Williams during a fishing session with the author. The Nene valley has been kind to this famous angler, who in 1996 dwarfed even this catch with a 40 lb-plus monster (see Chapter 9).

In the land of a giant

By now we have moved out of Cambridgeshire into Lincolnshire, although on the opposite bank of the Nene, from Wisbech down to the North Level outfall, we were briefly in Norfolk. This area was, within living memory, the fruit-growing capital of East Anglia. The countryside in these parts was a forest of fruit trees until some bureaucrat in Brussels decided that it would be in the interests of Europe for British housewives to buy tasteless French apples instead of the flavoursome varieties that the orchards around Wisbech and Marshland had been producing for generations!

The majority of these orchards have now been grubbed up now to provide yet more acres of cereal crops to add to the surplus grain mountains, yet remnants remain. You won't see them from the river, but travel along the Wisbech bypass in spring and you'll be delighted by the sight of apple and plum trees in blossom. Venture slightly south, east and north to the nearby villages of Upwell, Outwell, Emneth, Elm, Marshland and the Walpoles and you'll see even more.

It is in this area, too, that a legendary giant is said to have strode across the marshy, undrained fields. His name was Thomas Hicfric, or, more commonly, Hickathrift. Thomas was no mean ogre. He was a folk hero comparable to Robin Hood, only in the case of our local man there is circumstantial evidence to suggest that he actually existed – in particular his grave, a great oval slab of granite, in the churchyard of Tilney All Saints.

The tales of his exploits belong to the oral tradition, passed down to generations of wide-eyed youngsters, and therefore a bit hazy on specifics. It has been suggested that he may have lived in Saxon times, but others insist that his great feats were performed much later, in the 13th century. But never mind when he did them, let's look at what he actually did.

The son of a peasant, Thomas was born in **Terrington St John** and eventually grew to over 7 feet tall, which is hardly a giant in modern terms, but hundreds of years ago would certainly have stood him a good 2 feet taller than most of his contemporaries. In any case, it was his extraordinary strength rather than stature that made him a giant among mere men.

His notoriety began at an early age. Thomas was a strapping lad and by the time he reached his 13th birthday was a great deal stronger than any adult male, as one man found out to his cost when he rushed to assist the young giant to lift a huge bundle of straw on to his broad shoulders. Thomas was not aware of the presence of his would-be helper, who duly flew through the air and somersaulted over the wall of a nearby cattle yard when the burden was lifted with a shrug of those prodigious pectorals.

It was as he grew up that Thomas became not merely a strongman. After a tour of the Holy Land in the crusades with Richard Coeur-de-Lion, he returned to become a protector of the poor families who lived a precarious existence in the lawless Fens. He was the first man to be called upon when savage beasts threatened humans and livestock alike, and he was the scourge of robbers and ne'er-do-wells who lurked in the islands among the swamps.

One day, while driving a brewery dray along a lonely track, he was stopped by another giant who demanded money. 'Let's fight for it,' snarled Thomas, who promptly broke off a wheel and an axle from the dray – the former to provide a makeshift shield and the latter to supply the club with which he struck the blow that caused his assailant to fall dead to the ground. It subsequently turned out that the stricken robber had been plundering the local peasants for many years and Thomas duly redistributed that ill-gotten wealth to the needy.

Mind you, Thomas was not always a gentle giant, and locals quickly learned that it was prudent to keep out of his way when he was grumpy. One day he took out his frustrations by moving the tower at West Walton church, which stands close to the east bank of the Nene, 2 miles below Wisbech. I can think of no better explanation for the fact that, today, there is a clear 60 feet of open space separating tower and church building. Could it be that the ugly stone buttresses supporting this otherwise beautiful building were hastily erected after Hickathrift's fabled act of vandalism?

With such an awesome reputation, it is no surprise to learn that greedy lords of the manor who tried to prevent peasants from grazing their sheep on the plain at Marshland Smeeth soon retreated when the avenging giant intervened.

Much later in life, Thomas was playing a primitive game of cricket with some of his friends (an experience which must have left those hapless players feeling as inadequate as the current England team). During a break in play – probably to replace yet another splintered bat – his followers asked him where he would like to be buried. He picked up the ball, strode to the top of the nearest bank and hurled the ball as far as he could. 'Wherever it lands is to be my final resting place,' he boomed.

That ball must have taken some finding, for it landed a full 9 miles away, in **Tilney All Saints** churchyard. And that's where he is said to lie to this day – although residents of his birthplace argue that he was finally laid to rest in Terrington St John churchyard, where a coffin slab ornamented with a wheel, to commemorate that famous wheel-and-axle battle, can be found. Just to complicate matters, fragments of stone columns have been found in both churchyards – and are said to be Hickathrift's candlesticks.

Meanwhile, the point from which the ball was thrown, at Marshland St James, is still known as Hickathrift Corner. In the same area there is a Hickathrift Farm, Hickathrift House and even a row of 20th-century council houses named Hickathrift Terrace. Until recent years there was also a pond, known locally as Hickathrift's wash basin! That generous giant may have long gone, but his name lives on.

Queen of the Marshlands

The Hickathrift legend lingers too at **Walpole St Peter** church, where a stone figure on the exterior wall of the chancel is said to be of the giant. Two holes in the same wall are reputed to have been made by the devil kicking a football at the giant.

Locals call this church 'Queen of the Marshlands', and it is a major tourist attraction, its magnificent architecture somehow unexpected in such a small, quiet village. Of particular interest is the vaulted roof with its intricate carvings. The writer Dorothy L. Sayers, who spent her childhood in the Fens (her father was rector at Bluntisham), knew it well and later made it the setting for her book *The Nine Tailors*, featuring the stylish amateur sleuth, Lord Peter Wimsey.

Sayers, who died aged 64 in 1957, had a schoolmarmish appearance, but shocked some contemporaries with her frank views on sex. One of the first women to go to Oxford University, she began writing fiction to pay for her illegitimate son to be looked after. After several affairs, she eventually married the motoring correspondent of the *News of the World*.

Much earlier the village was the birthplace of Godric of Walpole, a pedlar-turned-hermit who was made a saint after travelling through Europe to Jerusalem. The village also gave its name to our first Prime Minister, for it was from here that the Walpole family took their name, duly recorded in the Normans' Domesday Book, although they had left by the time of Magna Carta in 1215.

King John's lost treasure

Magna Carta, of course, was signed under duress by the hated King John, who in the 13th century did such damage to the monarchy. Greedy John's reign was marked by monumental misjudgments and mishaps, but the greatest misfortune to befall him happened in the treacherous quicksands that once marked the estuary of the River Nene.

John was born in 1167, the youngest son of Henry II (1133-89) and Eleanor of Aquitaine (1122-1204). He became King in 1199, succeeding his brother, Richard I. No brotherly love was lost here. Treacherous John had tried to steal Richard's crown while he was abroad in the Holy Land, fighting in the crusades, but the attempt failed. When he was eventually crowned, it was in preference to his nephew, Arthur, who had a better claim to the throne. This provoked war with King Philip II of Spain, who supported Arthur. Meanwhile, he also upset the Pope when he refused to accept the pontiff's nominated archbishop, and fell out with the barons over their power and privileges. The pathetic King eventually climbed down on all issues, most notably the baron's demands, for which he was forced to sign the Magna Carta, which has been a principle of liberty for English folk ever since.

The year 1215 was truly John's *annus horribilis*. His oppression had brought civil war to the country and, higher up the Nene valley, the royal stronghold of Northampton Castle was besieged by the barons, although their efforts were unsuccessful. Later the townsfolk attacked the castle and, in retaliation, royalist forces destroyed a large part of the town.

Surely things couldn't get worse, John must have mused to himself. But they did. In October of that year John had been campaigning in East Anglia against the barons when he heard that a Scottish army was marching south. Setting off on 12 October from King's Lynn to repel them, he became impatient at the ponderous progress made by his overloaded baggage train, laden with his crown jewels and plunder, and went on ahead to await their arrival at Wisbech.

In those days the estuary of the Nene between Long Sutton and the Walpoles was a very different place. It was known as the Wellstream and carried the combined waters of the Nene and the Great Ouse, which then joined the Nene at Outwell. It was probably a mile or more wide, but at low tide it was possible to cross the shallow mudflats before the flood tide returned.

And it was here that the King's labouring baggage train got well and truly bogged down up to its axles in the quagmire, eventually to be overwhelmed by the incoming tide as it rushed in over the salt messages. Wagons, men and treasure disappeared without trace. John himself later went mad, and died the following year.

Never a trace was found of any of the King's belongings, which included the crown and other priceless regalia. Today the likely resting place is dry land. Somewhere below the rich silt fields between Walpole St Andrew and Cross Keys, close to the modern A17 trunk road, lies what must be the greatest lost treasure in the world. For centuries men have searched in vain for it, but even with sophisticated modern metal detectors, it remains lost. But who knows? Perhaps one day a lucky smallholder will dig his vegetable patch one day and unearth a fortune beyond his wildest dreams.

Although the route of the ill-fated baggage train is well documented, some adventurous eccentrics have decided that the King's treasure lies much further inland. Twenty years ago the colourful Len Warren declared himself King of Reach in Cambridgeshire and went to the highest court in the land to try to prove his title and secure independence for his remote parish. Alas, his legal arguments ended in failure . . . as did his excavations for King John's treasure, which he was convinced was buried there.

Grandad George

The true Fen Tiger was an independent sort, who would rather live by his wits than be subservient to a master. Such a man was my late maternal grandfather, George Banyard, whose daytime skills as a reed-cutter and thatcher were matched only by his roaring nocturnal capacity for hard drinking and poaching.

George despised men who shot for sport. His poaching was a means to an end – to provide food on the table for six hungry children – and, if a brace or two were surplus to his requirements, to bring in a few shillings for some ale at the local pub. It was, after all, very thirsty work.

Pheasants were the easiest targets and George didn't even need a gun. He would steal into the local orchards after dark and pluck the roosting birds off the low branches as easily as ripe bramleys. Poaching was a serious business in the depression-hit 1920s and the stakes were high. Daytime scrumping of apples by small boys earned a clip round the ear from the local bobby, but when George got caught by the village constable one night picking his feathered fruit he received a one-way ticket to Norwich Gaol. But then, those were enlightened times – a couple of generations earlier he would have been transported to Australia!

A couple of months of hard labour meant little to a man who had laboured hard all his life, but it must have hurt to be deprived of his beloved Fens. George carried on poaching, but made sure he wasn't caught again. His short spell behind bars merely reinforced his contempt for the ruling classes.

During the hard winter of 1947 George knew that a neighbour who had been laid off at a local farm could not afford Christmas dinner for his family, and decided to do something about it. At 4 am on Christmas morning he cycled into the fen, raided a local farmer's hen coop of two cockerels, scraped a couple of pounds of spuds from a potato grave and pulled up some Brussels sprouts from a field on the way home. These he left, anonymously, on his neighbour's doorstep. Ill-gotten gains or a sense of social injustice? I'll leave it for you to decide.

Revival of a vintage port

Our very last port of call is **Sutton Bridge**, notable for the final bridge over the River Nene, the famous Cross Keys swing bridge that carries the A17 over the river. The present steel girder structure, built in 1897 at a cost of £80,000, replaced an earlier cast and wrought iron bridge designed in 1850 by the great Victorian engineer Robert Stephenson. Both bridges initially carried the Midland & Great Northern railway line as well as the road over the river, but when the railway was closed in 1959 both sections were used for road traffic.

Sutton Bridge station opened on 3 July 1862 and was an important station on the former M&GN Spalding-King's Lynn line. Later, on 1 August 1866, it became a junction when a branch line was opened south to Wisbech and Peterborough. Together with the Peterborough-Blisworth line (see Chapter 5), this meant that railway lines shadowed the Nene for most of its length.

Today, sadly, the 100-year-old Cross Keys bridge sees no rail traffic, but it is as busy as ever and a testament to the longevity of Victorian engineering. From its central axis the hydraulically operated bridge swings

Low tide at the quayside at Sutton Bridge. The town's port, situated close to the mouth of the river, can handle cargo ships as heavy as 3,500 tonnes, while 1,500 tonnes is the limit at Wisbech, further upstream.

through 90 degrees to allow the passage of ocean-going vessels to and from the Port of Wisbech, 8 miles upstream. The bridge operator enjoys a marvellous vantage point in his bandstand-style control booth at the very top of the bridge. From his lofty position he can see the mouth of the river, now just 3 miles distant, and the long queues of fuming motorists caught in endless traffic jams on the main road below when the bridge swings aside for shipping!

Before efforts were made in the 1930s to revive the tidal channel of the Nene, the river was in a bad state and severe silting in the Sutton Bridge area led to the little town's decaying docks being abandoned in the 1920s. Amazingly, Sutton Bridge docks were resurrected in 1987 – and have been a commercial success ever since. The first ocean-going merchant vessel to be loaded there was the *Union Arrow*, bound for Belgium with a cargo of barley.

Before leaving the final settlement on the banks of the Nene, it is worth exploring this small town, and its near neighbour **Long Sutton**, which like others of their size can prove far more interesting than larger towns, with their inevitable cloned chain stores and burger bars. Small, family-run shops abound and I can personally recommend R. & W. Butchers in Sutton Bridge, which according to my taste buds produce the finest home-made pork bangers in East Anglia!

Beyond bovine belief

In these days of 'mad cow disease' and almost daily food scares, it is reassuring to know that at least some farm animals are reared naturally. Robin Savage, the owner of R. & W. Butchers, also runs a farm with his brother David, and I am pleased to report that his cattle are fed not on sheep's entrails but good old-fashioned grass.

Not ordinary grass, mind - the Savage brothers' herds roam the lush banks of the Nene upstream of Sutton Bridge. I've hinted before that Nene water has remarkable properties, but nowhere more, it seems, than in these tidal reaches, where its restorative powers are nothing short of unbelievable. Evidence of this came recently when a bullock - ie a castrated steer - swam across the raging current at flood tide for a romantic rendezvous with the Savages' heifers on the opposite bank.

The genitally challenged beast then spent two days at large in his new playground, as Robin and David faced the frustration of trying to catch half a ton of lusty beef in a field just 100 yards wide but a full 4 miles long. And I mean lusty. By the time its reign of ardour was ended, it had somehow served several heifers, who subsequently delivered a number of prime calves. Cynics may scoff that a careless vet had slipped with the secateurs when he had tried to prune the budding young bull - but we know better.

Birth of an empire

Long Sutton was, on 5 August 1858, the birthplace of Sir Richard Winfrey, a farmer's son whose political convictions built the foundations of a sprawling media empire. After studying to become a chemist, young Richard turned instead to Liberal politics and, to help the cause in the Fens, bought the *Spalding Guardian* in 1887 for the princely sum of £100. He was just 28 years old at the time.

From those humble beginnings he built a mighty press empire, and was five times elected MP for South-West Norfolk and once for Gainsborough. In 1913 he was elected Mayor of Peterborough and in 1919 bought the family home, Castor House, overlooking the river. He died on 18 April 1944, and three years later, in May 1947, his son, Pat Winfrey, incorporated the plethora of local newspaper companies under the East Midland Allied Press banner.

Until the mid-1990s EMAP owned newspapers the entire length of the Nene valley, from the *Daventry Weekly Express* at the source downstream to the Winfreys' first paper, the *Spalding Guardian*, covering the towns and villages around the mouth of the river. In between EMAP also held evening papers, the *Northampton Chronicle & Echo, Northamptonshire Evening Telegraph* and *Peterborough Evening Telegraph,* as well as the weekly *Fenland Citizen,* covering Wisbech and March. But from 1953 EMAP's interests had become increasingly centred around national leisure and lifestyle magazines and eventually the decision was taken to sell off all the company's provincial newspapers.

Happily, there was no shortage of buyers. Although EMAP lost its confidence in the regional press, other publishing companies share my own enthusiasm for local papers with their unrivalled values of community and continuity. Long may they all thrive and enrich our lives.

Scott's lighthouse

There's just half a mile to go now, and the very last buildings on the banks of the river are a pair of lighthouses, standing like a pair of tall, white identical twins – one on the west bank and the other on the east. They are redundant now, their days of guiding shipping through the treacherous shallows of the estuary over, but needless to say they have an historic role to play.

The lighthouse on the west bank, at Guy's Head, was once used by the late Sir Peter Scott as a base for wildfowling and, later, painting trips to the salt marshes. Born in 1909, the son of Robert (the South Pole explorer of 'Scott of the Antarctic' fame), young Peter was educated on the banks of the Nene further upstream at Oundle Public School, as already

The great naturalist Sir Peter Scott once lived in this lighthouse on the west bank of the tidal Nene, half a mile from the estuary.

mentioned in Chapter 4. The talented youngster was a budding skating champion as well as an Olympic yachtsman, but he will be remembered as the father of the wildfowl conservation movement. His Wildfowl Trust eventually set up the world-renowned Welney Wildfowl Refuge on the nearby Ouse washes.

Journey's end

One's arrival at the Nene estuary can be rather an anticlimax on a dull, overcast day, especially when the tide is out. There's a lot of mud and not much else. The tide will have ebbed to the far horizon and there's not a glimpse of the sea to be seen – such is the nature of this shallow sea. One doesn't really expect this epic journey down from the sources to end on such a flat note. And nor should one, for like the rest of the river this area is steeped in history and drama.

Return on a crisp, clear autumn day with binoculars and you can see the distinctive chalk and carrstone cliffs of Hunstanton as well as the soaring majesty of the fine Lincolnshire church known as the Boston Stump.

Then come back again on a winter's afternoon as a flooding tide is pushed in by a roaring northerly gale. Wrap up well, for the wind in these exposed parts rushes in from Scandinavia and cuts like a knife, but the exhilarating memories of the salt-lashed air and calls of countless thousands of wheeling seabirds will warm your soul for weeks.

The Wash is a great delta, formed by the accumulated mud and sand washed down from the uplands of the rivers that feed it. As well as the Nene, the Great Ouse, Welland and Witham all empty their muddy waters into it, and the suspended silts they have carried downstream eventually fall to the bottom to create the ever-shifting sandbanks and mudbanks that pose a constant challenge to the navigational skills of the shipping traffic that traverses it.

The last tributary of the Nene is the Lutton Leam, an artificial drainage channel that enters the river on the west bank a few hundred yards before the estuary. Unlike drains such as the North Level and South Holland, this is not a prolific fishery; it is contaminated by saltwater from the adjacent marshes and contains only eels.

In the days of sail the Wash was rightly regarded as a death-trap by sailors attempting to negotiate the twisting channels through the shallow banks. But still they came, risking their lives for the lucrative trade at the ports of Wisbech, King's Lynn and Boston. There were times, around the mouth of the Nene, when that trade looked like being lost. Over the centuries many eminent engineers were convinced that the constant problem of siltation would eventually render the Nene useless to navigation, yet each time that situation looked likely, a winter's flood would succeed in scouring away the silt and opening up the channels yet again.

Barely 30 years ago serious scientific studies were carried out into the feasibility of building a barrage across the Wash to turn it into a vast freshwater reservoir. Luckily they came to nothing and today the Wash is one of Europe's most important wildlife sites, and vast areas of the mudflats are now protected reserves. But it is not without its problems. Dredging for sea defences and over-enrichment of the mudflats by water washed down from the Nene and other rivers have been blamed for a calamitous decline in the numbers of shellfish and shrimps, which in turn have caused populations of some birds to plummet.

Surveys by the British Trust for Ornithology have found that numbers of oystercatchers have slumped from 45,000 to 15,000 in just seven years up to 1996. As their name suggests, oystercatchers feed on shellfish, and they are now coming inland in increasing numbers to seek food. They can be easily spotted in the shallow, muddy margins of the gravel pits and reservoirs throughout the Nene valley and have even overcome their customary shyness of humankind to feed on earthworms in gardens and parks.

The shellfish decline has also had an impact on the traditional fishing industry in the Wash. The cockles, mussels and shrimps for which the area was famous have been decimated, and the 400 full-time fishermen who work the area are now heading to Grimsby or the Thames estuary for catches.

It is probably too late to save the ailing British fishing industry from terminal decline, but there is a glimmer of hope for wildlife in the Wash. It has been chosen, along with 11 other sites in Britain, for special European Commission conservation funding as part of the Habitats & Species Directive. In common parlance, that means that the Wash will get some Euro-cash to pay for urgently needed scientific studies into its plight.

This is the end of the journey for the River Nene as it meets The Wash at its mouth on the South Lincolnshire coast.

7
The Old River

The brook o'er such neglected ground
One's weariness to sooth
Still wildly threads its lawless bounds
And chafes the pebble smooth

John Clare

The Old River

Look at a modern map, and the River Nene's course below Peterborough is easy to follow. It cuts a dead-straight swathe through the low, flat fields to Guyhirn,

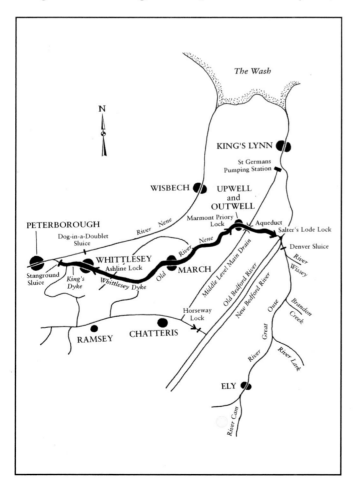

The Old River.

then veers sharply northward to Wisbech and Sutton Bridge before another straight channel discharges its waters into the Wash.

It's all so different from the natural meanders of the upper and middle reaches – and no wonder. That's because the modern course of the lower Nene bears very little or no resemblance to its original route through the undrained fens.

Look again at the map and, to the south-east of Peterborough, you'll find a twisting line of blue marked 'River Nene (old course)'. It makes it sound distinctly derelict, and that's exactly what it is. That abandoned scrap of our river's history is today no more than a minor part of the intricate drainage system of the Nene's near neighbour, the Great Ouse.

But it wasn't always so. In the Middle Ages the untamed and undrained Nene was a more powerful river than it is today. By the time it reached Peterborough it decided that it wasn't ready to surge straight to the sea by the most direct route, and opted instead for a sluggish, scenic journey through the Fens. Half a mile below the Town bridge, just downstream of where the modern Parkway flyover strides across the river today, is the point where the Nene took an abrupt right turn through Stanground and headed south past Farcet and Yaxley before emptying into a huge inland sea known as **Whittlesey Mere** and, until a century and a half ago, the largest freshwater lake in England.

Even greater in stature now, the Nene then headed east to **Ramsey**, picking up the waters of Ramsey Mere and smaller lakes along the way as it twisted through the quagmire to Benwick and **March**. At this point, even a thousand years ago, Man's hand was evident, for March stands on a raised ridge of gravel that the old

Right Whittlesey, once famous for the largest lake in southern England, is 150 years later better known for its brickworks.

course of the Nene traversed through a deep cutting. There is no way a natural river could have performed that feat, and it is widely supposed that Roman engineers diverted the Nene through March, nigh on 2,000 years ago. Unfortunately, today there is no trace of the pre-Roman route the river is supposed to have taken around the town, although it is believed to have looped north, where the modern **Whitemoor** high-security prison now stands. When the prison was built it was said to be impossible for inmates to break out – a boast comparable to the unfortunate statement that the *Titanic* was unsinkable. Whitemoor, of course, hit the headlines in 1994 when six prisoners escaped, including five IRA terrorists.

Before becoming infamous for its prison, Whitemoor was famous for one of the largest railway marshalling yards in Europe, built by the London & North Eastern Railway in 1925-33 and occupying 68 acres of land on both sides of the former Great Northern & Great Eastern Joint line to Spalding. This route crossed the modern course of the Nene at Guyhirn, but was sadly closed in November 1982, despite fierce opposition from locals. The earlier demise of many local branch lines as well as a drastic decline in freight in individual

Below A frosty morning on the Old River Nene at March.

wagons led to its inevitable closure, along with the associated engine sheds which, in 1960, boasted 103 steam locomotives and 80 diesels.

After March the river pushes on to **Upwell** and its near neighbour **Outwell**, where it was once joined by the combined waters of the Great Ouse and Wissey in a mighty tidal stream a mile wide, which swept in a north-westerly direction between Elm and Emneth before reaching **Wisbech** and a great estuary, surrounded by treacherous sandbanks and salt marshes. (An indication that all three rivers met the sea here comes from the old spelling of 'Wisbeach', which meant Wissey Beach, and is a name that was still in use at the turn of the century.)

The lost route we have just followed is very different to the featureless, functional channel Man has carved out for the modern River Nene. It is also 40 miles long, and to cover it in depth would be beyond the scope of this book. But the story of the Old River Nene is a fascinating one, involving as it does the transformation of the greatest area of wetland in England, so I can't resist making a brief detour to see just what we lost when the fens were drained.

Left It's hard to believe that this small, near-stagnant waterway was once the course of the powerful River Nene through the Fens.

Neat riverside gardens have sprung up alongside the Old River Nene at Benwick between 1975, when the first photograph was taken, and 1996, when the author returned to the same spot. Angler's Mail/author

An angler and a pleasure boat both venture out on to the frozen river between March and Upwell in January 1994. Neither appears to be making much progress.

Draining the Fens

Those arid fenland fields of grain, sugar beet and oil seed rape were until comparatively recently the wettest, muddiest parts of these islands. They were a vast, oozing delta, formed by the settling silts carried down from the uplands of Northamptonshire, Leicestershire, Bedfordshire, Buckinghamshire, Cambridgeshire and Norfolk by the rivers Nene, Ouse, Welland, Witham, Cam, Little Ouse and Wissey. They reached the Wash through ever-shifting quagmires of peat, mud and sand, which were dotted with huge lakes and intersected by muddy, meandering creeks that regularly inundated the whole region with both freshwater floods from the Midlands and saltwater surges from the sea (see Chapter 6).

The Fens cover a total of 680,000 acres – 2,000 square miles – and are almost 70 miles long from Lincoln to Cambridge and 30 miles wide at their broadest point between Huntingdon and Soham. The sodden nature of the Fens made transport over land very difficult if not impossible in wet, wintry weather when the whole area was often flooded. It is believed

that boats were used by the earliest settlers in Bronze Age times, and certainly the Romans and later invaders from the Scandinavian countries were adept boatmen as they traversed the Fens and made their way inland.

It was the Romans who made the first attempts to partially drain these wetlands. They built the Car Dyke from Lincoln to Cambridge, an artificial channel that bisected the Nene at Peterborough. It collected some of the flood waters from the uplands of Lincolnshire, Northamptonshire, Huntingdonshire and Cambridgeshire, and was also used as a navigable waterway. In its heyday the Car Dyke was 60 feet wide, but today it is no more than a shrunken reminder of its past glories. You can get a good view of this ancient waterway from the A47 Eye bypass, on the north-eastern outskirts of Peterborough.

Car Dyke partially solved the problems of freshwater floods, but the sea remained a constant threat to the marshlands around Wisbech. To hold back the worst tides, the Romans built a series of sea walls or banks. Again, remnants remain, particularly west of the tidal Nene at West Walton and Terrington St Clement, and north-east around Gedney.

As in so many things, the progressive Romans showed the way forward. But in the Dark Ages that followed their retreat from the British Isles, little further

Tame ducks forage for food on the Old River Nene at Upwell.

Outwell church stands on the Old River Nene close to the point where the Great Ouse once combined to produce a great tidal estuary a mile wide.

progress was made on the subject of draining the Fens. Those who lived there preferred them the way they were, despite the discomforts of what was a very harsh existence. Men walked on stilts to catch fish and fowl, living in thatched homes on the odd islands of clay and gravel that stood a few feet above the surrounding peat wetlands. They were hard men, reputed by outsiders to have webbed feet, and their aggression toward outsiders earned them the nickname Fen Tigers. Their idea of fun was bare-knuckle boxing matches and wrestling, in which the women also joined in, stripped to the waist and covered with lard.

Vast swarms of mosquitoes brought the constant menace of malaria and the dreaded ague – a malarial fever with successive stages of fever and chills, accompanied by uncontrolled shivering. Through the centuries and within living memory, fenmen drugged themselves with poppy tea, an opiate that eased the pain but caused hallucinations, madness and finally death.

The first successful attempt at drainage on a grand scale was carried out in 1490 by Bishop John Morton of Ely (later Cardinal and Archbishop of Canterbury). While at Ely he often travelled to stay at Wisbech Castle and saw at first hand the effects of flooding upon the district, as well as the problems caused to shipping by the silting up of the Nene outfall to the sea at Wisbech. An earlier Bishop of Ely had diverted the course of the Ouse to King's Lynn in the 13th century and the lack of flow into the Wisbech outfall made many believe it was in danger of drying up altogether.

Bishop Morton decided to drain part of the fen and improve conditions at Wisbech by excavating a new drain, 40 feet wide and 4 feet deep, from Stanground to Guyhirn. This drain, named Morton's Leam after its designer, is still in existence today and is shadowed by the modern course of the lower river, which runs parallel to it. From Guyhirn the Bishop also built another leam to Wisbech, which did indeed help scour out the silted outfall and make conditions easier for shipping. Again, the current course of the Nene between Guyhirn and Wisbech roughly follows that former waterway.

Morton was the first man to appreciate that artificial straight channels were the answer to draining the Fens. He was followed in 1605 by the Lord Chief Justice of England, Sir John Popham, who attempted to drain the Upwell area by ordering a 5-mile cut to be made from the Nene above Upwell to Nordelph on the Well Creek (the former course of the Ouse). That drain – Popham's Eau – still exists, although today it is bisected by the more recent Middle Level Main Drain. The section from Upwell to Three Holes has been enlarged through dredging over the centuries, but the section through to Nordelph must be much as it was when excavated almost four centuries ago.

But these early efforts pale into insignificance compared with the grand efforts on the next man on the scene, a Dutchman named Cornelius Vermuyden. Vermuyden, from the town of Maartensdijk in the province of Zeeland, had already made his name as a drainage engineer in his country of birth before he crossed the North Sea to Britain, where he enjoyed success draining Canvey Island, Dagenham Marshes, the Royal Park at Windsor, and Hatfield Chase in Yorkshire. In 1630 the Duke of Bedford, who owned great tracts of the Fens, offered him 95,000 acres if he could drain the whole of them. Vermuyden hesitated, but went ahead at the insistence of King Charles I.

The arrow-straight artificial waterways, which echo the canals of Vermuyden's native land, hastened the floodwater to the sea and, despite a war of attrition waged by the Fen Tigers, eventually succeeded in creating summer pastureland on what had been impossible terrain. The only problem was that the peat, which had acted like a great sponge, began to shrink and sink below the level of the rivers and drains cut through it. In the decades that followed, windmills had to be built to pump water from the cuts up to the level of the larger drains and rivers. These were later replaced by steam pumps, followed by diesel and, finally, electrically operated pumping stations. It is said that there were more than 700 operating windmills used to pump water at their peak in the 18th century.

Today, with drainage more efficient than ever, the peat continues to shrink. In summer it also tends to turn to a dry dust that can be blown away by high winds. A steel post sunk into the peat at Holme Fen,

The pumping station on the south bank of the river between Guyhirn and Wisbech shows the transition from steam engines (left) to electricity (right).

south of Peterborough, graphically measures that shrinkage. It shows that the level of the Fens in those parts has sunk an astonishing 18 feet in the last 150 years, and is said to be continuing to fall at the rate of 1 foot every 10 years. Much of these Fens are now well below sea level and it is not difficult to imagine the consequences of the rise in sea levels predicted by some scientists as a result of global warming.

Bog oaks

The shrinking of the fen peat has seen many interesting objects from the past resurface after thousands of years of being buried. Most notable are the fossilised trunks of great trees as much as 70,000 years old, dating back to drier times when the fens were a forest. As hard as iron after thousands of years of preservation in the peat, the trunks are capable of wrecking farmer's ploughs. When they are uncovered, it takes a great deal of effort with heavy machinery to haul them to the sides of the fields.

Known locally as bog oaks, they also include petrified oak, elm, Scots pine, yew, hazel, alder and willow. Some of the trunks are several yards in circumference and as much as 100 feet long. Many grew to 70 feet before putting forth their first branches, demonstrating that this primeval forest must have been very dense. Among them has been found the preserved bones of Celtic short-horned ox, Irish elk, mammoth, wild horse, cave lion, woolly rhinoceros, wild boar, narrow-toothed elephant, reindeer, lemming, musk sheep, bison, wolf and brown bear. The presence of this diverse and, in some cases, extinct fauna shows how very different these shores once were.

But what happened to them all? The answer lies in the trunks of the trees, which all lie on the same axis, in a north-easterly direction. It is reasonably assumed that the rising sea level eventually flooded the forest, and killed off the trees and animals alike, leaving just a ghostly forest of gaunt, skeletal trees that eventually were felled by a ferocious hurricane (remember 1987?) from the south-west.

Hereward the Wake

The lost forest of the Fens was already buried under yards of sodden peat by the time Hereward the Wake, the scourge of the Norman invaders of 1066, made the watery wastes his stronghold. The son of Lady Godiva and Leofric, King of Mercia, Hereward's home was at Bourne Castle, north of Peterborough. But after making his reputation on the battlefields of France, Flanders, Scotland, Ireland and Cornwall, he returned to his native Fens to fight a rearguard action against William the Conqueror's armies.

Skulking in the impenetrable, malaria-ridden reedbeds beyond Peterborough, Hereward proved impossible to overcome and became a symbol of dogged resistance and refusal to bow to tyrants. Thousands of Normans are said to have perished when he set ablaze the tinder-dry reedbeds through which they were marching in a bid to ambush him at Ely.

Yet even Hereward eventually bowed to the inevitable and returned to the simple life as Lord of the Manor at Bourne, still visited today by modern tourists to see the remains of his castle. He is believed to be buried at Crowland Abbey with his wife, Torfrida.

King Canute

Another historical figure who roamed these parts was King Canute (994-1035), best known in legend as the power-crazed monarch who ordered the tide not to come in, although the truth behind the legend wasn't quite like that.

Canute – also known as Cnut – was a Danish king of Norway and Denmark as well as England. His father, Sweyn, had been killed during the invasion of England in 1014 and Canute was his successor. Widely acclaimed as a wise and just ruler, Canute did not suffer fools. Fed up with his fawning couriers expressing the belief that there was no limit to his powers, he took them on a trip to the seaside to prove the contrary.

Although he could not tame the sea, he did, apparently, initiate early attempts to tame the River Nene. The King's Dyke, a short-cut on the Old River Nene between Horsey Toll and Floods Ferry, which bypassed the treacherous expanse of Whittlesey Mere, is said to have been excavated on his orders after he experienced a violent storm on that inland sea. On Jonas Moore's map of the area, drawn in 1650, it is marked out as 'Knute's Dyke'. This ancient cut, which can be easily seen from the A605 between Stanground and Whittlesey, is known in the latter town as the Briggate River.

Ghosts and gases

Some of the legendary figures of these parts were most definitely not the sort of creatures you'd like to bump into in some lonely reedbed on a fog-shrouded night. The most terrifying of all was Black Shuck, a giant spectral hound.

Also known as Old Shuck, this huge black dog, said to have one red eye in the middle of his head, has long been part of folklore throughout the Fens. Some say that the tale's origins came across with Norse invaders – probably from the fabled Hound of Thor. Fictional detective Sherlock Holmes's creator, Arthur Conan Doyle, heard the legend of Black Shuck while he was staying in Norfolk at the end of the 19th century, and based his *Hound of the Baskervilles* classic upon it. To see Shuck meant that you would die within a week. Old Fen folk would not venture out after dark for fear of sighting him, such was the power of the superstitions.

Or were they mere superstitions? There are still people out in the middle of the Fens who swear that they have heard Old Shuck's blood-curdling howls and will tell spine-chilling stories of people who have witnessed the hound, only to die soon after in mysterious circumstances. . .

Fen author John Humphreys tells the tale of a wildfowler out on a wild stretch of fenland on an equally wild, moonlit night. He chose that particular clump of waterlogged reedbeds to take advantage of an expected flight of wigeon, but in the back of his mind he knew he was alone on the site of a long-abandoned Roman settlement, which was said by locals to be haunted.

Suddenly the shape of a centurion appeared, complete with wooden spear, swaying gently before leaping and careering across the marsh in front of him. He fled the scene, but even as he looked back over his shoulder he could still see the ghostly apparition flitting about the boggy field. What he had seen, of course, was a will-o'-the-wisp, also known by Fen folk as a jack-o'lantern.

This particular shooter was not the first nocturnal visitor to marshland to be scared witless by the spontaneous combustion of marsh gas flickering across the sodden peat. 'Old Bushman' (actually a Northamptonshire parson) wrote in *The Field* in the middle of the 19th century:

'Vast must have been the extent of fen land when Ethelwold was king and the monastery at Crowland was founded. Many are the traditions of genii and kelpies inhabiting the fens at that time and the benighted traveller has trembled in his lonely journey over the dark, dank fen, as the sullen boom of the bittern shook the night air; or the deep, solemn note of the curfew bell from the distant abbey of Crowland borne upon the night breezes across the dreary fat, fell upon his startled ear. Benumbed with cold, his senses bewildered with fear, how many a one has risen again alive, or misled by the treacherous flickering light of the "will-o'-the-wisp dancing in murky night o'er fen and lake" has wandered out of his track, and the last despairing shriek of the dying man sinking below the surface was carried on the night breeze over the dreary marshes, where there was no one to hear it.'

The destruction of Whittlesey Mere

Imagine if you can this scene, 150 years ago. It is early morning and the eastern horizon is aglow from the rising sun, which we see from the window of our coach as we gallop south down the Great North Road from Wansford. We have already sped along the Nene valley past Stibbington, Water Newton and Alwalton, and now our horses are slowing as they climb the gradient up to where the Norman Cross roundabout is today. As we reach the top of the ridge, almost 120 feet above sea level, the low-lying wilderness of the old Fens stretches below us as far as the eye can see. And to our left, bathed in the pink blush of dawn, lies the great expanse of Whittlesey Mere.

That first glimpse of the old mere must have made many a seasoned traveller take a sharp intake of breath. The sheer beauty of the largest lake in southern England, surrounded by its wild, reeded fens, must have been a glorious sight to behold. Yet amazingly, a selfish and greedy handful of landed gentry stole this priceless part of our heritage. The magnificent mere was drained dry by these landowners in the grubby pursuit of profit, in the process destroying a valuable habitat for rare wildlife and robbing all Fenlanders and Nene folk of their birthright.

Can you recall the deplorable Earl Fitzwilliam of Milton, whom we met in Chapter 5 as he tried to prevent the construction of the Nene Valley railway line because his money was riding on another, rival line? Remember how he then greedily demanded more compensation than any other landowner along the route of the railway? Well, it will therefore come as no surprise that Fitzwilliam and his cronies, including Lord Sandwich, were the ringleaders of this gang of Victorian vandals.

But before we conduct our post-mortem into the death of our victim, let's look back at the better days when the might of the mere was too great to allow Man to meddle. First the facts. The great shallow lake, which averaged about 5 feet deep, was fed by the old course of the River Nene, which entered along the northern bank at Arnold's Mouth and left at the south-eastern corner. At its lowest level, in summer, it covered 1,600 acres – the size of the modern Grafham Water Reservoir, at nearby Huntingdon – while winter floodwater caused it to spill out across the surrounding Fens to cover over 3,000 acres, the size of Rutland Water. At its lowest ebb, Whittlesey Mere was four times the size of Hickling, largest of the Norfolk Broads.

The first written account of the mere dates back to the year 664, when King Wulphere of Mercia granted the fishing and fowling rights to the new monastery at Medeshamstede (Peterborough). Later, as already mentioned, King Canute sailed across it and was caught in a sudden freak storm, which were known locally as 'water quakes'.

The Middle Ages saw much commercial boat traffic upon the mere, with stone from Barnack, near Stamford, carried by barges to help build the abbeys at Ramsey and Sawtry. Later, following the dissolution of the monasteries ordered by Henry VIII, salvaged stone was taken to Cambridge to build Trinity and Corpus Christi colleges.

By the middle of the 17th century the mere became a popular outdoor playground, with thousands flocking there in summer for regattas and water picnics, and thousands more in winter for great skating competitions. Our patron poet, John Clare, often walked to the mere from his home at Helpston, where he studied the rare flowers and ferns around the fen margins and marvelled at the wildlife, which included the rare swallowtail butterfly as well as the extinct large copper. Great flocks of birds included the elusive bittern and great flocks of snipe. The latter inspired Clare to write the following:

Lover of swamps
The quagmire overgrown
With hassock tufts of sedge – where fear encamps
Around thy home alone
The trembling grass
Quakes from the human foot
Nor bears the weight of man to let him pass
Where thou alone and mute
Sittest at rest
In safety 'neath the clump
Of huge flag forest that thy haunts invest
Or some old sallow stump

It is no longer possible to fish Whittlesey Mere, which was drained in 1851, but this angler on the man-made Raveley Drain is trying his hand for roach on the edge of what was once the great lake.

The writer Charles Kingsley described in wonder the mere's wildlife:

'The coot clanked and the bittern boomed . . . while high overhead hawk beyond hawk, buzzard beyond buzzard hung motionless, kite beyond kite as far as the eye could see. Far off from the mere would rise a puff of smoke from a punt . . . then down the wind came the boom of the great stanchion gun: and after that sound, another sound louder as it neared . . . overhead rushed and whirled the skein of terrified wildfowl, screaming, piping, clacking, croaking, filling the air with the hoarse rattle of their wings, while clear above all sounded the odd whistle of the curlew and the trumpet note of the great, wild swan.'

But it was not to last. The profiteers prevailed and in 1851 the mere was pumped dry, using the powerful new Appold Pump that had been on display at the Great Exhibition at Crystal Palace the same year. The pump, with a diameter of 1.5 metres and driven by a twin-cylinder steam engine, discharged the waters of the mere at the rate of 1,652 gallons a minute from a new sluice erected at Johnson's Point, from where it was conveyed to the Bevills Leam drain.

The receding waters of the shrinking mere revealed hundreds of tons of fish, most of which were left to rot. Among the dying masses of roach, bream, tench, perch and eels was a huge pike said to weigh 52 lb, and which measured 55 inches long. It is accepted by many authorities as the biggest pike ever recorded in England. The same fish – or another of similar size – had been seen two years earlier by a young naturalist searching the shallow pools around the mere's reeded edges for the nest of a rare Savi's warbler. He was astonished to see the huge pike grab a fully grown swan by the neck, drag it beneath the surface and, apparently, devour it.

Also uncovered after the draining were skulls of wild boar and wolves, while deep beneath the peat was found the fossilised skeleton of a killer whale that had roamed this area hundreds of thousands of years earlier when it was beneath sea level. Out in the centre of the mere bed, and from more recent times, was a one-piece boat, cut from the trunk of an oak tree and measuring 27 feet long by over 3 feet wide. Nearby was a silver-gilt, boat-shaped vessel – probably a salt cellar or incense container. From the ram's head on its lid it was identified as coming from Ramsey Abbey and was probably lost out on the mere during a great storm as the monks attempted to flee from Viking raiders.

By 1853 fields of corn were growing where the great lake had been. 'The draining of the Huntingdon Fens alone added many thousands of acres to the cornlands of England, but, as a fenman, I lament the passing of that wild mere,' wrote the great naturalist Jimmy Wentworth-Day in 1954.

Three decades later, the Whittlesey-born writer and poet Edward Storey wrote in *The Spirit of the Fens* (Robert Hale):

'Look across the fields to where the setting sun once reflected in the waters of Whittlesea Mere and you will feel that the events of its history are not so long ago, or beyond the mind's reach. Just beneath the surface are the hidden places, waiting to be reborn.'

Poor John Clare had already spent a decade in a lunatic asylum by the time the mere was drained. Heaven knows what he would have written had he lived to witness the destruction of the wilderness he knew so well.

The scandal is that the drying out of the peat fenlands and the rise in sea levels predicted through global warning mean that the dry status of this area can only last a few decades. If the scientists have got it right, it will become impossible to keep these low-lying areas drained and, eventually, the water must return. The year 2000 will mark the 150th anniversary of the dark deeds that led to the draining of Whittlesey Mere. Wouldn't the restoration of that great lake make a magnificent project for the New Millenium?

Victorian profiteering, technology and disregard for the environment combined to waste Whittlesey Mere. Today its arid bed serves only as a means to grow yet more Euro-subsidised crops that we do not need. Would it not be appropriate for a new, environment-conscious generation to employ modern technology (and National Lottery funding) to reinstate the glorious 3,000 acres of water and wetland for future generations to enjoy? Let's bring back Whittlesey Mere . . . before Mother Nature beats us to it.

8

The tributaries:
Ise, Willow Brook and Harper's Brook

Where the gay river laughing as it goes
Plashes with easy wave its flaggy sides
And to the calm of heart in calmness shows
What pleasure there abides
To trace its sedgy banks from trouble free
Spots solitude provides
To muse and happy be

John Clare

The River Ise

The Nene's major tributary, the River Ise, rises close to the northern branch of its parent river near Naseby. But while the Nene runs south to Northampton, the Ise heads north-east, almost reaching the Leicestershire boundary as it skirts the villages of Arthingworth and Thorpe Underwood, before dividing the old shoe towns of Rothwell and Desborough.

Still heading east, the Ise runs through Rushton and on to the unspoilt village of Geddington before finally veering south through elegant Boughton Park. The first major port of call is Kettering, but the planners in this thriving town have always steered clear of building upon the river's broad flood plain. The Ise is a small river in summer, but floodwater in the winter months can turn it into a raging torrent.

On the outskirts of the town, near Barton Seagrave, the Ise feeds the boating lake at Wicksteed Park. In winter the lake is traditionally drained for maintenance

The unspoilt River Ise above Geddington.

and the fish stocks – which include specimen roach running to over 2 lb apiece – are temporarily flushed into the little river. Locals know this and enjoy superb sport in the winter months as they trot the miniature glides and pools for big roach as well as the river's indigenous population of chub and dace.

Emerging from beneath the new A14 road, the Ise runs parallel to the main London-Leicester railway line and opposite the prominent Weetabix factory before passing Burton Latimer and Finedon en route to Wellingborough and its confluence with the main river.

The Ise is a river of two parts. Above Geddington it is unspoilt and full of character, with natural meanders, shallow riffles and deep pools that have not been ripped apart by the dredgers of the unsympathetic river engineers who vandalised most of lowland England's rivers in the post-war period. Quite how the upper Ise escaped is a bit of a mystery, but as a result it is the only river in the Midlands with a natural, self-sustaining head of grayling. Crayfish, the natural barometers of water quality, are also present in this unpolluted haven, which boasts lush emergent water plants as well as a host of wild flowers in the adjacent meadows.

Left Monument to a Queen - the splendid Eleanor Cross at Geddington.

Below The old stone bridge and ford across the River Ise at Geddington.

Rushton's famous family

The Ise flows through **Rushton** beneath a bridge close to a weir. The village is best known as the home of the famous Tresham family, who built Rushton Hall more than 500 years ago and for two centuries played a leading role in the history of the county and, indeed, the country.

In the 15th century William Tresham and his son Thomas were both Speakers of the House of Commons; the Yorkist father was slain by Lancastrians in the Wars of the Roses and the son lost his own head after supporting Henry VI.

In the 16th century another Thomas Tresham was made Grand Prior of the Order of St John and was awarded a seat in the House of Lords by Mary Tudor. He died during the Spanish Armada and was succeeded by his grandson, 15-year-old Thomas, a Protestant who returned to the Roman Catholic faith of his ancestors. He was most famous for his buildings, which included the peculiar Triangular Lodge in the grounds of Rushton Hall, the market house at Rothwell and the unfinished masterpiece, Lyveden New Building, which today is a National Trust property.

After his death, his son and heir, Francis, became embroiled in the Gunpowder Plot. It was he who wrote the anonymous letter to Lord Monteagle, betraying Guy Fawkes, but he was nevertheless arrested and imprisoned in the Tower of London, where he died before he could be tried.

Memorials fit for a Queen

In an age when modern Royal marriages appear to fall apart so regularly, it is poignant to travel back to 17 December 1290, when Eleanor of Castile, wife of King Edward I, died suddenly at Harby in Nottinghamshire.

The King was so heartbroken that he called off a planned invasion of Scotland and instead returned south to London in a slow funeral cortège. At each stopping-off point along the 150-mile journey back to Queen Eleanor's eventual burial place at Westminster Abbey, Edward ordered that elaborate memorial crosses should be erected. They were duly built at Lincoln, Grantham, Stamford, Geddington, Hardingstone, Stony Stratford, Dunstable, St Albans, Waltham Cross, Cheapside and Charing Cross.

The two in Northamptonshire, together with the one at Waltham Cross, still survive. The **Geddington** monument, set in the middle of the timeless stone village on the banks of the River Ise, is the most impressive and complete. Visit it, and it is easy to recall happier days when Edward and his devoted wife – who is said to have risked her own life to save his by sucking poison from an arrow wound – travelled to the village

to stay in their lodge near the church, which they used as a base for hunting forays into Rockingham Forest between 1274 and 1279.

The Ise is crossed in the village by a narrow, four-arched bridge, dated 1784. Beside it is a ford, still used today by larger vehicles and, no doubt, predating the stone structure beside it.

Wicksteed's town

Kettering will always remember Charles Wicksteed, the son of a church minister who came to the town at the age of 24 and stayed for 60 years, during which time he became one its greatest inspirators. His made his fortune from engineering and spent much of it on the people of his adopted town, buying 250 acres of meadows on the outskirts to create a pleasure park, which predated the modern theme parks and today remains a popular attraction, drawing tens of thousands of visitors every year.

Willow Brook

The Nene's second-largest tributary, the Willow Brook, is unusual in that it suffers its worst pollution at its source, near Corby, and its water quality gradually improves as the effluents from the former steel town are watered down by clean, incoming brooks. It can never match the peerless water quality of its superior sibling, the River Ise, but the Willow Brook valley is nevertheless picturesque as it winds its way through the stone-built villages of Deene, Bulwick, Blatherwycke, King's Cliffe, Apethorpe and Woodnewton, finally joining the parent Nene below Fotheringay.

Town with a Scottish accent

Although mentioned in the Domesday Book as an iron-making centre, **Corby** was in Norman times little more than an isolated village surrounded by the dense wildwood of Rockingham Forest. It was best known for its bizarre Pole Fair, held every 20 years.

And so it remained through the centuries. Although situated on a rich seam of iron ore, surrounded by fuel from dense oak woods and standing at the source of a major tributary of the Nene, the Willow Brook, Corby never realised its true potential. Even during the iron-clad heights of the Industrial Revolution, Corby's furnaces were dwarfed by other foundries in the Nene valley. English scientist Henry Bessemer had invented the Bessemer Converter in 1856, which turned molten iron into steel by passing air over it, but Corby's ore was of a low grade, containing too much phosphorous to produce high-quality steel.

KETTERING, HIGH STREET.

Times have changed, but the modern pedestrianised Kettering High Street looks as busy today as it did in the days of horse-drawn carriages.

The pleasant grassy verges have given way to the provision of parking space since this pre-First World War photograph, but Kettering parish church's glorious 178-foot spire remains as impressive as ever.

However, Corby stood on 500 million tons of ore – at 26,000 acres it was one of the biggest ironfields in the world – and it was only a matter of time before technology found a way of converting it into the steel urgently required by a leading industrial nation. The man who invented the new process was a former solicitor's clerk, who studied chemistry in his spare time. Sidney Thomas discovered that by changing the lining of the Bessemer Converter, he could remove the phosphorous to produce steel as good as any in the world. The revolutionary new process had the added benefit of producing phosphorous-rich basic slag, which was valuable as fertiliser.

Time appears to have stood still in Corby in the early part of this century. In 1930 the quaint stone cottages that made up the village housed just 1,500 inhabitants. But Thomas's new steel-making process changed all that, and Corby was transformed from 1932 onwards as huge steel furnaces, factories and vast housing estates, were built. Overspill from Glasgow populated the new homes and worked in the new industry, with the result that even today, generations later, the predominant accent in this part of Northamptonshire is Scottish! In 10 years, Corby's population increased seven-fold, eventually settling at 50,000.

Huge open-cast quarries were dug around the town by giant excavators, and at night the glow of the giant furnaces could be seen for miles around. Corby's steel town was a true boom town until 1979, when the then nationalised steel industry was decimated by the incoming Conservative Government. Steel manufacturing in the town was closed down, a catastrophic blow to a single-industry community. But thanks to massive grants from the European Community, a host of fresh industries and businesses have since moved in and the newly diversified Corby is now looking stronger than ever.

orders of the 3rd Earl in 1703 by landscape gardener Vandermule, who dammed the Willow Brook for the purpose. In the 19th century the lake was the scene of the 'capture' of Northamptonshire's biggest-ever pike, a magnificent 42 lb 8 oz specimen that measured just half an inch shy of 4 feet long. Unfortunately it never graced the record books, as it was not landed fairly on rod and line, but shot in the shallows by a keen-eyed estate keeper. Until fairly recently, the stuffed and glass-cased predator was on display at the Wellingborough tackle shop of Arthur Cove (himself a famous trout angler).

The tragic Tryons

Just a mile downstream of Deene lies **Bulwick**, another village that bred important – and tragic – heroes of the British Empire. They were members of the Tryon family, of Bulwick Hall. Sir George Tryon died in 1893 along with 300 of his men while he was Commander of the Mediterranean Fleet. His flagship, *Victoria*, was sunk by the battleship *Camperdown* when the two ships collided during a flawed manoeuvre. The Admiral went down with his ship, his last reported words being 'It's entirely my fault'. It was a tragic end to a distinguished 45-year naval career, during which he had been the commander of the world's first iron-clad warship.

The brave Tryons also died prematurely on land, on the battlefield. Henry Tryon died at 25 in command of a night attack at Sebastopol, and five cousins were killed in the Great War. They are commemorated in the village's medieval church.

A further mile and a half downstream, at **Blatherwycke**, the brook is dammed again, this time to form the 54-acre expanse of Blatherwycke Lake. This picturesque stillwater is the largest estate lake in Northamptonshire and is believed to have been constructed in the 18th century. More recently it supplied the water for Corby's steelworks via a pumping station and underground pipelines.

In the Middle Ages, **King's Cliffe** was an important place, granted a charter for a weekly market and an annual three-day fair. It was well-known to Royal visitors, who hunted in the surrounding Rockingham Forest, and was in fact one of the three bailiwicks of the forest. Until 100 years ago the village was famous for wood carving and turning, but today its importance has greatly declined and no more than 1,000 people live there.

King's Cliffe's most famous son was William Law (1686-1761), a writer on theology whose pious views on life included the firm opinion that the theatre was the gatehouse to Hell and that actors and audiences alike were doomed to perdition. His best-known work, *A Serious Call to a Devout and Holy Life*, is believed to have influenced John Wesley's decision to found the

Willow Brook, pictured near Blatherwycke.

Cardigan's Charge

Below Corby the Willow Brook runs through **Deene Park**, which claims an important place in British history, having been the home of the Brudenell family since 1514. Here lived Edward Brudenell, who was made a peer by Charles I, only to be locked in the Tower of London by Cromwell during the Commonwealth. Happily the Restoration saw Charles II release him and make him the first Earl of Cardigan, the day after his own Coronation.

But the most famous of the family was the 7th and last Earl, of Balaclava fame, who led the ill-fated Charge of the Light Brigade during the Crimean War, yet still returned home a hero. He brought with him the horse that he had ridden during that disastrous charge and continued to gallop it around the fields and woods of Deene until he was killed in a riding accident. The horse lived on for a further four years; when it died, its head was preserved in Deene Hall.

The castle-like hall overlooks the park's most outstanding feature, its lake, which was built on the

A new gate and wall at the entrance of Apethorpe Manor in 1996 prevented the author from photographing the village church from the same vantage point as the earlier shot, circa 1910.

Methodist Church. Many people were impressed by his efforts, not least an anonymous stranger who walked up to him in London and handed him an envelope containing £1,000. Law used the stranger's donation to build a school for girls in Thrapston. Today he is buried beneath the shadow of the Norman tower of the church at King's Cliffe.

And so on downstream to **Apethorpe**, where the brook is dammed yet again to create a picturesque ornamental lake. The rush-lined water meadows of the brook in these parts have witnessed human settlement since at least Roman times, for traces of long-lost Roman buildings have been found here. Apethorpe Hall was the home of Sir Walter Mildmay, whom Henry VIII made commissioner for the receipt of royalties from the dissolution of the monasteries. Monuments to the Mildmay family figure largely in the village church.

The final port of call before Fotheringay and the Nene is **Woodnewton**, a small village that has boasted a church since Norman times, and judging by the unspoilt appearance of its mellow stone cottages, it looks as though it has changed little since. But appearances are deceptive. Its very name tells us that it was once all but isolated in the densest part of Rockingham Forest. Just as its handsome church has been altered and extended over the centuries, so has the great forest been reduced to mere fragments. The only thing that remains

constant in this pleasant piece of countryside is the Willow Brook itself, rushing sweetly enough over a gravel bottom, twisting between rushes, willows and overhanging alder and elderberry, before it is welcomed to the sluggish heart of its parent.

Harper's brook

The third tributary, Harper's Brook, also rises close to Corby, on the high ridge of ground near Desborough, to the south-west of the steel town. Unlike its neighbour, Willow Brook, it is not contaminated at birth and through much of its upper reaches wild brown trout can be found, although inadequate sewerage facilities in some villages en route do cause localised problems.

The course of the brook can be easily followed by road. From Stanion to Lowick it never strays more than a couple of hundred yards from the main A6116 Corby-Thrapston road. Below Lowick it executes a sharp curve to the east and runs parallel to the Lowick-Aldwincle road for three-quarters of a mile or so before skirting the Titchmarsh nature reserve and combining with Brancey Brook to join the parent Nene about half a mile downstream of Thorpe Waterville bridge.

Enter **Sudborough** from the Lowick direction and, as the road bends sharply to the left, you will see ahead of you an old toll house that was the home of one of Britain's greatest countryside writers. His name was Denys Watkins-Pitchford, but he wrote under the name of 'BB'.

With a pen-name derived from a size of lead shot, it is no surprise to learn that BB was a keen wildfowler who travelled the length and breadth of the country to hide in hedgerows and crawl across frozen marshes in pursuit of wildfowl. But to anglers he was better known as one of the founders of carp fishing.

Even the smallest tributaries can look impressive when in flood, as this picture of Brancey Brook, near Aldwincle, taken in January 1992, demonstrates. The same view in August 1996 shows the brook at normal summer level.

Almost a century separates these views of Brancey Bridge, pictured at the turn of the century and 1996.

BB would never have expected to be regarded as a great fisherman. His ability and level of technical expertise were, frankly, inadequate. No huge fish ever graced his line. But BB's ability to describe the atmosphere of angling in general – and carp fishing in particular – had few equals. In his writings it was possible to smell the watermint and hear the scolding moorhen as she fussed and chivvied her brood of youngsters around the water lilies. His description of a huge, chainmail-clad common carp breaking the oily surface film of a becalmed pool was enough to have any red-blooded angler reaching for his creel and rushing down to the lake.

Until the early post-war years carp were regarded as uncatchable by most anglers. It was said that they were too intelligent to be fooled by strong lines and big hooks, yet too strong to be landed on fine lines and small hooks.

But that supposed vicious circle did not deter the contemplative BB from trying. He caught very little, but the writings that resulted from his long, thoughtful vigils at countless rush-lined pools were inspirational to a new generation of anglers. Even today, second-hand copies of his classic *Confessions of a Carp Angler* remain much sought-after. Among the forward-thinking new breed of post-war anglers inspired by BB was the

The confluence of Brancey and Harper's brooks, near the Titchmarsh nature reserve.

newly demobbed Richard Walker, a brilliant engineer who set about inventing and manufacturing new tackle that would outwit the wary carp yet be sturdy enough to land it. Walker, BB and others formed an informal group known as the Carp Catchers Club, who pooled their experiences and began to travel to Redmire Pool, a farm lake on the Welsh border of Herefordshire that was reputed to hold the biggest carp in the country. BB failed to cause the carp any concern, but in September 1952 Walker smashed the British record by 10 lb with a 44-pounder.

The huge fish, later nicknamed Clarissa, was transported alive to the aquarium at London Zoo, where it lived out its days in front of millions of visitors until it died in 1971. It remained the British record until 1980, when a 51 lb 8 oz beauty was landed by Chris Yates – again from Redmire Pool.

That fish was still the biggest when BB passed away, in 1990, although it was beaten twice in the space of a month in 1995 from a gravel pit at Ringstead, just a few miles from BB's old home. It would no doubt have

This old tollhouse at Sudborough was the home of the famous countryside author known as 'BB'.

Main Street, Sudborough, photographed in 1927 and 1996.

Parish Church, Lowick, near Thrapston.

More than 70 years separate these views of Lowick Church, yet it remains unchanged - a bold sentinel overlooking Harper's Brook.

amused BB to know that a Nene valley gravel pit that didn't even exist during his heyday could produce such a huge fish. But even if he had still been alive, he would not have been interested in fishing for it, for the technological angling revolution that he and Walker had nurtured had progressed too far by then.

The carbon fibre rods, electronic bite alarms and high-protein baits employed as routine by modern carp catchers would have left BB bemused as he tapped his briar pipe out on the handle of his old cane rod. This brave new world, where tens of thousands of eager and competitive young carpers equipped with millions of pounds worth of tackle set out each day to prove themselves, simply isn't in the simple spirit of the early pioneers. No matter how many big ones they land, they are unlikely to derive the same joy from the waterside as BB enjoyed while he was catching very little.

Indeed, BB had turned his back on the big fish scene many years before his death. He felt more content wandering along the banks of the nearby Harper's Brook and enjoying the company of the modest fish and creatures that lived there. BB's literary career had begun in 1949 with the publication of an enchanting book entitled *Be Quiet and Go A-Angling*. Between then and his much-lamented passing he was a prolific writer on fishing, shooting and the countryside for many publications – some illustrated with his own exquisite woodcuts.

In *Fisherman's Folly*, published three years before his death, he wrote about Harper's Brook in his inimitable style:

'Standing on the old stone bridge the other day and looking over at the brown stream where the minnow shoals were spawning, I began to think about this little stream, how it has run down the centuries way back into the mists of time. Trees die, as does all life, but this bright water runs eternally, truly as old as the hills.'

The church of a would-be assassin

The Middle Ages were troubled times in which England was constantly at war and kings were insecure on their thrones. When Henry of Bolingbroke dethroned Richard II in 1399 to become King Henry IV, friends of Richard were aghast and plotted to assassinate the usurper at Windsor Castle. But their attempt at regicide was foiled and the conspirators were executed in December that year.

Among them was Sir Henry Greene, lord of Drayton Manor, whose lands at **Lowick** stretched down to the fertile meadows of Harper's Brook. Sir Henry therefore died long before the completion of the magnificent perpendicular church he had commissioned, but his son Ralph continued the good work and his grandson, another Henry, built the magnificent lantern tower that dominates the landscape in this part of the valley. All three men were buried in the church, and although the son and grandson are celebrated with magnificent sculpted tombs, the traitor Henry's grave is without a monument.

Ironically, Drayton Manor later became the home of the Mordaunt family, one of whom, in 1605, was arrested and thrown in the Tower of London for a year, accused of being involved in the Gunpowder Plot to assassinate another unpopular English king.

9
Fishing

The firs look dark on Clifford hill
The river bright below
All foamed beneath the water mill
While beauteous flowers do blow

John Clare

Anglers' paradise

The lonely mill of which Clare wrote has been long since demolished. It used to stand close to where thousands of pleasure-seekers now enjoy the water-based entertainment offered by Billing Aquadrome. What was once an ugly sequence of holes ripped out of the ground by gravel extractors, has now been flooded and re-colonised by nature to provide a setting in which thousands of people can have fun.

It is the same story the length of the valley. Nobody appreciates that more than anglers – and no river in the land better captures the essence of angling than the gentle, meandering Nene. It boasts not the might of the majestic Severn, Britain's longest watercourse, nor the sheer power of the relentless salmon spates of the kingdom's Celtic corners. Slow and ponderous though she is, the Nene does not flow to sea with the stately swagger of Old Father Thames, the river of the capital (and the only one granted a masculine suffix). Like most other rivers the Nene is, of course, female and would blush at such a crass comparison.

Yet while anglers on the Severn, Thames, Wye and Tweed bemoan the ever-declining fish stocks, fans of the Nene smirk silently as they celebrate their good fortune. The fact is that the fishing is very good – and getting better.

The non-tidal Nene and its tributaries contain (in descending order of size) carp, pike, barbel, zander, bream, eels, tench, chub, perch, brown and rainbow trout, roach, rudd, grayling, dace, ruffe, gudgeon, loach, sticklebacks and minnows. The tidal reaches and the estuary also hold flounders, bass, sea trout, smelt, mullet and even stray salmon. Oddities like geographically challenged sturgeon have, in the past, lost their way from the Caspian Sea and ended up by mistake in the Nene.

The great leveller

But forget this bizarre catalogue of diversity. Anglers do not flock to the Nene to pursue rarities; most return time and again to their favourite haunts to catch Britain's favourite fish, the roach. Like the Nene itself, the roach is a gentle, modest specimen.

Just why anglers love roach is a mystery. Plain and silvery, it does not boast the speckled splendour of the trout, nor the striped swagger of the bristling perch. It is not a spectacular fighter, nor does it grow to a prodigious size. The record roach, from the chalk-rich River Stour in Dorset, stands at 3 ounces over 4 lb – and the very biggest Nene specimen would be hard-pressed to achieve much more than half that weight. The best chance of a big roach is from the unspoilt River Ise, which regularly produces 2 lb-plus samples.

But what the Nene lacks in quality, it more than makes up for in quantity. No river in Britain holds more roach than the Nene, which contains vast shoals of this silvery, red-finned species. An average sample from our river scrapes in at 4 ounces, while a venerable specimen of a pound and a half is certain to provide the excuse for celebratory drinks in the nearest pub. But to sneer at such small fry is to miss the point. The Nene, you see, is a great leveller.

There is nearly 100 miles of the River Nene to choose from, of which there is barely a yard without a resident roach or two with a taste for bait. Here is a river where the average angler can confidently set out his stall without the embarrassment of returning home with a dry keepnet.

Competition anglers love the Nene and its roach. When they draw their numbers from the hat to determine which spot they'll fish, they know that on

A typical catch of roach from the River Nene at Woodford by angling journalist Simon Roff.

this river the end result is less of a lottery than on most others. Match anglers like to see the best man win – or at least stand a chance.

The reliable roach is a fish for all seasons. You can catch it in the height of a heatwave and the shivering depths of a freeze-up. Fine lines, small hooks, boiled hempseed, maggots and their pupae (known to anglers as casters) are the keys to success.

But some anglers prefer bigger fish. Instead of banking on the odds-on roach, they risk all on the weightier outsiders like bream, tench and carp.

Hump-backed heavyweights

Bream are different from roach. They don't spread out evenly through the river, but instead concentrate in specific areas. Wide, slow and deep stretches are best, and it is not unknown for a renowned bream hole to keep on producing the goods for generations. These spots are worth knowing, for bream grow to a decent size and when they are in a feeding mood a

heavyweight catch is on the cards. Slab-sided Nene bream seem to start at 2 lb, average almost 4 lb and grow to 9 lb or more. When fish like this get their heads down to tuck into your groundbait, a netful of 100 lb or more is possible.

Some places on the Nene are synonymous with bream. Splash Lane at Castor is favourite, but Peterborough Embankment is a winner in winter and Yarwell Mill, Islip island, Wadenhoe and Pilton are all real hot-spots. To catch them, lace your groundbait with casters and worms and fish a leger or feeder rig to present your bait hard on the bottom. The latter, incidentally, should be what anglers call a cocktail bait – a combination of any two of the following: casters, red maggots, worms, sweetcorn or bread. Switch them around and experiment until you discover which pairing the picky bream prefer.

River bream grow big, but their stillwater cousins grow even bigger. The hump-backed bream is a ponderous creature that avoids the strenuous activity of swimming against the current as much as possible. In the gravels pits along the river it can conserve its energy and pile on extra pounds. The pits in the Thrapston area have produced bream to 13 lb.

Great match catches

The Nene is noted for its huge bream shoals and in 1995 produced the biggest haul ever taken in a five-hour match on the river. It came during the annual Nene Championships and weighed 131 lb 6 oz.

Many pundits thought that record was impossible to beat, but Kirkby-in-Ashfield angler Roger Parnell came agonisingly close in September 1996 with a 127 lb 8 oz 8 dr catch from Islip island. He beat 449 other anglers with that catch and would have broken the river record too but for the fact that he lost four bream during the course of the match. Any one of them would have been enough to earn him his place in the record books.

Such catches from the middle reaches of the river were unheard of until a few years back. For most of this century pollution from below Northampton was detrimental to fish stocks, and for big bream catches most anglers headed for the Peterborough area, where the effluent was more diluted. It was not until 1950 that the National Federation of Anglers deemed the Nene good enough for their annual All-England National Championships, an event that was won by the host team, Peterborough Angling Association, with an aggregate weight of 62 lb 5 oz 12 dr for the 12-man side. The individual winner needed just 15 lb 4 oz for a gold medal.

The 1951 Rivers (Prevention of Pollution) Act was criticised in some quarters as being toothless, but it must have had some effect upon the Nene, for in 1959, when the prestigious NFA match was again staged on the river, the winning team (Bedford) landed 86 lb 1 oz 4 dr and the top individual caught 57 lb 8 oz 8 dr – the second-heaviest haul ever taken in the 53-year history of the event.

In the early 1970s the rules were changed, with the team event decided by points rather than aggregate weight, and the sides split into divisions, with their matches fished on different venues. By the time the Division One National was eventually fished on the Nene, in 1975, the individual winner, Michael Hoad-Reddick from Rotherham, won with 63 lb 7 oz of bream from a swim at Stibbington.

A local world champ

The very last single-division National Championship was fished on the River Severn in 1971 and was won by Peterborough maestro Robin Harris with a 40 lb 5 oz catch. In doing so he achieved a unique feat by becoming the only man ever to win both World and National Championships. Robin had taken the world crown two years earlier, in West Germany in 1969, when he was only the second Englishman ever to win the gold medal.

No angler could ever rival Robin's float fishing skills. His mastery of the running line was perfection itself, but his dominance faded later in the 1970s when English anglers finally learned the continental pole-fishing techniques that have dominated match fishing ever since.

By coincidence, another Nene valley angler, Wisbech's Brian Lakey, won the penultimate All-England, fished on the Middle Level Drain near Upwell in 1970, while Whittlesey's John Hart won the first-ever Division Two National, on the River Welland in 1972.

Tench in the lilies

Tench are generally regarded as a species that thrive best in muddy, stagnant pools, but they have adapted well to the sluggish Nene and can even be found in the fast-flowing backwaters and weirpools.

A fish of the warmer months, tench prefer to feed early in the morning and late in the evening. The best spots to catch them are close to lilies – especially where they grow in profusion in the old dead arms left behind where the river was straightened in the past. They like nothing better than nosing around in the deep layers of silt for bloodworms, the underwater larvae of mosquitoes and midges.

To attract tench into your swim, it is worth stirring up the muddy bottom with a rake-head attached to a length of rope. The natural food thus disturbed acts as a magnet to inquisitive tench, which will also feed more confidently under the cover of coloured water. The rake is also useful for clearing a narrow, lily-free channel in which to play the hard-fighting fish. Tench fight hard and to risk fishing for them with line weaker than 4 lb breaking strain is to invite disaster in the jungles of tough lily stems and roots.

Nene tench average 4 lb apiece and grow to over 7 lb. The best bait to tempt them is sweetcorn, straight from

Bernie Smith of Stoke-on-Trent nets a good bream during the Division One National Championships on the Nene above Peterborough in 1975. Today this stretch of river is part of the Nene Valley Country Park. Angler's Mail

Tench grow big in the rich gravel pits that line the Nene valley, as Peterborough angler Mick Smith discovered when he landed this beautiful trio scaling 8 lb 9 oz, 7 lb 12 oz and 7 lb 5 oz in a short evening session.

the tin with the juice saved to flavour your groundbait. Again, the biggest samples are generally found in the stillwaters. Sywell Country Park, near Wellingborough, has achieved national prominence for its huge tench, which average close to 7 lb apiece and run to over 10 lb. There are probably more big tench in this 100-acre former reservoir than any other water in the country, and the venue can be fished either on a day ticket or a value-for-money season ticket from Wellingborough Nene Angling Club.

Catching tench from the rich, weedy waters of Sywell demands specialist tactics. These big fish can break light tackle with ease, so stout gear is called for – line of around 8 lb breaking strain is the norm here. Legering is banned at this venue, but a heavy float rig with plenty of shot anchoring the bait hard on the bottom is a good compromise. Specialist tench anglers use baits known as boilies – hard, round balls of high-protein goodness, laced with fish-attracting flavours. These are

deadly, but by no means essential to success. Sywell tench also enjoy the fare eaten by tench elsewhere – simple baits like bread, sweetcorn and worms all catch fish.

The much-maligned pike

As the bream and tench have already demonstrated, most fish from lakes grow bigger than their river counterparts. That's because stillwater fish don't have to waste valuable calories fighting against flowing water. Therefore, if you want to stand a chance of catching a huge pike, the gravel pits, reservoirs and near-stagnant drains of the Nene valley are the best bets. But that doesn't mean that the river itself isn't worth trying.

Fish that have spent their lives in running rivers may not attain the bulk achieved by their lazy lake cousins, but they do develop extra muscle that makes them fight a lot harder. In short, they are great fun to catch.

The biggest pike ever recorded from the Nene itself weighed 28 lb 12 oz and was caught by a young Peterborough angler three or four years ago. The biggest recently weighed 26 lb and came from Wellingborough locks early in 1997. That's well shy of Britain's biggest known pike, the infamous 40-pounder known to dwell in a riverside gravel pit near Fotheringay, but without doubt there are pike over the 30 lb mark waxing fat on the rich roach and bream shoals of the Nene.

Piking in the river is never boring. There is an apparently unending supply of smaller pike averaging 6 lb that will provide exciting action all day long. And interspersed among them are odd bigger fish over the 10 lb mark that add spice to any session. The most exciting way of catching these fish is with artificial lures. Commonly known as spinners, these baits include lures made from plastic, wood and metal. What each has in common is an ability to imitate the action of a wounded live fish if worked correctly and thoughtfully by the angler. And there is nothing a crafty pike likes better than an easy-to-catch wounded fish.

Livebaiting – the act of impaling a live fish on the hook – is outlawed by most angling clubs these days. However, the alternative natural method, legering a deadbait for the scavenging pike, can be boring. The exciting answer is to explore the river with artificial lures, fooling the pike into believing that the inanimate object on the end of your line is alive. I promise you won't be disappointed.

The sheer numbers of pike in the Nene make them unpopular with some anglers, who believe they threaten the stocks of other fish. Indeed, water bailiffs in the Oundle area have even been instructing visiting anglers to destroy all the pike they catch. *On no account pay heed to this ignorant advice.* The presence of so many predatory pike in the Nene is an indicator of the healthy state of the fishery. Mother Nature is capable of maintaining her own natural balance without meddlesome interventions.

The pike has, in less enlightened times, been known as the water-wolf or freshwater shark. And like the saltwater shark, it has suffered from man's fear of the unknown. There are 300 species of shark in the world, only 15 of which have ever been reported as attacking humans. Shark attacks on man are very rare – an average of 100 per year – yet 100 million shark are slaughtered by man per annum. The shark's ridiculous demonisation in the 1975 film *Jaws* planted the bad-guy image in our psyche. As a result, the subject of the film, the great white shark, is now threatened with extinction.

The shark is a superb predator that should be admired. So too is the pike, which plays an invaluable role in maintaining the balance of nature in our rivers

Pike have a reputation for being savage predators, and in the past were usually killed by their captors. Happily the more enlightened modern anglers go to great pains to return their catches safely - in this case Hertfordshire enthusiast Eddie Turner even kisses a prized 30 lb-plus pike farewell as he slips it back gently into a gravel pit at the Bluebell Fishery complex above Fotheringay.

and lakes. Bigoted fishermen who say 'the only good pike is a dead one' should be expelled from the sport. Those who say 'pike eat fish, therefore there'd be more fish for me to catch if pike were killed' are using a flawed equation and need educating.

The presence of that fabulous 40-pounder in Bluebell Lakes is a tribute to the enlightened views of the dedicated anglers who have been fortunate enough to land it. Each of them have carefully returned it to its gravel pit home. The first captor of this fish was Corby angler Derek McDonald, who tempted it on a home-made spoon back in 1992. Since then it has been caught on several occasions, peaking in weight at 41 lb when Peterborough angler Colin Bailey landed it in 1995. Its latest capture was on 14 February 1996, when footloose fisherman Nige Williams became the seventh angler to catch it.

Staffordshire-based Nige is regarded as Britain's leading pike angler, with six specimens over 30 lb and another 62 over 20 lb in an illustrious predator-hunting career spanning 20 years. But until St Valentine's Day 1996 there was always one ambition left unfulfilled – a 40 lb pike.

The fishing tackle dealer had scoured the British Isles, travelling tens of thousands of miles across Ireland, Scotland and Wales in search of the ultimate prize. He

This 40 lb 12 oz pike, landed by Wolverhampton angler Nige Williams on 14 February 1996, is the largest known pike in Britain. It was taken from Kingfisher Lake - a former gravel pit beside the River Nene.

came agonisingly close on several occasions, most notably in 1992 when he boated a 39 lb 8 oz monster during a trip on Kent's Bough Beech Reservoir. But to an angler obsessed, a fish falling half a pound short of the mark just wasn't good enough. It was like a top athlete running the mile at a fraction over 4 minutes. Happily, Nige finally achieved his dream on the banks of a small gravel pit beside the River Nene. The massive, pot-bellied female measured 48 inches from the tip of its huge jaws to the fork of its tail. More important to 37-year-old Nige, it thumped the spring balance down to 40 lb 12 oz.

Later, Nige recalled, 'The lake had been iced-up for two weeks, but had just thawed. The weather forecast predicted a mild, south-westerly wind and I reckoned conditions were ideal for the big pike to feed. I just had a hunch that I might catch it.'

To make that hunch pay off, Nige made the 180-mile round trip from his home in Coven Heath, Staffordshire, arriving on the bankside at 7.15 am. At 3 pm he contacted the fish for which he had been waiting, and

the 40-pounder turned out to be the biggest caught in Britain that year – just as it had been the previous season, when Colin Bailey landed it.

The days of a pike stew for a local family are long gone. Conservation-minded modern anglers like Nige and Colin treat their catch lovingly and ensure that no harm comes to them before they are gently returned to the water. This means that the giant pike of Kingfisher Lake is free to renew its reign of terror on the lesser inhabitants of its watery domain – and could be even heavier if another angler is fortunate enough to tempt it.

Perch and zander

The pike is not the only predatory fish to dwell in the Nene. It shares the river with the smaller but no less impressive perch and, especially in the lower reaches around Peterborough, it suffers competition from an illegal immigrant known as the zander.

The perch is probably the most colourful and impressive-looking fish in our waters. The bold, black-striped sides, erect spiny dorsal fin and vermilion tail and lower fins combine to make the perch a larger-than-life character. It is also the first fish most young anglers encounter. Small perch are bold biters and care nothing for the clumsy presentation of the

This handsome 2 lb perch fell to Brixworth angler Graham Billing during a trip to Pitsford Reservoir.

inexperienced fisherman. As long as the hook is baited with a worm, a little perchlet will almost certainly oblige.

It is when the perch grows bigger that it becomes of more interest to the angler. At around 1 lb it is worthy quarry, at 2 lb magnificent. Perch to 3 lb are present in the Nene, although bigger specimens are likely to exist in the gravel pits. Large numbers of fine perch over 2 lb are present in Pitsford and Ravensthorpe reservoirs, where they are often caught by mistake by trout anglers. On the main Nene, swims to close to bridges, locks and other man-made structures are favoured by perch. So too are rushes and reedbeds, although in truth perch are present virtually throughout the system.

Worms and maggots are the tried and tested baits for perch, and your chances of success are enhanced by the rather messy procedure of chopping up the worms and flicking in a few free offerings. The scent will attract perch – along with the Nene's ever-present eel population, of course. When using maggots, opt for those dyed red, as the perch have a definite preference for baits of that colour.

But as true predators, perch eat small fish. Small livebaits – gudgeon, minnows and bleak – are deadly offerings, but more fun can be had with miniature artificial baits. Little bar spoons like those from the

Mepps family are excellent, and their effectiveness can be further enhanced by fixing a tag of red wool to the trailing treble hook for the perch to aim at. Although perch do not have sharp teeth, it is best to use a short wire trace to cope with the awesome dentistry of the pike, which is also sure to intercept your spinners.

The zander is a native of continental Europe and was unknown in British waters until 1878 when the Duke of Bedford imported 23 German specimens, which were placed in his lakes at Woburn Abbey. There they thrived and bred, and some of their offspring were removed to other stillwaters in the vicinity. But it was not until nearly a century later that the former Great Ouse River Board received permission to remove and stock some into their breeding ponds in Suffolk.

The Area Fisheries Officer in those days was Norman McKenzie, a man raised on the wild trout and salmon rivers of the north – and a man who regarded the coarse fish of the lowlands as boring. He was intensely disliked by many of his staff, including his head bailiff, Cliff Cawkwell, who thought his boss was a frightful snob. On 18 March 1963 McKenzie made the controversial decision to release 100 young zander into the open waterways of the Great Ouse system. Three died on the journey from Bury St Edmunds to the Relief Channel at Stow Bridge in West Norfolk, but the 97 survivors were destined to change Britain's freshwaters for ever. Ironically, it was Cliff Cawkwell who was put in charge of the task. He reluctantly carried out his boss's order, but the forthright bailiff – a wonderful man I have known since boyhood – warned that it was an act of folly. He was proved right.

Within a decade the prolific predators had bred and spread throughout the Fens of Cambridgeshire. Sluices and other physical obstacles did not stop them penetrating the Nene system, via the lock at Stanground that connects the Nene to the drains of the Middle Level system. It is thought that irresponsible, mischievous anglers probably transplanted live specimens to other stretches of the Nene.

By 1984 there was a population explosion of small zander, particularly upstream of Orton. Since then numbers of the new predator have stabilised and fewer are present, although individual specimens are larger than they were 15 years ago. Weirs, locks and old mills make the Nene a difficult river for fish with a wanderlust, but zander have nevertheless been reported as far upstream as Thrapston.

Although irresponsible introductions of alien fish are illegal and can pose a threat to native species, the zander does not seem to have caused any damage in the Nene, and the best thing anglers can do is enjoy catching them. If you are determined to catch a Nene zander, the best area to try is around Ferry Meadows, near Peterborough, where fish over the 10 lb mark are regularly recorded.

At the time of writing, Britain's current record zander stands at 18 lb 12 oz, taken from the lower reaches of the River Severn in March 1992 by Birmingham angler Ray Armstrong. The species was illegally stocked into this river at around the same time as the River Nene. If the Nene received the same attention as the Severn from predator anglers, there is no reason why it could not produce a specimen to at least challenge that record.

Carp

The hardest fish in the Nene to catch is the carp, but for some perverse reason it is my favourite. Perhaps that's because the Nene is the very best carp river in the

This flooded gravel pit below Ringstead is known as the Mid-Northants Carp Fishery and, during 1995, twice broke the British carp record.

country – and every one landed can be considered something of a personal triumph.

There are huge carp weighing over 30 lb in the Nene that have never been caught by an angler. I know – I've seen them with my own eyes, just feet from the bankside, swimming disdainfully over a carpet of bait that I'd laid down in the vain hope that it would lead to their downfall. Carp fishing is never easy and blank returns are more common than red-letter days, but every hard-won success is at least a minor victory.

My biggest from the Nene was 2 lb shy of the 30 lb mark, but who could complain at catching a magnificent 28 lb common carp? It fought like a tiger

before finally submitting and allowing me to admire its golden, chainmail-scaled flanks for a few moments before gently returning it back to its watery world.

I sat, soaked, through a September thunderstorm for that beauty, plus another of 16 lb a few minutes earlier. A year later in the same swim, near Oundle, I enjoyed an incredible two-hour session in which I managed to land carp of 25 lb 8 oz, 19 lb and 15 lb without mishap. Occasions like that make up for the times when I've ham-fistedly missed my only bite of the day or, even worse, not had so much as a sniff from the discerning carp. It's enough to make you tear your hair out in frustration.

It's high summer and the author has found success in his quest for carp from a weed-choked backwater of the river near Oundle.

This is the author's biggest carp from the River Nene - a 28 lb common that had probably never seen another angler's bait.

The author was thrilled to land this 17 lb mirror carp from the river in June 1994 . . . but his smile was even wider a few months later when he managed to catch the same fish, this time weighing 23 lb 12 oz.

Carp, you see, don't actually *need* anglers' baits. You can throw in a supermarket trolleyful of luncheon meat, sweetcorn and bread, but these perverse creatures would rather slobber around in the evil-smelling mud on the bottom rooting out the larvae of mosquitoes. There's no accounting for taste, I suppose.

Thankfully, carp occasionally appreciate a change of diet. But to take advantage of this infrequent trait on their part, you need to be patient. Forget about fishing for a while – just throw in copious quantities of free offerings every evening for a couple of weeks to allow the suspicious carp to allay their fears and start feeding confidently on the new food source. It sounds like some kind of bizarre pagan sacrifice, turning up every night to throw in your gifts to the underwater gods. But believe me, it works. After a week or so of slinging in a bucketful of bait you might even be rewarded by the glorious sight of happy carp, rolling and leaping on the surface to show their appreciation of your generosity.

Don't let that fool you into running for the rods – control yourself, for heaven's sake! All this self-sacrifice is worth it. Abstinence makes the carp grow fonder.

If you are very rich or foolish, you can achieve this marvellous state of affairs by arriving every night and piling in cans of sweetcorn or expensive proprietary carp baits. Alternatively, you can take the cheaper option of baiting up with inexpensive grains and pulses purchased in bulk from your local seed merchant, which are equally effective once soaked and boiled. Maize is excellent, and maple peas – which I used to catch that 28-pounder – are even better. Almost as good is plain boiled wheat, which costs around a fiver for a half-hundredweight sack and with which I've baited to tempt plenty of big carp from the Nene.

Finally the big day arrives. You've religiously baited up your chosen pitch for a fortnight, the trap is set, and now's the time to spring it. Throw in just half the normal quantity of free offerings, then cast out so that your hookbait lands smack-bang in the middle of all that free grub. Finally, make sure you don't walk under any ladders or step on the cracks of paving stones before you start fishing. It would also help to have a rabbit's foot handy. The carp should do the rest . . . but you never know.

A cut above the rest

The Nene enjoyed a head start over other British rivers when in 1948 it became the first to be stocked with carp. These fish flourished, especially in the warm-water overflows of the old coal-fired power stations at Northampton and Peterborough. It was the latter – known, prosaically, as the Electricity Cut – that produced the country's first-ever 30 lb-plus river carp, more than 30 years ago. The first big carp, weighing 20 lb 6 oz, had been landed there by a local angler, Don Barnes, in 1959. By the 1960s anglers from all over the country were flocking there, particularly in winter when the warm water from the power station's cooling towers drew the carp like a magnet.

The cut, situated on River Lane, was only a quarter of a mile long, but on freezing cold winter nights carp enthusiasts often lined it, shoulder to shoulder. Those who could endure the elements (and hordes of rats) were often rewarded with big fish. In 1964 Grantham angler Stan Hill recorded a 31 lb 12 oz carp, which was bettered two months later by local teenager Peter Harvey, who banked a 33 lb 12 oz monster. Just weeks later the same fish at the same weight was caught by Londoner Peter Hemingway.

All those big fish were caught in winter, usually at night and mainly on the fashionable bait of the day – namely part-boiled potatoes. But Londoner William Beta bucked the trend on 16 June 1965 when he fished the cut in broad daylight and landed the biggest carp of all on a piece of cheese. That fish weighed 34 lb 4 oz and was never beaten from the cut (although it has since been bettered by a 38-pounder to a Peterborough angler from the North Bank of the Nene a few miles downstream).

On 1 January 1966 a young Peterborough angler, Elliott Smith (later Symak), landed a 22 lb carp that was the first of seven over 20 lb he landed while fishing with a local student, David Moore. That duo's catches dominated the cut until the power station closed in 1970. Today Elliott is a well-known carp expert and fishery owner, while David is recreation development manager for Anglian Water, in charge of the prestigious trout fisheries at Rutland Water, Grafham Water, Pitsford and Ravensthorpe.

I have my own fond memories of the Electricity Cut. One Saturday afternoon in September 1967, as a fishing-mad 11-year-old, I was dropped off there by my father and brother-in-law while they walked another quarter of a mile along London Road to watch Peterborough United play at home. I'm not sure what the Posh scored that day, but by the time they had

This lily-fringed bay on the middle reaches of the Nene is home to some big carp.

returned I had netted my first-ever roach, rudd and bleak on float-fished maggots and – excitement of excitements – had witnessed a fellow angler land a modest mirror carp.

Once the power station closed and warm water ceased to be pumped into the river, the carp population spread out and today the fish can found throughout the Nene. The best places to locate them are in wide, lily-fringed bays and around bridge structures. Immediately below Oundle Bridge, where the canal-like Town Wharf meets the main river, is a classic river carp swim that has produced scores of 20 lb-plus specimens, summer and winter. It is controlled by Coventry & District Angling Association, whose bailiff issues inexpensive day tickets on the bank.

Chub and barbel

The gentle pace and muddy bottom of most of the River Nene does not provide the ideal habitat for the chub and barbel, which prefer a more powerful flow over a clean, gravel riverbed. But the backwaters and streamy channels that bypass many of the locks and sluices along the river provide just that combination – and are the best places to try for those species.

The biggest Nene chub I have ever weighed and

witnessed went a shade over 5 lb and was landed by accident by former World Champion Ian Heaps, who was fishing for roach with fine tackle on a Kettering, Thrapston & District Angling Club stretch of the river close to the bridge at Thorpe Waterville. Successfully beating that specimen on a tiny size 22 hook and frail 1 lb line was a real test of angling skill and one that certainly brightened a bitterly cold January day at the riverside.

That particular fish was caught in open water, which is unusual, for most chub generally lurk close to the sanctuary of cover, in the form of underwater roots, weedbeds and reedbeds. Overhanging trees that offer a roof over their heads as well as tasty windfalls in the shape of grubs and insects are also favourite areas.

The best chub fishing I've enjoyed on the Nene has been at Castor backwater, a stretch controlled by Peterborough & District Angling Association. Three-pounders are commonplace here, along with a

A bleak January morning in 1995 was well worth the endurance of former World Champion Ian Heaps when he landed this cracking 5 lb chub on light pole-fishing gear from the Nene near Thorpe Waterville.

sprinkling of better fish over the 4 lb mark. The best time to see them is on a bright, summer's day when the water is low and clear. Wear polarising sunglasses to cut out the surface glare and you will see chub aplenty cruising slowly between the bulrushes and feeding on items of food swept down by the current.

Another good place to try is Willow Creek, a half-mile stretch of wooded backwater in the heart of the Bluebell Fisheries complex near Fotheringay. I've seen photographs of chub to well over 5 lb landed here, and fish topping 6 lb are rumoured. The chub certainly grow to a bigger-than-average size in these parts, for a few have found their way into the adjacent gravel pits, where specimens of over 6 lb have been weighed and witnessed. Unfortunately, stillwater chub are very tricky customers to catch and success is more likely on moving water.

River chub have long been known as the most obliging fish that swim, and their catholic tastes are legendary; they will eat anything remotely edible. But they are also easily scared, and will steadfastly refuse to feed if they are startled by a sudden heavy footstep or shadow falling across the water. Be stealthy in your approach and lull them into a false sense of security by allaying their suspicions with plenty of free offerings.

Bread is as good a bait as any. In the summer chub readily accept floating crust from the surface, so position yourself upstream of a known chub lie and start flicking in bits of bread. It won't be long before bow-waves appear below the surface as the ever-hungry chub get stuck into the new food source. Once they are feeding confidently, it is time to attach a piece of crust to your hook and allow it to drift down the surface with the current, until it too is snaffled.

Bread is also a good bait in winter, but with the water coloured and fish less inclined to feed on the surface, different tactics are required. At this time of the year it is better to prime a swim with mashed bread first and give it a rest for half an hour or so before legering a lump of bread in the spot. If feeding chub are present, you should get your first bite within minutes, if not seconds.

Winter is also the time that chub move out of the main river into the smaller tributaries. Harper's Brook, which joins the Nene above Aldwincle, is a good venue in the colder months when it is carrying a foot or two of extra water. Most of the chub in this venue are on the small side – a 3-pounder is a whopper here – but the lack of quality is compensated for by quantity.

Although chub have always been commonplace, barbel were Nene rarities until 1993, when the former National Rivers Authority (now the Environment Agency) began a breeding programme at its Calverton hatchery near Nottingham to produce thousands of young barbel. These have been stocked into strategic

A roving approach through the thick undergrowth on Harper's Brook pays off in summer, when decent chub can be successfully stalked.

points along the river from Northampton to Peterborough and should provide superb sport in the next decade, especially if they grow to the size of native specimens.

The biggest Nene barbel on record is a 12 lb beauty landed from the weirpool at Orton Staunch in 1969. Its captor was a local student, legering for chub. Apart from that monster, barbel to 10 lb have been caught from the Ringstead area and another of 9 lb rumoured a few years back from the streamy water below Elton Mill.

Barbel fishing demands a no-nonsense approach. They are powerful fighters that use the strong current of their preferred habitat to their advantage, so tackle up with line of at least 6 lb breaking strain and strong, forged hooks. The best bait is luncheon meat, fished over a tasty carpet of boiled hempseed. The thousands of tiny seeds will keep any hungry fish occupied in your swim for a long time. Barbel experts sometimes bait up with a gallon of more of this inexpensive bait, which is believed to contain scented oils that are irresistible to barbel and capable of drawing them hundreds of yards upstream.

Eels and dace

These two species have absolutely nothing in common . . . except for the fact that they are neglected by anglers. The eel is all too often regarded as a bait-grabbing nuisance that leaves your hook and line in a tangled, slimy mess, while the dace is usually ignored by anglers chasing bigger fish like roach and chub. But both species have their fans. The eel is popular with match anglers in the early summer, when the roach and bream often refuse to feed and anything at all is welcome. The small eels they are likely to catch are usually less than 1 lb in weight and known rather disparagingly as 'bootlaces'. There are also a handful of anglers who specialise in the capture of big eels – python-like creatures that fight like fury and are more often found in landlocked stillwaters. These big fish of 4 lb or more usually venture out to feed only under the cover of darkness, when they scavenge for dead fish or any other available animal matter. Both worms and deadbaits are excellent offerings for these fish, which have been recorded from local gravel pits to 7 lb. The British record stands at over 11 lb.

The eel is certainly the most interesting fish to swim in the Nene, for every single eel present in the river first had to make an incredible journey of thousands of miles from the Sargasso Sea, off Bermuda. It is to there that each one also returns on adulthood to spawn and die, leaving yet more tiny recruits to head back to Europe and wriggle up the River Nene.

Many anglers despise the serpent-like eel, which is netted in its thousands every year by commercial fishermen supplying the lucrative jellied eel market. It is certainly a tasty, nutritious fish. But unless you want to take one or two samples for the table, I urge you to return what you catch unharmed to complete its incredible life cycle. The Nene would be a poorer place without the enigmatic eel.

A lot of anglers catch whopping great dace without ever knowing it. A big dace looks very much like a small chub, for which it is often mistaken. It is not that difficult to differentiate between the two. The chub has a more robust appearance, larger mouth and deeper coloration. The surest way to tell the difference, however, is by examining the anal fin. On the chub it is convex, on the dace concave – simple as that.

The biggest dace are usually found in the smallest waterways. The clear-flowing upper reaches of the Nene and its tributaries are ideal habitats for dace to grow to a decent size. I've enjoyed splendid sport with dace to 10 oz in Harper's Brook below Lowick, where float-fished maggot and bread baits on fine tackle are all you need to explore the overgrown, miniature watercourse.

Most of these streams are not controlled by angling clubs, but seek permission from the local farmer or landowner before you fish them.

Trout and salmon

In the days before the Nene was canalised and polluted, migratory sea trout and salmon would have left their feeding grounds in the sea and forced their way upstream every year to spawn in the river of their birth. Today the occasional sea trout – and even the odd wandering salmon – still braves the dirty tidal river, but is thwarted in its upstream quest by pollution and man-made barriers.

However, the upper reaches of the Nene above Northampton still hold wild brown trout, supplemented by escapee rainbow trout from the reservoirs in the area. The Ise above Kettering is the only river in the Midlands to hold stocks of the trout's near relative, the grayling, along with good trout.

But for the best trout sport, anglers turn to the reservoirs and gravel pits. Pitsford and Ravensthorpe Reservoirs, controlled by Anglian Water, hold a good head of stocked brown and rainbow trout, as do privately run gravel pits like Ringstead Grange and Elinor, which are controlled by the Foster family. The latter also contain farmed salmon for anglers who cannot afford the ridiculous price of wild salmon fishing on the exclusive salmon rivers of Scotland.

The most interesting development on the game fishing scene in recent years has been the advent of river trout fisheries, at Wadenhoe and Perio Mill. Both are situated on pleasant mill streams off the main river, where farmed rainbow trout and odd brownies are regularly stocked to provide an intriguing challenge.

Tiddlers

The Nene contains vast shoals of gudgeon, game little fellows of an ounce of so apiece that look very much like miniature barbel. Like their much bigger cousins, they prefer streamy, clear water over a gravel bottom.

Much the same size, bleak are slender, silvery fish that generally inhabit the surface layers. They are

Inexperienced anglers often have difficulty differentiating between small chub (left) and dace. The larger mouth, chunkier build and bronze coloration of the former are usually a giveaway.

The humble gudgeon may be small in stature, but it is ever-present throughout the Nene and always willing to bite.

Boat and bank anglers compete for an early season trout on an artificially stocked gravel pit at Ringstead.

found in profusion below most locks, bridges and other structures. In 1972 Surrey angler Ray Mumford won the coveted Gladding Masters Championship on the Nene with a catch of bleak that weighed half an ounce over 14 lb. That haul was the talk of the angling world at the time, for it comprised a staggering 752 of the tiddlers in just 5 hours, with Ray often catching at the rate of a fish every 6 seconds. Ray, who now lives at Luton, was a controversial figure at the time with his continental-style pole techniques, but time has proved his theories and modern match anglers today use the very same methods that Ray was using 30 years ago.

Ruffe, a close – but much smaller – relative of the perch, are found in slower, muddier reaches. A 4 oz ruffe is a specimen to be proud of, but in 1996 the river between Thrapston and Oundle reputedly produced two record-smashing mini-monsters of 6 oz or so. These fish caused some debate in *Angler's Mail*, with experts believing that they were quite probably immature zander, which look quite similar. If both were cases of mistaken identity then it is indeed ruffe justice for the anglers concerned. . .

The extinct burbot

Mention cod to most folk and they conjure up a mouth-watering picture of a tasty, white-fleshed sea fish, fried in crispy batter and served up with chips. But the deep-sea-dwelling cod has many close relatives, and the River Nene was once one of the country's strongholds for the only freshwater member of the cod family, the mysterious burbot.

Even in its heyday, the burbot – also known as the eel-pout – was a rarity for anglers. It lived in holes under the bank and only ventured out at night to scavenge on dead fish and other animals that had sunk to the bottom of the river. It was also fussy about its habitat and breeding requirements. In order to spawn, the burbot required very cold winter temperatures when the surface of the river was frozen solid.

Nene burbot probably died out in the early years of the 19th century due to the canalisation of the river and subsequent loss of habitat. Warm water from the discharges of factories and power stations would certainly have been the final straw. The burbot did, however, linger on in the Fens until about 25 years ago. The last reported captures were from the Old West River near Cambridge and the Great Ouse Relief Channel at Denver Sluice around 1970. It is now believed to be extinct.

The burbot - the only freshwater member of the cod family - was once commonplace on the Nene, particularly around the former Whittlesey Mere. Today, sadly, it is extinct.

Permits and licences

Before you can go fishing you need to buy an Environment Agency rod licence from your local Post Office. The 1997 price is £16 for adults.

Also remember that the fishing rights to every stretch of water, whether it is a river or a lake, belong to somebody. Although some landowners and local councils allow free fishing, most stretches are either under private control or owned by an angling club. *Do not under any circumstances go fishing without a licence or permit – you are breaking the law and liable to hefty fines.*

Commercial coarse fisheries like the Heyford Fishery at Upper Heyford and the Bluebell Lakes complex near Fotheringay offer day tickets, as do most of the trout waters in the valley. Some angling clubs also sell day tickets, but annual membership is usually very reasonable, and better value for money.

The best source of information on the fishing available locally is from one of the tackle shops in the area, who usually sell club membership as well as day tickets. Consult *Yellow Pages* for the shops in your area.

Angling clubs controlling stretches of the Nene and its tributaries include Northampton Nene AC, Northampton Castle AA, Wellingborough Nene AC, Kettering & Thrapston DAA, Rushden & Higham Ferrers AC, Irthlingborough & Raunds AC, Oundle AA, Ringstead AC, Peterborough DAA, March DAA, and Wisbech DAA.

✂10✂
Messing about on the river

By hedgerow side and field and brook
I love to be its partner still
To turn each leaf of nature's book
Where all may read as will
And he who loves it not destroys
His quiet and makes life a slave
His soul is dead to loves and joys
His own heart is their grave

John Clare

Man has long appreciated the value of waterborne transport, and the River Nene has thus seen human activity for as long as mankind has dwelled in the valley. Once an important artery for freight and passenger traffic, today the Nene is a playground for anybody who wants to get afloat and mess about on the river.

The Nene is the perfect river for boating enthusiasts. The gentle current makes is safe and easy to navigate, and while civilisation is never far away, there are wonderful, unspoilt areas where you really do feel that you have the river all to yourself.

The river as a highway

The River Nene today is bisected by important rail and road routes. Main-line expresses head north from London's Euston, St Pancras and King's Cross stations to roar over the river, while the M1, A5, A6, A14, A1, A47 and A17 bridge crossings rattle with the constant clatter of heavy trunk traffic. In contrast, the placid Nene looks a peaceful backwater. But it wasn't always so. The river has been an important communications route for people and cargoes since earliest times and it is only since the Second World War that that role has dwindled.

The Romans were probably the first to exploit the Nene in a businesslike fashion. They recognised the importance of water as a means of transport and excavated a network of canals for that purpose. One already mentioned, the Car Dyke, connected the Nene at Peterborough to Lincoln, and remnants of this waterway – now almost 2,000 years old – still exist to the north of the city. The present A5 (Watling Street) and A1 (Ermine Street) were also built by the Romans, and it is certain that the latter's crossing of the Nene at Wansford around AD 50 must have made use of the river to reach the important industrial area of Durobrivae a few miles downstream, near modern-day Castor.

Later the Nene would have been used by Danes and Vikings to penetrate inland beyond Northampton, but navigation in anything other than very small craft with a shallow draught would have been very difficult due to the presence of shallows, rapids and other obstacles.

The Nene we see today from Northampton downstream is very different from the natural river before Man implemented changes. The dredgers have long since ripped out the areas of ankle-deep gravels (which were once natural fords and useful crossing places) and straightened most of the tortuous curves. Throughout the Nene valley are little dead arms of

water, often still connected to the main river, which are actually parts of the old course. A few of the older ones may be natural oxbow lakes, but the vast majority are the scraps that were left over when the navigators decided to create short-cuts. Good examples abound in the meadows between Thorpe and Pilton, and the dried-up remains of an old course, plus a landlocked oxbow, can be clearly seen from the hill at Wadenhoe church.

The flow of the river, unhindered by locks and unaffected by abstraction, was also much more powerful. To get an idea of what the old Nene looked like, stand on one of bridges over the faster-flowing backwaters in summer and see the clumps of gravel-loving bulrush and streamer weed waving in the pacey current. That, albeit on a bigger scale, was the old Nene we have lost.

Until the 18th century the accepted limit of navigation from the sea was Alwalton, 6 miles upstream of Peterborough. Periods of high water may have made it possible to progress further inland, but this was the exception rather than the norm. Enterprising souls did, however, take advantages of flood conditions to reach much further upstream. The wet autumn of 1648 left the unsurfaced roads of the area impassable, but a boat-owner and two hired hands succeeded in transporting 3 tons of cheese by river from Peterborough to Higham Ferrers. Their task was achieved only by arduously manhandling both craft and cargo around 16 obstructions, but they still succeeded in transporting the goods cheaper than could have been done over land. This manhandling of boat and cargo was known as portaging. It was back-breaking work that was also very time-consuming. In dry weather, horse and cart along the rutted roads of Northamptonshire was a quicker means of getting goods moved inland.

Below Peterborough, however, it was a different story. The deeper, broader river was tidal and high tides twice a day meant that bigger vessels could ply their trade in the lower reaches. Sea-going ships could reach Sutton Bridge from The Wash, and usually Wisbech, although the treacherous mudbanks in the twisting channel between those ports made the so-called Capital of the Fens a place many wary ship-owners preferred to avoid. Instead, fen lighters were used for the task.

These lighters were believed to be descended from Viking craft. They were around 50 feet long, 10 feet wide and had a shallow, flat bottom that only drew a little over 3 feet of water when fully loaded with 20-odd tons of cargo. Gangs of five lighters were normally tied together. A single square mast, hinged to allow passage under low bridges, was connected to the first lighter to take advantage of windpower. Otherwise horses and plain manhandling were the only means of propulsion and, in drought conditions, it could take the toiling lightermen a month to travel from Wisbech to Peterborough. It is no wonder that these early lightermen had a reputation for hard drinking. They also had a justified reputation for fighting and pilfering, but their appearance at local riverside taverns was welcomed by the locals who knew that the generosity of the lightermen was legendary and the ale usually flowed free.

Like the barge-owners of later years, the lightermen lived on their craft, but they did not bring their families with them. There was no proper living accommodation on board – usually just a crude wooden cab on the leading vessel – and these hard men lived rough and ready, enduring the elements with just a thick coat and an otterskin hat.

The dream becomes reality

In the 1650s a pamphlet was published seeking financial backing for a scheme to make the Nene navigable beyond Alwalton to Northampton. Nothing came of it, although the townsfolk of Northampton were desperate for such a scheme to come to fruition. The cost of transport meant that coal in the county town was twice as expensive as the purchase price in Peterborough. This fact was of little interest to rich landowners along the valley who resented the intrusion of commercial boat traffic and objected accordingly. In earlier decades their strident voices would have probably killed the argument, but these were times of great change that even the landed gentry were no longer able to contain. The Nene was about to change for ever.

In 1714 an Act of Parliament was passed leaving the way clear to develop the river above Peterborough, but nothing happened because of legal technicalities. It had to be re-drafted and it was not until 1724 that a further Act was passed and work finally began. By the late 1730s the Nene was navigable as far upstream as Thrapston. The apparent success of Dutch engineer Cornelius Vermuyden's new scheme to drain and tame the Great Ouse fens in the late 1740s encouraged entrepreneurs – then known as adventurers – to look again at the feasibility of opening the Nene yet further to commercial traffic. A third Act was duly passed in 1756 to push the head of navigation a further 25 miles to Northampton. By this time coal prices in the town had rocketed to 7½ times the amount paid in the coalfields of Warwickshire, just 40 miles away.

Yorkshire engineer John Smith was put in charge of the project and by early 1860 Wellingborough was reached. To mark the occasion, on the last day of March that year a gang of five lighters delivered around 72 tons of coal from the North East. It had taken them less than two days to travel the 12½ miles from Thrapston, negotiating seven new locks and two navigation weirs en route. The latter were known as

A boat queues to use Wadenhoe Lock in high summer.

staunches, because they literally staunched the flow of the river. They were artificial dams, constructed at the downstream end of a length of troublesome shallows to deepen the water and hence aid navigation. Removable boards within the dam were raised to allow the passage of boat traffic, which was either arduous or very rapid, according to whether you intended to travel upstream or down! The primitive staunches were later replaced by proper locks, but the name lives on at places like Orton Lock above Peterborough, which is still known to locals as Orton Staunch.

Northampton was finally reached on 7 August 1761. The *Northampton Mercury* noted the occasion thus: 'No less than thirty-eight barges, laden with coals and other merchandise, and adorned with flags and streamers, came up with the greatest ease to the public wharf at the South Bridge.' Cannons were fired, church bells pealed in celebration – and the price of fuel in the town was halved virtually overnight. The successful navigation of the Nene from the sea to the county town laid the foundations for the latter's prosperity in the decades to follow as wharfs were built and warehouses and industry began to spring up along the riverside.

Passenger traffic on the river was also important

during this golden era. Unsprung coaches provided a bumpy, uncomfortable ride on the rutted roads of the period, while boats were altogether more comfortable. Pleasure boating also became more popular in this period, both on the river and on the unspoilt expanse of Whittlesey Mere, until it was drained in the middle of the 19th century.

Northampton's position as a major trading centre was reinforced towards the end of the century as engineers brought the new Grand Junction Canal ever nearer to the town. The main canal reached Blisworth in 1796 and in 1815 the Northampton spur connected the new artery to the navigable Nene. Ironically, Northampton's new connection via the Midlands canal network lessened the importance of the link, via the Nene, to the sea. It was cheaper to transport coal from the Midlands than it was to ship it by sea, but although the Nene's commercial significance was reduced, it continued to play an important – although ever-lessening – commercial role for another 150 years.

The decline of water transport began with the dawn of the railway era. George Stephenson's Stockton & Darlington Railway of 1825 heralded a new technology that enthused the Victorians in the early years of the Industrial Revolution. Within five years the Liverpool & Manchester Railway was even more spectacularly

A family group happily splashing in the Nene at Wadenhoe Lock in 1929, just before the old-style gates were removed during the navigation modernisation of the 1930s. The well-intentioned works were aimed at boosting commercial traffic on the river, but it was too late. Today, the characteristic 'guillotine' lock gates are used only by pleasure craft. Peter Hall/author

Right High summer, and a traditional narrowboat passes the Wadenhoe alder wood SSSI as it makes gentle progress downstream.

successful and projected new canals, including one crossing Northamptonshire, were aborted in favour of the rapidly growing railway network. It was Stephenson's son, Robert, that engineered the first railway along the Nene valley (see Chapter 5). The writing was on the wall, all right, and by the middle of the century, with Northampton and the major towns of the Nene connected to the rail network, this rapid new mode of transport was obviously set to overtake the sedate, old-world pace of the waterways. By the end of the century railways had taken much of the long-distance heavy freight away from the rivers, but a certain amount of co-operation existed, as demonstrated by the sidings and wharf at Woodston, upstream of Peterborough. Road transport was at this time still unreliable.

Steam tugs were introduced to modernise and speed up the passage of the old gangs of lighters, which had remained virtually unchanged since Viking days, but it was too late. The death knell had already sounded.

Yachting and windsurfing facilities are available on many of the large gravel pits along the Nene, including here at the Nene Valley Country Park at Ferry Meadows, above Peterborough.

A brief renaissance

Commercial boat traffic was at a low ebb early this century, but it enjoyed a brief renaissance in 1930 when the Nene Catchment & Drainage Board was set up under the forward-thinking chairmanship of George Dallas to revitalise what was considered in some quarters to be an under-used resource. The single body had sole responsibility for the river from source to sea, and its responsibilities included drainage as well as navigation. New steel locks were installed, along with a tidal sluice near the Dog-in-a-Doublet inn on the North Bank between Whittlesey and Thorney. This, combined with the dynamiting of awkward gravel shallows at Northey, downstream of Peterborough, was intended to allow Peterborough to become an inland port of similar importance to Norwich on the River Yare.

Improvements by the new Catchment Board meant that by 1938 small seagoing vessels began to ascend the river as far as Peterborough. A tanker, the 229 bhp diesel-engined *Constance H*, moored at the city's embankment on 20 January of that year. She was 36 metres long and had a draught of 2 metres – twice the maximum that the old lightermen could have afforded. She was registered at Hull and belonged to the Yorkshire-based firm of John Harker Ltd. At Peterborough she was loaded with 150 tons of creosote and set off back via the North Sea to Middlesbrough, complete with her adapted funnel and mast, both of which could be lowered to allow passage beneath the low bridges at Guyhirn and Wisbech.

Later a 32-metre ship, *The Peterborough Trader*, began her regular trade carrying cargoes of bricks from the brickworks that encircled the city at that time. Millions more bricks were also carried in the opposite direction inland and on to the canal system beyond Northampton to provide building materials for the expanding industrial towns of the West Midlands. Traditional canal longboats and new steel-hulled craft were pressed into surface for this task until the late 1940s, when commercial river traffic faded into insignificance.

In the meantime, in the desperate early years of the Second World War, water transport had been looked upon favourably as a possible last resort by an increasingly beleaguered Government, which saw rivers and canals as a viable alternative to the vital rail network then at constant risk from German bombing campaigns. But after hostilities ceased in 1945 and Britain enjoyed a post-war boom that embraced roads – including the projected new motorways – as the mode of transport in the future, waterways again faded from the political agenda.

Commercial boat traffic finally died at the end of the 1960s. The last commercial operations to use the river were Whitworths Victoria Mill at Wellingborough and quarries at Wansford. From the latter, stone was shipped downstream to constantly shore up the erosion-threatened mud banks of the tidal channel in the Wisbech area. They met very little traffic, for by this time Peterborough's aspirations as an inland port were forgotten as a new Development Corporation was formed to take advantage of overspill population and industries from London.

Apart from the continued importance of Wisbech and, later, Sutton Bridge as modern ports serving commercial sea traffic, the Nene was no longer a vehicle for the transportation of freight. But the unexpected affluence of a the leisure-orientated post-war generation saw a remarkable transformation of the river into a watery playground. Unlike some inland canals, which fell into disuse and subsequent dereliction once commercial traffic ceased, the flood-prone River Nene had to be kept in good order.

While sensible early settlers from the Iron Age onwards had shown admirable prudence by building their settlements on high ground away from the river's treacherous flood plain, later generations had been more foolhardy and erected their homes and factories

A colourful array of boats on the Nene at Ringstead.

on low-lying land subject to inundation. For this reason the early canal-style locks had already been replaced by 'guillotine' steel gates that could be permanently raised in times of flood to allow excess water off the uplands to proceed downstream as rapidly as possible. The infrastructure therefore remained in place, and the Nene's potential as a pleasure-boaters' paradise was never in doubt.

Makeshift transport

Out on the undrained Fens below Peterborough, two centuries ago, boats were an essential mode of transport. The local experts – the so-called slodgers – could knock up a punt from any scraps of wood available. This was essential, because very few trees grew in the bleak, windswept Fens.

Two long planks, between 13 and 17 feet long would form the sides, while cross joists between 3 and 4 feet would be nailed across the bottom to form the basic skeleton, to which any scraps of timber would be nailed. The whole lot would then be coated inside and out with hot pitch or tar to provide a degree of waterproofing. The whole vessel would then be launched, and water would swell the wood to make it more or less watertight. It was usually the latter, and

Left Fancy a 'des res' by the river? The owners of these houseboats moored above Titchmarsh Mill overlook the gravel pits that make up one of the best wildlife sanctuaries in the valley.

constant baling would be necessary to reduce the ever-rising level of muddy water slopping around the bottom boards. Nevertheless, these makeshift, flat-bottomed craft were ideal for their task of slipping through shallow water and reedbeds and, with judicious repairs, would sometimes be pressed into service by successive generations. A willow pole cut from the local withy bed supplied the propulsion and, in expert hands, would make these ponderous great craft fly across the rivers and meres.

They were working punts, designed for carrying freight and people as well as the important task of bearing the huge punt guns, which could kill upwards of 20 birds in a single firing.

The Fenland Ark

A century ago the Fens in winter were a wet place to be, and local clergymen were concerned that their parishioners in the more desolate settlements were deterred from attending church by the floodwater that made many of the unmetalled droves and muddy tracks impassable.

The Rev Horatio Broke, who became vicar of Holme in 1895, refused to be beaten by the elements and decided that if worshippers could not get to church, he would take the church to them. In 1896 he commissioned the famous Stanground boatbuilder, William Starling, to build a floating church at a cost of £70 – a very considerable sum in those days. Archdeacon Vesey of Huntingdon blessed the new

floating church on 5 April 1897, and dedicated it to St Withburga. It inevitably became known locally as the Fenland Ark.

The enterprising parson used the old course of the Nene and connecting drains and lodes to reach isolated communities like Wood Walton, Ramsey St Mary, Ponders Bridge, Farcet and Yaxley. The boat remained in service for 7½ years, and 70 people were baptised in it.

In 1904 the Fenland Ark was towed 14 miles to Welches Dam and handed over to Rev F. G. Guy of Manea, but its popularity waned. Eventually it was renovated as a summer house-boat, named *The Saints Rest*, and moored at Orton Staunch by its new owner. Sadly it sank a few years later and was abandoned.

Nene navigation

The navigable stretch of the Nene, from Northampton to the sea, measures 91 miles and is part of over 250 miles of rivers in East Anglia under the control of the Environment Agency (formerly the National Rivers Authority). British Waterways controls the connection, via the Northampton Arm of the Grand Union Canal, to the Midlands canals network, while the Middle Level Commissioners take responsibility for the old course of the river and artificial cuts by which it is possible to cruise from Peterborough to the Great Ouse.

Pleasure boating on the Nene is more peaceful than major navigations like the canals, Norfolk Broads and rivers like the Thames, but there are plenty of facilities for boaters, including marina services at Billing, Thrapston, Oundle and Stibbington. Moorings are available throughout the navigation, together with pleasant riverside pubs, towns and villages.

The Nene offers a connection to the Grand Union Canal, which is pictured here on the high embankment which crosses the upper river near Weedon.

Oundle Marina is situated conveniently close to the ancient market town. The famous spire of St Peter's Church can be seen in the background.

Floods remain a feature of the Nene most winters and the familiar 'guillotine' locks are raised to allow the excess water to flow downstream unhindered, as in this shot of Lilford lock. In these circumstances, no attempt should be made to navigate the locks.

A speed limit of 7 miles per hour is in force throughout most of the river, which should be negotiated with care, especially when there is a chance of floodwater. The 37 locks between Peterborough and Northampton are also used to help with flood control, when the pointing doors are chained open and the vertical gates raised. At these times no attempt should be made to navigate through the locks. However, such conditions are rare – at least in the summer months – when many boaters find that operating the locks is part and parcel of the fun of exploring the river. All vessels using the Nene must be licensed by the Environment Agency, who supply keys to operate the locks, as well as full instructions.

Passage through the Dog-in-a-Doublet sluice to the tidal reaches is by prior arrangement with the lock keeper (phone number below). The tidal river down to Wisbech and the sea can be treacherous, especially during spring tides, and should only be navigated by experienced boaters. The tidal river is controlled by the Port of Wisbech and the Port of Sutton Bridge.

A safer and more interesting voyage is through the Fens, via Stanground Sluice, on to the King's Dyke, Old River Nene and Well Creek to the Great Ouse, which opens up the possibility of exploring this river through to Ely, Huntingdon and Bedford, or branching on to the River Cam as far as Cambridge.

Useful telephone numbers

Environment Agency (Orton Goldhay, Peterborough)	01733 371811
Billing Aquadrome	01604 408181
Thrapston Mill Marina	01832 732850
Oundle Marina	01832 272762
Stibbington Boatyard	01780 783144
Dog-in-a-Doublet Sluice	01733 202219
Middle Level Commissioners	01354 653232
British Waterways (Blisworth)	01604 858233
Port of Wisbech	01945 582125
Port of Sutton Bridge	01406 351530

11
The nature of the Nene

Birds fluttered round the water's brink
Then perched their dabbled wings to dry
And swallows often stooped to drink
And twittered gladly by

John Clare

A rare treat

No matter how well you think you know the Nene valley, there is always something new lurking just around the corner. Michelle and I got a pleasant surprise recently when we were entertained by a pair of otters cavorting playfully up and down a steep, grassy bank. Apparently oblivious to our presence, they then obligingly slid into the river, bow-waving to our very

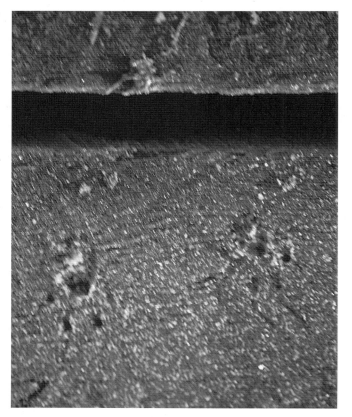

feet before disappearing into their holt, beneath an impenetrable tangle of hawthorn.

I won't tell you exactly where these shy, secretive creatures are living, because there are undesirable elements who would seek them out and destroy them. Thirty years ago men and hounds were still hunting otters, driving them to the edge of extinction, and today there remains the odd trigger-happy individual retard who sees his shotgun licence as a right to decide what shall live and what shall die. Sadly there also remain country folk who regard any predatory creature as vermin, and take aim accordingly. In truth, the real vermin are at the other end of the gun. . .

I later returned to the otters' holt, suitably armed, but failed in my mission to 'shoot' them. My weapons were, of course, a 35 mm camera and 300 mm telephoto lens. This time the elusive duo scampered over a footbridge before I was within shooting range, but they kindly left their footprints in the hoar frost of the wooden planks of the bridge, which I gratefully photographed.

The otter's status as a protected species ought to allow it to re-colonise the Nene, but you cannot be sure. The cormorant is a protected species, but a handful of reckless fishery owners have recently begun taking the law into their own hands by shooting what they hysterically describe as the 'Black Plague'. What emotive nonsense! Cormorants are merely moving inland because mankind, aided and abetted by the European Common Fisheries Policy, has succeeded in virtually exhausting their food source at sea. Those birds need fish to survive; fishermen – myself included –

The author has so far failed in his bid to photograph the pair of otters living on the middle reaches of the river, but he did take this snap of their footprints in the frost after spotting them scampering across a footbridge early in the morning.

do not. It would be a very mean-spirited angler who begrudged a fish meal to any fellow creature whose life depended upon it.

Frustrated fishermen who cannot bear the truth – namely that the efforts of a mere bird are more successful than their own – should sell their tackle and find a new hobby. Angling is at present perceived by the general public as a slightly dotty, yet harmless, activity. Selfish support for the unlawful destruction of creatures that the vast majority of the population value will shift that perception and dump anglers in the same boat as shooting clubs and huntsmen. And that leaky boat is heading for the falls even as I write this.

Hunting, meanwhile, is defended by some as part of the rich, colourful pageantry of the countryside. Foxes and hares are a pest, say the supporters, and therefore must be controlled. A pest to whom, exactly? Farmers, of course. But farmers also say that rabbits are their biggest pests – and the fox, along with persecuted birds of prey like the buzzard, are the most efficient forms of control for rabbits and young hares. The truth is that hunters go a-hunting because they enjoy it. They like galloping across fields in funny clothes and justify it all by insisting that it is sporting.

When H. E. Bates wrote *Down the River* in 1937, otters as well as foxes were still allowed to be hunted for fun. This is what the finest Nene valley writer of the 20th century had to say about it:

'If I were to get up from this chair, arm myself with a stick and beat the nearest dog to the point of death, I should earn the contempt of all decent men and the penalty of the law on top of it in the shape of fines or imprisonment. And no one would question the justice of it and no one would listen to my pleas that it was sport. . . But the law of this country, still too often framed on the assumption that property is higher than life, especially if it is the property of the rich and the life of the poor, has no objection, no condemnation and no penalty for those . . . who have nothing better to do than incite one set of animals to rip out the living guts of another. Such repugnant bloodiness in a so-called civilised age and country make me wish, sometimes, that the laws of England could be framed, for a change, behind the walls of a madhouse.'

Need I say more?

The last emperor

Today, when regular church attendance is seen as a minority activity, it is very easy to underestimate the influence of the old-time preachers. In the rural communities of old the local clergy were usually the only available source of articulate information, and their words were taken seriously. Religiously, even.

The debatable principle of Man's ascendancy over his fellow animals has had a profound effect upon the world we live in. We are all much poorer as a result of this flawed religious philosophy. Don't get me wrong: I'm not trying to pillory the parson here. In truth, the Nene valley can boast its fair share of enlightened clergymen who fought tooth and nail for the common man. Some, as we have learned, were even great men whose shining influence would illuminate us all. But there were also downright fools with too much time on their hands, and of them there were some who could not resist meddling with nature. One even succeeded in pushing rare butterfly species to the verge of extinction.

The Rev William Bree (1823-1917) was curate of Polebrook for 15 years, from 1847. When he arrived the purple emperor and large blue were commonplace in the parish, while at nearby Barnwell Wold the black hairstreak and chequered skipper were frequently seen. Unfortunately Bree was a fanatical collector whose prime leisure activity involved scouring the local meadows armed with a net in order to 'preserve' his captures. The irony that preservation on Bree's terms meant exterminating the unfortunate insects in order to impale them on the mounting boards of his trophy cabinets was lost on him.

Worse was to follow. Bree was a generous soul, pleased to share his happy hunting grounds with others of a similar disposition, who rode in from all over the country and descended upon the neighbourhood to add rare butterflies to their own collections. By the time he was made rector in 1862 he was, through his own selfishness, largely responsible for their extermination. Happily, Bree's calling took him to Warwickshire a year later and he went on to become Archdeacon of Coventry. No nature lover in the Nene valley can lament his departure.

The large blue, purple emperor and chequered skipper are all now extinct in Northamptonshire. The black hairstreak lives on, thanks to the efforts of a new generation of nature lovers who work tirelessly to ensure that its habitat is preserved. The best place to enjoy its presence is at the Glapthorn Cow Pasture nature reserve, where it is now free to flit among the borders and rides without being pursued by pathetic parsons.

'The new Norfolk Broads'

Throughout this book we have wallowed in nostalgia, but it should be clear by now that not everything in the past was better, no more than all in the present is in some way poorer. You cannot stamp hard on the brakes of Progress to perform an emergency stop; to do so would create chaos. The answer is to influence progress so that the quality of our lives and environment do indeed get better.

Even before humans began to assert their influence along the Nene valley, things were changing. When the last Ice Age began to retreat 14,000 years ago, giant elk roamed what was then a spartan tundra. With their huge antlers – 10 feet from tip to tip – the elk must have been an impressive sight, yet within a few thousand years they had died out. The warmer climate had encouraged thick forests to grow in place of the rich, open grazing the elk required to provide enough calcium to maintain those incredible antlers. Even if the elk had survived, those same antlers would have made it impossible for these unlikely leviathans to negotiate the thick undergrowth of the forests.

We are still in an Ice Epoch – a series of four Ice Ages that started two million years ago and that have been named by geologists as the Pleistocene. At times a third of the earth's surface has been covered in ice, but we are currently in a warm inter-glacial period. If predictions about the 'greenhouse effect' and global warming are

Environment Agency staff in action, conducting a test netting on a gravel pit beside the Nene near Thorpe Waterville.

Right A glorious angler's sunset over the same gravel pit near Thorpe Waterville. Just a decade ago, this beauty spot was an ugly quarry, but nature soon heals the scars of mineral extraction.

accurate, future generations will see yet more changes in this part of the world.

Meanwhile, assuming that the Nene valley does not become as arid as a desert, we can learn from mistakes made in the past to create a wonderful environment for humans and wildlife to live in harmony. There is already a small but tireless band of unsung heroes working towards that very aim. Local councils, the Environment Agency, English Nature, the Countryside Commission and various wildlife, farming and angling interests all have more or less the same target in their sights.

The most imaginative of these is the Nene Valley Project, launched in 1990 to implement Northamptonshire County Council's Nene Valley Management Plan. 'We aim to conserve and develop the Nene valley's landscape and wildlife, whilst improving opportunities for countryside recreation,' pledged Nene Valley Project Officer Steve Brayshaw at the launch of its first newsletter in the autumn of 1994. Steve certainly got the project off to an exciting and energetic start by adopting a positive stance on gravel extraction

along the Nene corridor and hinting that the lakes and wetlands thus created could be the basis of a new Norfolk Broads.

Rather than concentrating on narrow, specific issues, the project has taken a broad view of the Nene valley. Countryside Stewardship schemes have ensured that hundreds of acres of meadows along the river will be farmed in traditional, environment-friendly ways, while hedging plants and willows have been provided free of charge to parish councils and landowners in a bid to enhance the landscape. There are even plans to create large areas of flooded reedbeds to attract rare birds like the bittern, a shy cousin of the heron, which has not bred in the Nene valley since Whittlesey Mere was drained 150 years ago.

Too often in the past nature reserves and countryside management have been hijacked by wildlife fanatics who deter ordinary folk from sharing the facilities on offer. This is most certainly not the case in the Nene valley, where everybody is catered for, including boaters, canoeists and anglers. You see, it is possible for us all to enjoy it in harmony.

A better, cleaner river

Of course, none of this would have been possible without the work – and millions of pounds – almost literally poured into the Nene and its tributaries in recent years to make the valley a better, cleaner place. The Environment Agency, which in 1996 took over the role of the former National Rivers Authority, is performing a sterling service by fighting pollution and improving habitats for the fishes, birds, mammals and insects that live here. In this they have been helped by Anglian Water, whose investment in improved effluent discharges has transformed the water quality.

Official figures show that water quality in the Nene has improved by a staggering 39 per cent in the five-year period between 1990 and 1995. That is a remarkable performance and is the reason why stretches of the middle Nene, once regarded as a waste of time from an angler's point of view, are now teeming with fish. The knock-on effect for all nature lovers, of course, is that the return of the fish means more kingfishers, herons and, of course, otters.

As recently as 1990 the Nene turned green every summer due to algae blooms produced by a combination of hot weather, nitrate-based fertilisers running in off the land and excess phosphates that flowed unchecked from sewage works. Nobody has been able to do anything about the hot summers, and some farmers stubbornly refuse to cut back on the amounts of chemicals with which they contaminate their land (and our food), but the sewage works have succeeded in stripping phosphates from their treated discharges and the Nene in summer is now clearer and cleaner than even the oldest residents of the valley can recall.

This coincides with the emergence of a new breed of river engineers. In the bad old days after the Second World War, rivers were seen as aquatic highways along which water was hastened down to the sea as quickly as possible. They were heartlessly dredged and straightened to that purpose, and their bare, featureless channels were thus made inhospitable to the many creatures that once lived along them. The new generation does things differently, and today the damaged rivers are actually being restored to re-create the diverse habitat that was destroyed by their predecessors.

Left A proud swan and her cygnets, pictured on the duckweed-encrusted Mortons Leam, which runs parallel to the Nene near Whittlesey.

Right A fine spring day near Brancey Bridge, Aldwincle, and a pair of mute swans forage for the emerging aquatic vegetation which will flourish in the coming months to provide food for their young cygnets.

Some excitable anglers and extremist environmentalists mutter darkly about conspiracy theories and make absurd claims about the Environment Agency fiddling the figures and covering up pollution levels. Sewage works, meanwhile, are rumoured to open up the floodgates under the cover of darkness so nobody knows how much muck is discharged into the river. What utter nonsense – and a deplorable slander upon the integrity of organisations and individuals who are working tirelessly to make our river better. Give 'em bouquets, not brickbats.

A closer look at wildlife

The great thing about the Nene valley and its wild creatures is that you can enjoy them at your own pace. There is no rule to say that you must hike 20 miles along the Nene Way laden down with telescope, binoculars and tripod . . . although some seem to prefer it that way.

A bird does not have to be a rarity to be appreciated. Every day hundreds of people, young and old, enjoy the simple fun of going down to the river and 'feeding the ducks' – an all-embracing term which usually covers swans, moorhens, coots and assorted species of gulls, and, of course, ducks. And why not? The Nene valley is lined with nature reserves where you can indeed simply feed the ducks . . . or seek out the scarce species of fauna and flora for which the area is famous. By chance the course of our river follows part of the route from the Wash to the Severn estuary that is used as a natural flight path by tens of thousands of migrating birds. And the more wetlands and attractive places we create en route, the more tempted they are to linger a while.

Here are some of the best places to see rare birds, enjoy the scenery or simply enjoy the Nene valley countryside at its very best:

● Badby Woods, near Badby: Close to the western source of the river, this 181-acre deciduous woodland is privately owned. It is best visited in spring, when the leafy glades are carpeted with bluebells.

● Pitsford Reservoir, off the A508, south of Brixworth: Anglian Water-owned water supply reservoir of 700 acres, incorporating a 194-acre reserve controlled by the Northants Wildlife Trust (NWT). Famous for rare visiting water birds, including the occasional osprey. This is also an SSSI, but access is restricted.

● Kingsthorpe Nature Reserve: Northampton Borough Council owns this 25-acre area of water meadows,

Left These ancient alder woods on the steep slope down to the river below Aldwincle are an important SSSI.

Inset The profusion of pink flowers and interesting foliage make the Himalayan Balsam a pleasant plant to encounter along the banks of the Nene. But this specimen at Wadenhoe, like all others, is an unwelcome alien that threatens native plant species.

river, ponds and mill races along the unspoilt northern arm of the Nene above Northampton. Access from Mill Lane.

● Lings Wood, headquarters of the NWT, off the A4500 4 miles east of Northampton: 56 acres of mixed woodland, grassland and ponds.

● Sywell Country Park, near Earls Barton on the Mears Ashby-Washbrook road: Disused 68-acre reservoir, which once supplied nearby Rushden and Higham Ferrers with water. Its future was once in doubt and there were even proposals to use it as a landfill dump, but the County Council bought it in 1983 to provide a picturesque amenity for all. Anglers, birdwatchers, dog walkers and families out for a picnic can all celebrate this environmental victory over commercial vandalism.

● Irchester Country Park, on the B570 south of Wellingborough and the county's most popular country park, under County Council control. Old ironstone workings with woodland areas and nature trails, plus picnic meadows. Visitor centre, ranger service, toilets and disabled access, which includes facilities for the visually impaired.

● Higham Ferrers Pit, close to the A45: Another NWT former gravel pit, with healthy stocks of waterfowl, some rare.

● Kinewell Lake Nature Reserve, Ringstead: 50 acres of flooded gravel pits, plus 80 acres of adjacent meadows, planted with trees and shrubs by a Trust set up by the local Parish Council. Unlike most gravel pits along the valley, this pit is connected to the Nene, allowing fish to migrate between river and lake, thereby benefiting both. It is named after an ancient spring that was submerged by the flooding of the old quarry.

● Denford Churchyard: 1 acre of grassland, pond, scrub, springs and mossy and lichen-covered walls, controlled by the NWT.

● Titchmarsh Local Nature Reserve, between main A605 and Aldwincle village: Around 200 acres of former gravel pits, wetlands, meadows and one of the

Titchmarsh Decoy, originally built by Lord Lilford in the 19th century, is now part of a diverse nature reserve.

biggest heronries in the county. Also skirted by the Nene, Brancey Brook and Harper's Brook. Over 200 species of birds have been recorded at this NWT-controlled reserve, which boasts excellent hide facilities.

- Barnwell Country Park, near Oundle: 37 acres of former gravel pits, a backwater of the river, reedbeds and grassland. Visitor centre, ranger service, toilets and disabled access.

- Glapthorn Cow Pastures, between Glapthorn and Upper Benefield: 69 acres of 200-year-old woodland and blackthorn thickets, noted for nightingales and the black hairstreak butterfly (NWT).

- Short Wood, between Glapthorn and Southwick: Over 50 acres of ancient and secondary woodland, particularly noted for bluebells in May, which are said to be the best in the county (NWT).

- Bedford Purlieus, 2 miles west of Wansford and owned by the NWT: 46 acres of ancient woodland (a fragment of the old Rockingham Forest).

- Thorpe Wood, on the western outskirts of Peterborough: Over 20 acres of ancient coppice and woodlands, with associated birds and plant life (NWT).

- Nene Park, Peterborough: Huge area of river meadows, gravel pits and woodland as well as leisure and water sports facilities, controlled by the Nene Park Trust. Served by the preserved Nene Valley Railway.

Luxury home . . . for newts

In less than a generation, Peterborough has grown from a small cathedral city to the fastest-growing city in Europe. Following the first London overspill developments of the 1960s, subsequent decades saw surrounding areas of green meadows and farmland transformed by bulldozers and builders into thousands of acres of houses and factories.

That development is continuing apace today, with the city's southern township currently under construction on the disused brickyards to the south of the Fletton Parkway. From a distance, and to the uninitiated, that lunar landscape of old clay workings and heaps of spoil appeared to be an ugly blot on a barren landscape. But to those who bothered to take a closer look, the old brickworks were a rare haven for wildlife.

Mother Nature had reclaimed the clay wasteland and the population of rare creatures included Europe's largest known population of greater crested newts, which thrived in the labyrinth of shallow pools and overgrown ridges left behind by the giant diggers. They were threatened by the new township, but developers have found £2 million to pay for a 100-hectare nature reserve on part of the old brick workings to which 15,000 great crested newts have been moved. It has already been designated a Site of Special Scientific Interest (SSSI) and is now controlled by English Nature, whose newt expert, Andy Bascombe, says, 'We are very keen that we do the right thing for the newts and we believe that this site is probably the most substantial contribution to great crested newt conservation in the UK.'

The newts' luxury new home includes around 100 pools that date back to the 1920s when the area was excavated for brickmaking clay. Since then many of the pools have been colonised by fish, but fish and newts don't mix – the fish eat the newts' eggs – so the fish had to go. Netsmen from the Environment Agency moved in in the summer of 1996 to trap vast shoals of rudd, tench and perch and move them on to other waters in the area, including the South Holland Drain near Sutton Bridge, where the native fish population had declined through saltwater seeping in from the tidal Nene.

Just as Peterborough has changed so much in a generation, so has Britain's amphibian population. As little as 30 years ago every pond, ditch and dyke held a healthy population of newts. It was every little boy's birthright to catch them in jam jars, marvelling at their bristling, prehistoric appearance before returning them to their watery homes. Today it would be technically illegal for a schoolboy even to attempt to catch a newt. As an endangered species they are protected under the Wildlife & Countryside Act, introduced by the Government in 1981. Some would argue that it's a shame that the legislators did not tackle the root cause of the newts' demise – development, habitat destruction and the poisonous agricultural chemicals that we still allow our farmers to pour over the crops we are destined to eat. Most are absorbed by the crops while the surplus seeps into the soil and, through drainage systems, into ditches, streams and ponds. Europe's Common Agricultural Policy is costly to us, the taxpayers, but creatures like the great crested newt pay the highest price of all.

Happily the untainted grasslands along the flood valley of the Nene are a rare stronghold for newts, and many small ponds and ditches still hold healthy populations. A good place to see them is at Barnwell Country Park, where countryside rangers have excavated purpose-built pools for newts and other amphibians.

A detour to Rutland

An unspectacular pumping station at Wansford marks the point where a great deal of the River Nene's water is diverted to make a secret journey north. An underground pipeline takes millions of gallons of water below Clare country and Lincolnshire through to Britain's smallest county, where it helps to replenish the massive public water supply reservoir known at Rutland Water.

Although only opened in 1977, Rutland is already designated a globally important wetland habitat for birds, with 240 species recorded there during the last two decades. It is regularly home to 10,000 wildfowl. Despite its prime status, owners Anglian Water are trying to improve Rutland as a wildlife habitat by creating areas of reedbeds and – most exciting of all – attempting to re-introduce the osprey to England as a

Although situated in Britain's smallest county, massive Rutland Water is topped up by water diverted from the River Nene at Wansford. Although only flooded two decades ago, it is already a stronghold for rare bird species and is now home to ospreys, imported from the Scottish Highlands.

breeding bird for the first time in 150 years. Osprey chicks from Scotland are being imported to Rutland in a five-year project jointly organised between Anglian Water, the Highland Foundation and the Leicestershire & Rutland Wildlife Trust.

No doubt there will be a minority of unthinking anglers who will complain about the presence of another fish-eating bird at this venue, which is also an important trout fishery. But the angler writing this would be only too pleased to catch a few less fish if it meant seeing those magnificent birds of prey return to this part of the world.

The upper Nene also supplies water to Pitsford Reservoir, via another underground pipeline – this in addition to a large number of natural springs; the valley that was flooded when Pitsford was created was known locally as the Field of Three Hundred Springs.

And finally . . .

We've almost arrived at the end of our journey, and I hope that during the course of our jaunt you've shared my love of the Nene, its valley, its people and its past. But although our pilgrimage is now virtually complete, the river's meanderings are far from over. The Nene will still be bubbling from its sources and spilling into the sea long after we have all turned to dust.

So although it would seem appropriate to close this chapter with a sentimental description of the setting sun reflecting on the lapping ripples of the river, this is no time for maudlin farewells. This isn't that sort of book. Our journey may be drawing to its conclusion, but the River Nene most definitely is not. There's life aplenty in the old girl yet and, having dwelled so long in the past, it is time to look forward and, perhaps, even help to shape the future.

At this point I can't resist returning to Steve Brayshaw's vision of the Nene valley as a new Norfolk Broads or, to be exact, *Northamptonshire* Broads. Norfolk's Broadland has, effectively, gained National Park status in recent years, just like tracts of the North Yorkshire Moors, the Lake District, Snowdonia, Dartmoor and the Peak District. All have more or less been pickled for posterity, and have been preserved in this way because of their unique natural beauty. Because each is unique, none is typically English. And because they have been mounted like taxidermists' subjects, their appeal is no more than glass-cased.

The countryside cannot be held in suspended animation. The theme of this book has been irresistible change, whether by unstoppable forces like the glaciers of successive Ice Ages, or by the hand of Man. The Norfolk Broads would never have happened were it not for humans cutting peat for fuel in the Middle Ages and creating excavations that were subsequently flooded to

Above The wide open spaces of Pitsford Reservoir are a playground for anglers, boaters and bird watchers.

Below Ravensthorpe Reservoir, which is fed by the upper tributaries of the Nene, is a haven for geese, ducks and other wildfowl.

Right The pastoral perfection of the Nene valley remains little changed in centuries and, with a little luck, will stay this way for future generations.

create the landscape we enjoy today. They are a lucky accident.

Progress cannot be un-invented. But through experience of the past we can learn and make the present a better place. That is already happening in the Nene valley.

This valley is essentially English. It is as if someone has taken everything that is good about our land and spread it evenly along the course of the Nene. From source to sea the river is a vibrant, living ribbon that threads together the Midlands and East Anglia, town and city, village and hamlet, uplands and fenland, forest and field. Industry and agriculture, urban and pastoral, are seamlessly blended by the Nene in such a way that you struggle to see the joins.

Somehow this valley has survived all that mankind has thrown at it and yet come up smiling. Why not mark that feat by turning our thriving vale into a living National Park? Is it not time to celebrate the modest Nene that has done so much to shape our landscape, lives and even the history of the modern world?

And what about the river itself? The Nene deserves some long-overdue recognition. It should be the centrepiece of every settlement along the valley.

Northampton should be ashamed of the way it has turned its back on the river for centuries, when it ought be the pride of that great county town. Where are the signs in the town centre directing visitors to the river? Peterborough, on the other hand, seems to have made more of an effort – it has at least dipped its feet into the water, and the scruffy riverside areas are being tidied up now, so perhaps the cathedral city can escape with a mild reprimand.

Only Wisbech, so far downstream that it's almost coastal, ever took pride in its river, and upon its north bank built as fine a row of Dutch-inspired houses as you'll ever find outside Holland. Sadly the Capital of the Fens has done little since. The ramshackle area between the town's two bridges looks as though it could collapse into the river at any time.

The Nene and its connected waterways have the potential to become the greatest watery playground in England. The river itself, from Northampton to the sea, plus thousands of acres of gravel pits and the old course of the Nene through the Fens, together amount to a gleaming paradise that would put the Norfolk Broads in the shade. Inaccessible Broadland, isolated on the east coast of Norfolk, with its shanty town developments and crowded, polluted waters, is not even in the same class.

The entire Nene valley enjoys excellent road communications, picturesque villages and thriving towns. You can enjoy the river by boat or by foot – and if the Nene Valley Railway is ever extended you could even appreciate it by train from Peterborough to Northampton. Bring back Whittlesey Mere and the system would boast a wetland nature reserve second to none. It's never too late to rectify the mistakes made by our forefathers.

Money is not the problem – there seems to plenty of cash in the National Lottery coffers, for example. Where have they gone, those imaginative, swashbuckling schemes for which Britain was once famous? In this book we have met many of the great and good from the Nene valley who strode into the wider world with vision and verve. Surely another will come along soon with a blueprint for the world much closer to home?

In the meantime, as we await the Nene's new messiah, let's return for the last time to the verse of the old master, John Clare:

Flow on winding river in silence for ever
The sedge and flags rustle about in a bustle
You are dear to my fancy thou smooth flowing river
The bulrush bows calm and there's peace in the
   hustle.

Index

à Becket, Thomas 41-2, 45
Achurch 64, 72, 76
Adams, John 22, 72
Aldwincle 62, 65, 66, 143-5,
    182, 185
Alwalton 98, 100, 134, 168
Angler's Mail 168
Anglian Water 161, 182-3, 187
Apethorpe 143
Arbury Hill 17, 19
Arthingworth 137
Ashton 80, 82, 92
Askham, John 45-6

Badby 17, 19-20, 183
Bailey, Colin 155, 156
Banyard, George 122
Barbel 151, 161-2
Barnabee 96
Barnwell 77, 79, 96
    Country Park 79, 186
    Mill 80
    Wold 179
Barratt, William 37
Barton Seagrave 137
Bascombe, Andy 186
Bass 151
Bates, H. E. 33-4, 48-51, 179
'BB' (Denys Watkins-Pitchford)
    143-50
Becket's Park 41-3
Beeching, Dr Richard 49, 99
Benwick 129
Bessemer, Henry 139
Billing 175
    Aquadrome 44
Billing, Graham 157
Bittern 64, 135, 182
Black Death 32
Black hairstreak butterfly 179
Blatherwycke 142
Bleak 165
Bluebell Fisheries 85, 162, 166
Bog oaks 133
Boston 124
Boughton Park 137
Brancey Brook 64, 143-5, 147
Brayshaw, Steve 180, 187
Bream 47, 110, 119-20, 151-3
Bree, Rev William 179
Bringtons, the 26, 28
Brixworth 30
Browne, Robert 72

Bulwick 142
Burbot 165
Burton Latimer 138
Buzzard 179

Canute, King 133-4
Car Dyke 130, 167
Cardigan, Earl of 142
Carlsberg Brewery 32, 37-40
Carp 44, 52-5, 84, 110, 146-7,
    151-2, 158-60
Castile, Queen Eleanor of 138-
    139
Castle Ashby 96, 99
Castor 96, 100, 152, 162, 167
Catfish 85
Catherine of Aragon 108
Cave, Margaret 117
Cawkwell, Cliff 157-8
Chambers, John 105
Charles I 24-5
Chequered skipper butterfly 179
Chichele, Henry 51
Chub 85, 110, 151, 154, 161-2,
    164
Church, Bob 44
Clare, John 7, 12, 32, 36, 45-6,
    51, 82, 87, 100-104, 109,
    119, 135-6, 137, 151, 167,
    178, 190
Clarkson, Thomas 117
Clay, Ron 44
Cogenhoe 45
Conan Doyle, Arthur 134
Conway, Michelle 18, 72, 178
Corby 12, 139, 140-141, 143
Cormorants 178
Cotterstock 85
Coypu 93
Crayfish 138
Cromwell, Oliver 11, 24-5, 34

Dace 110, 151, 163-4
Dallas, George 172
Daventry 19
Daventry Weekly Express 124
David, Earl of Huntingdon 45
de Kirkton, Roger 56
Deene Park 142
Denford 56-7, 185
Desborough 137, 143
Diana, Princess of Wales 28
Dimock, Dr 119

Ditchford 47, 49, 96
Dog-in-a-Doublet sluice 110-11,
    113, 172, 177
Draining the Fens 130-3
Dryden, John 65, 85

Eaglethorpe 92
Earls Barton 45, 185
Ecton 45
Edward I 139
Eels 44, 110, 151, 163-4
Eleanor, Queen 138-9
Eldernell 113
Electricity Cut, the 160-1
Elgoods Ales 37, 114-5
Elizabeth I 90
Elm 120
Elton 93, 96, 163
EMAP 124
Emneth 120
Environment Agency 55, 110,
    162, 166, 175, 177, 180, 182-
    3, 186
Everdon, Little and Great 20

Fenland Citizen 124
Ferry Meadows (Nene Park)
    100, 158, 172, 186
Finedon 138
Fitzwilliam, Earl 96, 99-100,
    134
Floods 119
Flore 22
Flounder 151
Fotheringay 50, 82, 87, 90-1
Foxes 179
Franklin, Benjamin 11, 45
Fuller, Thomas 34, 65

Geddington 137-8
Gedney 130
George III 20
Glapthorn Cow Pasture 179,
    186
Gloucester, Duke of 77
Goosetree 113
Grafham Water 134, 161
Grahame, Kenneth 92-3
Grand Union Canal 20, 32, 44,
    96, 99, 175
Gray, Thomas 20
Grayling 151
Great Doddington 45

Great North Road 96, 134
Greene, Sir Henry 150
Griggs, R. & Co 37
Gudgeon 151, 164
Guyhirn 114, 131, 132, 172

Hall, Peter 70-71
Hamill, Michael 72
Hares 179
Harper's Brook 64, 143-50,
    162-4
Harrington, James 24
Harris, Robin 153
Hart, John 153
Helpston 101-4
Henry II 41, 121
Henry VIII 11
Hereward the Wake 11, 133
Heyford Fishery 22, 166
Hickathrift, Thomas 120-1
Higham Ferrers 13, 48-50, 54,
    168, 185
Hill, Octavia 116
Hoad-Reddick, Michael 153
Hollowell Reservoir 19, 44
Hunsbury Hill 32
Hunstanton 124
Hunt, Thomas 67

Ice Ages 10, 180
Inwood, Cyril 44
Irchester 47, 50, 185
Irthlingborough 33, 51-2, 96
Irthlingborough & Raunds
    Angling Club 166
Ise, River 47, 137-9
Islip 12, 58, 62-3, 152

John, King 56, 121
Joyce, Mary 102-3

Kay, Duncan 53
Kettering 13, 137, 139-41
Kettering, Thrapston & District
    Angling Club 162, 166
King's Cliffe 142-143
Kingsley, Charles 136
Kingsthorpe 183
Kirby, Edmund 49-50
Kislingbury 22, 24

Lakey, Brian 153
Large copper butterfly 135

Law, William 142
Laxton, William 84
Lewis, Cecil 84
Lilford 50, 74, 77, 176
Lilford, Lord 64, 76, 96
Lings Wood 185
Loach 151
Long Sutton 122-3
Lowick 62, 143, 149-50, 164
Lutton Leam 125

Mackeness, Sam 44
Manfield, Philip 37
March 126-7
March & District Angling
    Association 166
Marshland 120
Marshland Smeeth and St James
    121
Mary Queen of Scots 82, 87,
    89-91, 108
Mauntell, Sir Walter 22
Meads, Sid 119-20
Mid-Northants Fishery 52-3
Middle Nene Cruising Club 64
Mildmay, Sir Walter 143
Milton Ferry 100-1
Mink 92
Minnow 151
Mole 113
Moore, David 161
Morton, Bishop John 131
Morton's Leam 111, 131, 182
Mullet 151
Mumford, Ray 165

Naseby 17, 19, 24, 137
Nassington 93
Nene (Old Course) 12, 126-36,
    177
Nene Catchment & Drainage
    Board 110, 172
Nene Valley Project 180
Nene Valley Railway 96, 99,
    186, 190
Nether Heyford 22
Newnham 20
Newts 186
North Bank 110
North Brink, Wisbech 114-5
North Level Drain 120
Northampton 13, 18-19, 30-44,
    96, 99, 122, 167-9, 190
Northampton, Battle of 33
Northampton Chronicle & Echo
    49, 124
Northampton Nene Angling
    Club 31, 166
Northamptonshire Evening
    Telegraph 124
Northamptonshire Wildlife Trust
    183-6
Northey 172

Old Shuck 133-4
Orton 158, 163, 169, 175
Osprey 64, 187
Otters 178
Oundle 80, 82-5, 96, 159, 161,
    175-6
    School 82-84, 99, 124
Oundle Angling Association
    166
Outwell 120, 122, 127

Peckover, Jonathan 116
Perch 151, 156-7, 186
Perio Lock and Mill 85-6, 164
Peterborough 96, 99, 102-5,
    108-10, 126, 130, 168, 172-3,
    186, 190
Peterborough & District Angling
    Association 152, 162, 166
Peterborough Evening Telegraph
    124
Pike 82, 84-5, 110, 120, 151,
    154-6
Pilton 74, 77, 168
Piper, John 84
Pitsford Reservoir 19, 44, 157,
    161, 164, 183, 187-8
Polebrook 80
Popham, Sir John 132
Porter, Roddy 54
Purple emperor butterfly 179
Pyel, John 51-2

Quincey, Joshua 72

Ramsey 126
Randolph, Thomas 20
Ravensthorpe Reservoir 19, 44,
    188
Reeds, Chris 110
Reynolds, Bob 44
Richard I 121
Richard III 89
Ringer, Geoff 31
Ringstead 52, 54, 147, 163,
    173, 185
Ringstead Angling Club 166
Ringstead Grange Fishery 53-4,
    164
Roach 110, 138, 151-2
Roff, Simon 152
Rothschild, Charles 80
Rothschild, Dr Miriam 80
Rothwell 137
Rudd 151, 186
Ruffe 151, 164
Rushden 13, 49-50
Rushden & Higham Ferrers
    Angling Club 166
Rushton 137, 139
Rutland Water 134, 161, 187

St Kyneburga 100
St Werburgh 20

Salmon 151, 164
Sanderson, Frederick 84
Sandwich, Earl of 79, 134
Savage, Robin 123
Sayers, Dorothy L. 121
Scarlett, Robert 108
Scott, Sir Peter 84, 124
Short Wood 186
Shrive, Dick 44
Sibson 96
Silverlock, Ken 22
Skittles, Northamptonshire 72
Smelt 151
Smith, John 168
Snipe 135
South Holland Drain 120, 186
Spalding Guardian 124
Spencers, of Althorp Park 26,
    28, 30, 31
Squire, Thomas 62
Stanground 110, 177
Stanion 143
Stanwick 52, 54
Stephenson, Robert 96, 99, 123,
    172
Stibbington 96, 134, 175
Stickleback 151
Stoke Doyle 16, 77, 79
Storey, Edward 136
Stowe 21
Sturgeon 151
Sudborough 143, 147-8
Sutton Bridge 84, 123, 168,
    173, 177, 186
Swallowtail butterfly 135
Swans 182
Symak, Elliott 161
Sywell Country Park (and reser-
    voir) 19, 154, 185

Tench 64, 151-3, 186
Terrington St Clement 130
Terrington St John 120
Thorney Abbey 112-3
Thorpe Underwood 137
Thorpe Waterville 64, 67, 96,
    143, 162, 168, 180
Thorpe Wood 186
Thrapston 56, 58-61, 96, 158,
    168, 175
    Lagoon 62
Tilney All Saints 120-1
Titchmarsh Mill 64, 174
Titchmarsh Nature Reserve
    143, 146, 185
Townsend, Peter 67
Trailly, Sir Walter 55
Tresham family 139
Trout (brown and rainbow) 44,
    151, 164-5, 187
Trout (sea) 110, 151
Tryon family 142
Turner, Eddie 155
Turner, Patty 102

Turpin, Dick 20, 96
Tydd Gote 120

Upper Heyford 166
Upton 24
Upwell 120, 127

Vermuyden, Cornelius 132, 168

Wadenhoe 64-5, 67-8, 70-71,
    164, 168, 170, 185
    King's Head 67, 72
Walker, Richard 147, 150
Walpole Cross Keys 122
Walpole St Andrew 122
Walpole St Peter 121
Wansford 20, 93-6, 99, 134,
    167, 173, 186-7
Ward-Hunt, George 67
Warmington 91
Wash, The 124-5, 183
Washington, George 11, 22, 25-
    8, 56, 62
Water Newton 96, 100, 134
Watling Street 20, 167
Watts, Trevor 65
Weedon 20-1, 175
Weetabix Ltd 138
Wellingborough 13, 45-7, 50,
    96, 138, 168, 173
Wellingborough Nene Angling
    Club 154, 166
Wellstream 122
West Walton 93, 130
Weston Favell 44
White, Alex 54-5
Whitemoor 127
Whittlesey 111, 113-4, 127, 182
Whittlesey Mere 12, 126, 134-
    6, 169, 182, 190
Whitworths 45, 173
Whyt, Robert 113
Wicksteed, Charles 139
Wicksteed Park 137, 139
William the Conqueror 11
Williams, Nige 120, 155-6
Willow Brook 138-43
Willow Creek 162
Winfrey, Sir Richard 124
Wisbech 19, 62, 37, 93, 99,
    109, 114-20, 127, 168, 172-3,
    177, 190
Wisbech & District Angling
    Association 166
Woodford 55-6
Woodnewton 143
Woodston 172
World Conker Championships
    82

Yarwell 93
Yates, Chris 147

Zander 110, 151, 156-7